THE COMPLETE GUIDE TO PERSONAL DIGITAL ARCHIVING

THE COMPLETE GUIDE TO PERSONAL DIGITAL ARCHIVING

Edited by
Brianna H. Marshall

facet
publishing

Published by Facet Publishing,
7 Ridgmount Street, London WC1E 7AE
www.facetpublishing.co.uk

Facet Publishing is wholly owned by CILIP: the Chartered Institute of
Library and Information Professionals.

First published in the USA by
the American Library Association, 2018.
This UK edition 2018.

British Library Cataloguing in Publication Data
A catalogue record for this book is available from the British Library.

ISBN 978-1-78330-266-6

Printed and bound in the United Kingdom by Lightning Source.

Contents

PART I
LEARNING ABOUT PERSONAL DIGITAL ARCHIVES BEST PRACTICES

PART IV
SOCIAL AND ETHICAL IMPLICATIONS OF PERSONAL DIGITAL ARCHIVES

BRIANNA H. MARSHALL,
EDITOR

Preface

I FIRST BECAME INTERESTED IN DIGITAL ARCHIVING for purely personal reasons. From childhood on, I displayed the tendencies of an obsessive, legacy-oriented collector and organizer of cherished mementos. It started with my decision to catalog movie ticket stubs in elementary school. Years later when I got a cell phone, I meticulously hand-transcribed texts in a notebook, lamenting the lack of tools to automate this process. Witnessing the loss of years of family photos due to hard-drive failure was a wake-up call for me that things could and often did go wrong in the digital world. I couldn't avoid technology, so I might as well embrace it. As a teenager, I figured out how to transfer files from dusty floppy disks to recover long-forgotten poems and stories. In college, I tracked down photos dug out of relatives' attics, digitized them, and tested workflows for storing and sharing these new digital images. It probably wasn't a surprise to anyone when I turned my organizational inclinations into a career and became a librarian.

In my first professional job, I was privy to all the trappings of a domain filled with information professionals: fancy scanners, metadata standards, and a frequent assumption of technical literacy. I found myself reciting best practices for data management to researchers and academics—often just digital file management basics like file organization, naming conventions, and storage and backup tips, and I was continually floored by the immediate positive impact these practices could have. However, I also found myself increasingly concerned about my own (and to a broader extent my profession's) ability to translate our rapidly developing standards into useful practices for the everyday user.

At home, I struggled through planning and executing my own digital archiving projects. I was all too aware of my own missteps, and was frequently guilt-ridden when I deflected from the supposed standards to speed things along. I felt mildly fraudulent, as if my credibility as an information professional would be revoked if anyone found out about the admittedly small ways I was cutting corners. I found similar frustrations and self-doubt reflected in my conversations with others, from family members to kindred spirits in the scrapbooking community. Almost everyone was overwhelmed, leaving abandoned projects in the wake of their procrastination.

It soon became apparent that managing digital information was the glue that bound my personal and professional life together. Suddenly, everywhere I looked people needed help wrangling their digital stuff! That realization was the impetus for this book. My hope is that it will help information professionals become not just informed but also *excited* to pass along critical skills so that users will have less painful and more fruitful journeys in personal digital archiving (PDA). I am convinced that sharing even simple principles for how to store, share, and preserve digital objects will benefit our users in both their personal and professional lives.

Personal digital archiving is relevant to information professionals, organizations, and institutions of all types. Empowering individuals often means enabling communities to document their experiences in new ways, potentially with the long-term outcome of this material making its way into an archive. As I reviewed the chapters in this book, I found myself inspired by the work that is underway. Information professionals in diverse roles are increasingly taking the mantle of personal digital archiving advocacy, developing new models for outreach, programming, and services.

There is still a lingering sense of the grassroots nature of PDA in libraries and archives, though year by year I am excited to see it being written about to a greater extent. This book joins excellent recent writing on PDA, including Donald Hawkins's *Personal Archiving: Preserving Our Digital Heritage,* Cal Lee's *I, Digital: Personal Collections in the Digital Era,* and Melody Condron's *Managing the Digital You.* My favorite is perhaps the Library of Congress's *Perspectives on Personal Digital Archiving,* an open-access electronic publication that includes a rich array of stories and narratives about PDA. I highly recommend these books and hope that this volume will be a useful addition to the existing literature.

From the outset, my intention has been for this book to be used as a primer for information professionals who aren't quite sure how to approach personal digital archiving yet. I wanted the book's chapters to feel informed yet personal, like anecdote-filled conversations with brilliant colleagues. The chapters are intentionally practitioner-focused so that after finishing this book, readers will feel ready to start conversations and make amazing things happen within their communities. Enjoy!

CHELSEA GUNN

Introduction

Putting Personal Digital Archives in Context

THE TERM PERSONAL DIGITAL ARCHIVING (PDA) refers to the collection, management, and preservation of personal and family materials created in digital media. These materials can include digital photographs and videos, documents, e-mail, websites, and social media content. For information professionals, PDA encourages collaboration with their publics, with the goals of supporting digital information fluency and assisting individuals in their efforts to preserve their personal and family digital records. In many ways, PDA has grown out of and in response to previous movements and theoretical paradigms in archival and information science history. This chapter sets out to introduce some of these areas—namely early archival theory, personal information management, digital curation, and the digital record life cycle—in order to situate current PDA practices and scholarship within a larger historical and theoretical framework. A contextual understanding of PDA is especially helpful for us as we begin to imagine how this growing area of focus may impact the larger field of information science, and those of us working within it, as we move forward.

Information professionals have a stake in the PDA discussion not only because any number of the digital records currently being created by private individuals could one day be acquired by our repositories, but because we ourselves create vast and diverse personal digital archives of our own. As a result of this dual perspective, it has been observed that our own personal practices often deviate from our professional standards.[1] With our feet firmly planted in both worlds, we are uniquely positioned to see that the best practices we adhere to in professional settings simply do not always comply with the myriad ways we create, use, and save records in our day-to-day lives. The current PDA landscape creates a space for considering issues of personal information management in conjunction with professional archival and records management practices in new and interesting ways.[2] Exploring collaboration and conversation across these disciplinary areas of focus is increasingly necessary as information professionals from different areas find themselves at the same table—and often, occupying multiple seats at that table.

It is, of course, impossible to provide a comprehensive overview of each of the various approaches to and influences on PDA in a single chapter. Rather, what follows is intended to serve as a brief introduction to the professional literature in several areas that are particularly relevant to the current personal digital archiving landscape in order to place current PDA efforts in context, and to point to opportunities for further learning. This introduction begins with the treatment of personal papers in early archival theory and practice, and moves into practices associated with personal information management and digital curation, followed by discussions around the record life cycle and points of archival intervention. It ends with some observations about how PDA, which has grown out of the aforementioned areas of focus, may be signaling changes in the information professions, with particular emphasis on archival outreach, interdisciplinary collaboration, and conceptions of objectivity in the archives.

PERSONAL PAPERS IN ARCHIVAL THEORY

The personal papers of individuals and families from periods throughout history can be found in many archival repositories today. But personal papers have occupied a somewhat tentative position in archival theory and practice throughout the history of the profession. Before elaborating further, it is helpful here to define what is meant by personal archives or papers, and what has distinguished them from other archival records. Public archives refer to collections comprised of records from government and other public institutions, ranging from the federal to the local. These are defined as being systematically created and collected in the course of regular operations, often using mandated, consistent conventions.[3] Personal archives, which have often been defined as a subset of the broader category of private archives, have historically been defined by what they are not; which is to say, by their failure to meet the criteria of public archives as set forth by early archival theorists.[4] An accepted professional definition identifies personal papers simply as:

> (also personal records, private papers), n. - 1. Documents created, acquired, or received by an individual in the course of his or her affairs and preserved in their original order (if such an order exists).—2. Nonofficial documents kept by an individual at a place of work.[5]

Traditionally, the private archives of an individual or family have been made up of such record types as diaries, correspondence, commonplace books, manuscript drafts, scrapbooks, photographs, and all variety of ephemera. Today, individuals continue to create these familiar records, but it has increasingly become the case that personal archives are hybrid, consisting of both analog and digital materials. These personal archives might then also include e-mails, social media profiles, multimedia files stored on hard drives or cloud storage accounts, personal websites, and so forth. The introduction of these materials to the archives has required that archivists rethink traditional approaches to the appraisal, preservation, and access of personal papers.

The influential archival scholars Hilary Jenkinson and T. R. Schellenberg considered personal records to fall outside of the purview of proper archives ("proper archives" being those generated in the course of government or corporate activity) for a variety of reasons, tellingly referring to them instead as personal manuscripts, a term that persists to this day.[6] Both Jenkinson and Schellenberg considered these collections to be better suited to the custody of libraries, museums, or historical societies, and indeed, personal archives are still to be found in all of these institutions. But, as Rob Fisher has written, by distinguishing private from public records, and explaining the exclusion of the former from archival theory, both Jenkinson and Schellenberg did have their fair share to say, if implicitly, on the subject of personal papers.[7] This distinction between the public and private archive has continued to impact modern archival theory and practice, as archivists have had to formulate new approaches to personal records. While personal papers have long been collected by a variety of cultural heritage organizations, the exclusion of these materials from early literature has resulted in a disconnect between archival theory and the actual professional practices of archivists working with personal collections.[8]

For Jenkinson, the primary reasons for excluding these types of personal records from archival theory and practice were their potentially faulty provenance and the subjectivity of the records themselves.[9] Personal collections could pass through the hands of many creators before making it to the archives, and the collections could consist of records whose creator was unverifiable; these factors, in addition to the unreliable nature of personal narrative, threatened the objectivity of the historical record produced by the personal collection. For Schellenberg, a primary reason for excluding private records from archival repositories was that of evidence, which personal papers, in his estimation, could not adequately provide.[10] Professional conceptions of subjectivity and objectivity—of archivists as well as of archives—have changed significantly in the history of the archival profession. Modern approaches to archives increasingly reject the notion that objectivity or neutrality in the archives is either possible or desirable, but for Jenkinson and Schellenberg, archival records were intended to reflect, objectively, the activities of public administrations. Sue McKemmish revisits the idea of evidence in her work on the value of personal records in "Evidence of Me," connecting personal records with the establishment of collective memory, placing greater historical value on the very subjectivity of the personal record. The subjective accounts of many individuals provide a more nuanced (and perhaps more truthful) perspective than does a single dominant narrative of history.

In part, it can be challenging for contemporary information professionals to theorize personal archives because they are so unique to their creators. Where public archiving practices can be standardized according to the terms of government or corporate records management, personal archiving practices may be orderly and consistent, entirely chaotic, or anywhere in between, depending on the practices of the individual.[11] Yet in spite of the diversity of records and their organizational structures, personal archives are not simply a haphazard assemblage of disparate materials; they reflect the life and context of the creator.

Today, many—if not most—archives have adopted what is referred to as the "total archives" approach—one that assumes custody of both public and private archives within the same institution. And for some archivists and researchers, it may be these private or personal collections that drew them to the archives in the first place. These collections have, as Catherine Hobbs has written, an "intimacy . . . not present in the collective, corporate, formalized record-keeping system."[12] And while in the past, the paucity of literature that is focused on personal archives has been lamented, scholarship on this area has flourished in recent times.[13] In addition to the richness and intimacy of personal archives, the rise of born-digital records can be credited with contributing to the increased interest in personal archives.

PERSONAL INFORMATION MANAGEMENT

The increasing rate at which records are created in hybrid and digital forms has required information professionals to reconsider traditional approaches to archival processes and procedures. Often, personal collections, while still in the custody of their creators, have been subject to a form of benign neglect that is often explained by way of the "shoebox metaphor."[14] As the name suggests, the shoebox metaphor is a model in which individuals might store personal papers or records that they consider valuable in a shoebox, perhaps under a bed or in a closet. Untouched, these items remain stable and are generally in good physical condition when the box is eventually accessed, even if years have passed (provided, of course, the box was not stored in damaging environmental conditions like high heat or humidity). However, two important aspects of the shoebox metaphor are complicated by the presence of materials created and stored in digital forms: first, in the shoebox model most, if not all, items are collocated in a single physical space; and second, fragile physical items benefit when left alone, not subjected to the wear and tear of regular use. But a personal digital archive is likely to be distributed across many locations: perhaps on e-mail account servers, hard drives, old computers, and multiple social media platforms, to name only a few of the myriad possibilities. And as scholarship in digital preservation has demonstrated, if digital objects are left alone for too long, with neither updating nor migrating, they are liable to be significantly degraded, if not lost completely.[15] In thinking through the complications posed by the introduction of digital records to the shoebox metaphor, we begin to see how personal information management (PIM) and digital preservation methods stand to benefit PDA.

Some scholars have suggested that "archival literature about personal archiving mainly revolves around the management and care of personal papers [that have been acquired by collecting institutions] and thus lacks the individual focus" of PIM behaviors associated with archiving.[16] PIM is defined as "the practice and study of the activities people perform to acquire, organize, maintain, retrieve, use and control the distribution of information items such as documents (paper-based and digital), web pages and e-mail messages for everyday use to complete tasks (work-related or not)," and it is primarily concerned with the relationship between the creator and the record, rather than the relationship between the record and the archives.[17] PIM scholarship examines the information seeking, information storing, and usage of individuals working with active records. Considering PIM alongside archival practice, then, enables us to take a more holistic view of the record in all stages of its life cycle, considering creation and active use as well as preservation.[18]

Intersectional work across the areas of archives and PIM creates a space to address more comprehensively the challenges of managing and preserving personal digital archives in a variety of contexts. While private or personal papers are now considered to be significant to collecting archives, it is also important to bear in mind that for many individual creators of records, the imagined or intended publics of their personal collections are not necessarily the archives and researchers; rather, they may be relatives, friends, or community members. Regardless of the intentions for future use, the knowledge and skills of the information professional nonetheless remain important factors for the preservation of personal collections. The more a collection's imagined uses and users are understood, the easier it will be to tailor a situation-specific preservation strategy for it. Emphasizing education and outreach around PIM for individuals and communities preserving collections for their own purposes relieves those interested in PDA of the notion that accession into a professional archives is necessarily the end goal of preserving personal records.

As personal archives have been created more frequently in digital formats, and in greater quantities, information professionals have been given cause to reimagine traditional approaches to their work in order to meet the needs of personal digital collections, including the incorporation of PIM scholarship and methods and the inclusion of citizen archivists.[19] In this reimagining, archivists are encouraged to learn about and work with record creators, assisting them in the creation of stable, well-organized, and accessible personal digital collections. In this area, the work of researchers like Catherine C. Marshall has been extremely revealing, particularly in regard to better understanding how private individuals store, update, and migrate their digital files, or, in many cases, how they don't.

RECORD LIFE CYCLES AND THE ARCHIVAL INTERVENTION

In some respects, just as archival theory began with public records and has been adapted to suit private records, practices related to digital archives and preservation have been developed for institutional or public records and subsequently adapted to meet the needs of the everyday digital assets of private individuals.[20] Richard J. Cox has written that growing concerns around digital preservation would likely direct increased attention to personal papers.[21] Indeed, this does appear to be the case. Cox uses the examples of digital photographs and camera phones to illustrate this point. As the practice of using digital or cell phone cameras has grown, so too has the availability of software designed to help individuals store, manage, and share their personal digital photographs. Likewise, information professionals and technologists have developed and maintained digital image preservation standards that continue to address emerging equipment and file formats.[22]

As discussed above, PDA workshops and tutorials create a space in which information professionals can communicate those standards and best practices to users based on their current PIM strategies and level of comfort with technology. This increased emphasis on public outreach and education has underlined a professional debate about the proper point in the record life cycle at which information professionals ought to intervene for preservation purposes. For those new to the concept, the records life cycle comes from records management and digital curation. It has been illustrated with a cradle-to-grave metaphor, encompassing creation, classification, use, storage, and disposal.[23] This concept serves as a critical reminder that digital records are almost constantly in flux; they are created, used, edited or revised, saved, and sometimes deleted. Using the record life cycle model, we can consider the specific features and requirements of our records at each stage more precisely. In this framework, records are not static or stagnant; rather, they occupy many forms and may have many different needs between the time when they are created and the time when they are either preserved or destroyed.

Archival records, for the most part, arrive at a repository at an inactive stage in their life cycle, and in some cases, at specific points designated prior to their creation. Those inactive records are then maintained and often made available to researchers according to predetermined schedules. Personal records may be acquired at a greater variety of stages in the records life cycle, and may have any number of privacy or legal restrictions based on the materials themselves and the instruction of their creators. And as previously noted, with digital records in particular, "if archivists waited for the individual creator to approach the archive, records would be lost, a collection would be incomplete."[24]

For this reason, many have advocated for intervention earlier in the life cycle of the personal record. This, early-intervention advocates suggest, will better ensure the long-term viability of the digital object. Some go further, suggesting that it is important to intervene prior even to the creation of digital records. If digital materials are created with preservation in mind, creators will choose the most sustainable file formats, documentation practices, and storage solutions. The idea of early intervention recalls Marshall's assertion that archiving must be intentional, not merely a side effect of record creation and use.[25]

Some researchers and practitioners of archives have warned against early intervention on the part of the archivist, however, because it has the potential to influence or altogether change records in unanticipated ways, thereby compromising the integrity of the evidence they provide.[26] This was of particular concern to Jenkinson, who put considerable stock in the objectivity of archival records.[27] Similar arguments have been made about the very existence of the archive itself, suggesting that if we know about the archive, we create and self-edit our records with posterity in mind. In fact, this is a concept that persists beyond any formal sense of the archive, much less the digital archive. Thomas Mallon has written of diaries, for example, that perhaps we always write in our diaries with some reader in mind, even if that reader is an unknown figure in the future.[28] While debates about the optimal points of intervention will likely continue, it is probably safe to suggest that those engaged in PDA see the value in providing the public with the skill set required to create personal digital records that will be accessible at least during their own lifetimes, if not beyond.

IMPLICATIONS FOR STUDENTS, EDUCATORS, AND PRACTITIONERS

The growth of the personal digital archiving movement poses a number of potential questions and opportunities for current and future information professionals. Building upon the theoretical frameworks, methods, and skills described in this introduction will be not only useful but necessary for librarians and archivists moving forward within a new paradigm of digital and hybrid personal collections.

One significant implication of the growing emphasis on PDA outreach is that librarians and archivists will likely work more and more in direct collaboration with their publics. Librarians and archivists, as both creators of digital personal records and professionals trained in information behavior, digital preservation, and archival management, are uniquely poised to work with members of the public, and to assist them in making the best possible choices for saving their own personal digital collections. This gestures toward a continuing shift from historical models of the librarian or archivist as a "gatekeeper" of information toward a more user-focused approach to collections.[29] Providing public outreach and education is, of course, far from being a new responsibility for many information professionals; nonetheless, the nature of PDA workshops, labs, and instruction sessions thus far demonstrates a very open form of communication between archives in particular and their publics. In these settings, individuals may learn strategies and techniques from the professionals, but at the same time, the professionals have an invaluable opportunity to learn directly from individuals how they create, use, and save the digital objects that matter to them. If the preservation of digital objects begins at their point of creation, as has been suggested, a comprehensive PIM-archival approach is especially beneficial, since it considers all stages of the record life cycle.

PDA also requires information professionals to take a flexible, scalable, and collaborative approach to their work. Collaboration with researchers and practitioners from other disciplines and information professionals from other areas of focus is a critical component of an effective outreach strategy. Information professionals in these roles must meet people where they are and help them develop practical, tailored strategies that will work for them. In other words, the best PDA strategy is not necessarily the same preservation policy adhered to within professional archives, but rather the preservation policy that an individual can consistently implement and sustain. This may mean incorporating new skills and technologies that are geared toward the casual individual user rather than the professional archivist into information science curricula or continuing education workshops where they are not already taught—for example, creating a digital oral history, personal photo management, or community organizing. Preserving the digital records of many individuals with many disparate goals requires not only a solid grasp of current and past personal computing technologies, but a variety of soft skills, from public speaking to asking helpful questions to presenting information in a clear, concise manner.

Work in the area of PDA also has, perhaps most meaningfully, the potential to continue to challenge professional notions of the objectivity and neutrality of both archivists and archival records. The notion, supported by Jenkinson and other early archival theorists, that archivists should assume a professional position free of subjectivity has been largely rejected by modern archival scholarship. Working directly with record creators and potentially influencing their processes is a departure from the more passive, neutral custody described in early professional manuals. As Sue McKemmish has written, through preserving the records of individuals, we collaboratively build the record of a community.[30] The more we know about our publics, the better we are able to meaningfully partner with and support them. As we work with and learn from our constituents, we stand to learn more about our personal and professional practices and biases. Through this work, we may begin to better identify and address existing gaps and silences in the archives.

CONCLUSION

While we can't predict what the future holds for the personal digital archiving labs, workshops, and tutorials that have begun to emerge at institutions throughout the country, our turning to previous moments and movements in the history of archives and records management, PIM, and digital curation gives us some insight into the evolution of professional practice and theory. Thinking about PDA as one area of focus within a dynamic, evolving field lends us a framework for considering how current practices may lay the groundwork for new developments in libraries and archives. Through this lens, we can see PDA workshops and labs as a current iteration of the archival profession's ever-evolving treatment of personal archives. We can also see how archivists continue to expand our practice to incorporate concepts and strategies from other subsets of information science. PDA provides us with opportunities to reconsider personal digital archives from the perspectives of individual record creators as well as those of professionals in many specialized areas of information science, and to make new meaning in the middle ground of these points of view.

NOTES

1. Devin Becker and Collier Nogues, "Saving-Over, Over-Saving, and the Future Mess of Writers' Digital Archives: A Survey Report on the Personal Digital Archiving Practices of Emerging Writers," *The American Archivist* 75, no. 2 (2012): 499.

2. Christopher A. Lee and Robert Capra, "And Now the Twain Shall Meet: Exploring the Connections between PIM and Archives," in *I, Digital: Personal Collections in the Digital Era* (Chicago: Society of American Archivists, 2011), 29–77.

3. Richard Pearce-Moses, "Archives," in *A Glossary of Archival & Records Terminology* (Chicago: Society of American Archivists, 2005).

4. Mikael Korhonen, "Private Digital Archives—Lost Cultural Heritage?" in *Essays on Libraries, Cultural Heritage, and Freedom of Information,* ed. Dorrit Gustafsson and Kristina Linnovaara (National Library of Finland, 2013), 84.

5. Richard Pearce-Moses, "Personal Papers," in *A Glossary of Archival & Records Terminology* (Chicago: Society of American Archivists, 2005).

6. Sir Hilary Jenkinson, *A Manual of Archive Administration* (London: P. Lund, Humphries, 1937); T. R. Schellenberg, *The Management of Archives* (New York: Columbia University Press, 1965).

7. Rob Fisher, "In Search of a Theory of Private Archives: The Foundational Writings of Jenkinson and Schellenberg Revisited," *Archivaria* 67 (2009): 2.

8. Fisher, "In Search of a Theory," 4.

9. Fisher, "In Search of a Theory," 9.

10. Riva A. Pollard, "The Appraisal of Private Archives: A Critical Literature Review," *Archivaria* 47 (2001): 139.

11. Korhonen, "Private Digital Archives—Lost Cultural Heritage?" 84.

12. Catherine Hobbs, "The Character of Personal Archives: Reflections on the Value of Records of Individuals," *Archivaria* 47 (2001): 127.

13. Rodney G. S. Carter et al., "Perspectives on Personal Archives," *Archivaria* 76 (2013): 1–5.

14. Amber L. Cushing, "Highlighting the Archives Perspective in the Personal Digital Archiving Discussion," *Library Hi Tech* 28 (2010): 305.

15. Peter Williams, Jeremy Leighton John, and Ian Rowland, "The Personal Curation of Digital Objects: A Lifecycle Approach," *Aslib Proceedings* 61, no. 4 (July 5, 2009): 354.

16. Cushing, "Highlighting the Archives Perspective," 302.

17. William Jones and Jaime Teevan, eds., *Personal Information Management* (Seattle: University of Washington Press, 2007), 3.

18. Lee and Capra, "And Now the Twain Shall Meet."

19. Jan Zastrow, "Crowdsourcing Cultural Heritage: 'Citizen Archivists' for the Future," *Computers in Libraries* 34, no. 8 (October 2014).

20. Catherine C. Marshall, "Rethinking Personal Digital Archiving, Part 1: Four Challenges from the Field," *D-Lib Magazine* 14 (2008).

21. Richard J. Cox, *Personal Archives and a New Archival Calling: Readings, Reflections and Ruminations* (Duluth, MN: Litwin Books, 2008), 178.

22. Library of Congress, "Recommended Formats Statement," www.loc.gov/preservation/resources/rfs/.

23. Gordon E. J. Hoke, "Records Life Cycle: A Cradle-to-Grave Metaphor," *RIM Fundamentals,* September-October 2011.

24. Cushing, "Highlighting the Archives Perspective," 304.

25. Marshall, "Rethinking Personal Digital Archiving, Part 1."

26. Rachel Onuf and Tom Hyry, "The Personality of Electronic Records: The Impact of New Information Technology on Personal Papers," *Archival Issues* 22 (1997): 43.

27. Jenkinson, *A Manual of Archive Administration.*

28. Thomas Mallon, *A Book of One's Own: People and Their Diaries* (New York: Ticknor & Fields, 1984), xvi.

29. Korhonen, "Private Digital Archives—Lost Cultural Heritage?" 87.

30. Sue McKemmish, "Evidence of Me," *The Australian Library Journal* 45, no. 3 (January 1, 1996): 174–87, doi: 10.1080/00049670.1996.10755757.

BIBLIOGRAPHY

Becker, Devin, and Collier Nogues. "Saving-Over, Over-Saving, and the Future Mess of Writers' Digital Archives: A Survey Report on the Personal Digital Archiving Practices of Emerging Writers." *The American Archivist* 75, no. 2 (2012): 482–513. www.jstor .org/stable/43489633.

Carter, Rodney G. S., Rob Fisher, Carolyn Harris, and Catherine Hobbs. "Perspectives on Personal Archives." *Archivaria* 76, no. 0 (2013): 1–5.

Cox, Richard J. *Personal Archives and a New Archival Calling: Readings, Reflections and Ruminations.* Duluth, MN: Litwin Books, 2008.

Cushing, Amber L. "Highlighting the Archives Perspective in the Personal Digital Archiving Discussion." *Library Hi Tech* 28 (2009).

Fisher, Rob. "In Search of a Theory of Private Archives: The Foundational Writings of Jenkinson and Schellenberg Revisited." *Archivaria* 67 (2009).

Hobbs, Catherine. "The Character of Personal Archives: Reflections on the Value of Records of Individuals." *Archivaria* 47 (2001).

Hoke, Gordon E. J. "Records Life Cycle: A Cradle-to-Grave Metaphor." *RIM Fundamentals,* September-October 2011.

Jenkinson, Hilary, Sir. *A Manual of Archive Administration.* New and revised edition. London: P. Lund, Humphries, 1937.

Jones, William, and Jaime Teevan, eds. *Personal Information Management.* Seattle: University of Washington Press, 2007.

Korhonen, Mikael. "Private Digital Archives—Lost Cultural Heritage?" In *Essays on Libraries, Cultural Heritage and Freedom of Information,* edited by Dorrit Gustafsson and Kristina Linnovaara. National Library of Finland, 2013.

Library of Congress. "Recommended Formats Statement." www.loc.gov/preservation/ resources/rfs/.

Mallon, Thomas. *A Book of One's Own: People and Their Diaries.* New York: Ticknor & Fields, 1984.

Marshall, Catherine C. "Rethinking Personal Digital Archiving, Part 1: Four Challenges from the Field." *D-Lib Magazine* 14, no. 3/4 (March 2008). doi: 10.1045/march2008 -marshall-pt1.

———. "Rethinking Personal Digital Archiving, Part 2: Implications for Services, Applications, and Institutions." *D-Lib Magazine* 14, no. 3/4 (March 2008). doi: 10.1045/march2008-marshall-pt2.

McKemmish, Sue. "Evidence of Me." *The Australian Library Journal* 45, no. 3 (January 1, 1996): 174–87. doi: 10.1080/00049670.1996.10755757.

Pearce-Moses, Richard. "Archives." In *A Glossary of Archival & Records Terminology.* Chicago: Society of American Archivists, 2005.

———. "Personal Papers." In *A Glossary of Archival & Records Terminology.* Chicago: Society of American Archivists, 2005.

Pollard, Riva A. "The Appraisal of Private Archives: A Critical Literature Review." *Archivaria* 47 (2001).

Reyes, Vanessa. "We Created It, Now How Do We Save It? Issues in Preserving Personal Information, A Review." *Preservation, Digital Technology & Culture* 42, no. 3 (2013): 150–54. doi: 10.1515/pdtc-2013–0020.

Schellenberg, T. R. *The Management of Archives.* New York: Columbia University Press, 1965.

Williams, Peter, Jeremy Leighton John, and Ian Rowland. "The Personal Curation of Digital Objects: A Lifecycle Approach." *Aslib Proceedings* 61, no. 4 (July 5, 2009): 340–63. doi: 10.1108/00012530910973767.

Zastrow, Jan. "Crowdsourcing Cultural Heritage: 'Citizen Archivists' for the Future." *Computers in Libraries* 34, no. 8 (October 2014).

PART I

Learning about Personal Digital Archives Best Practices

SARAH SEVERSON

1

Archiving Digital Photographs

OVER THE COURSE OF THE TWENTIETH CENTURY, photography established itself as a ubiquitous technology in our daily lives. From the introduction of the Kodak Brownie camera in 1900 to the invention of the instant
Polaroid cameras of the 1970s, and then the introduction of digital cameras in
the 1990s, photography in all its forms has become one of the most popular
ways to document our everyday personal histories. Now, thanks to the rising
popularity of cell phone cameras, more and more people have a camera with
them wherever they go, dramatically increasing the number of photographs
we take. A study by InfoTrends projects that the number of photographs
taken in a year will reach 1.3 trillion in 2017.[1]

With numbers like these, there is a real concern about how we're going to
manage and save all of these images for the future. Vint Cerf, chief evangelist
at Google, warns of a potential digital dark age,[2] a future where it will be difficult to read historical electronic media because they were left in obsolete or
obscure file formats. The sheer amount of photographs now being produced
makes older print-based archival practices, like hand-selecting or keeping everything, impractical. Digital collections are increasingly easy to lose,

compared to their analog counterparts. A single computer failure can wipe out an entire digital photograph collection, destroying years of a family's carefully curated memories. There is also the very real danger of accidents happening when migrating data from an old computer to a new one. Another practical concern is how easy it is to lose context for what is shown in photographs: now that we can no longer sit down and write on the back of a photo, it's harder to keep valuable contextual information associated with a photograph. Finally, even with precautions taken against all these hazards, there is still the risk of hardware obsolescence making a digital collection inaccessible in only ten or twenty years, let alone a hundred years.

THE ROLE OF THE INFORMATIONAL PROFESSIONAL

The Library of Congress reports that questions about archiving personal photograph collections are among the most frequent questions they receive.[3] This demonstrates that people are aware of the urgent need for archival work, and they want to be more involved in archiving their own digital collections. There are also amateur and professional photography communities that have a vested interest in managing and preserving their photograph collections. They have collectively created an extensive body of literature documenting their work to that end. These range from personal websites with extensive blog posts detailing personal systems to the American Society of Media Photographers' Digital Photography Best Practices and Workflow, an initiative funded by the Library of Congress.

As such, it's important that the library and archives community knows how to support personal digital archiving processes, and also that we share this knowledge with the general public. The nature of library and archival work equips us professionals with unique perspectives and insights into the preservation of electronic records. It is important that we share this knowledge to raise awareness of the importance of preservation and, hopefully, help more people to start their own personal digital archives before so much material accumulates that they are overwhelmed by the task.

Simple steps can be taken to help people adopt practices that will help them to better manage their own digital archives. The most important thing in archiving digital photographs is developing a workflow that addresses the capture, organizing, and storing of photographs. This chapter will look at best practices in personal photo archiving, as well as tools and processes which can be used and implemented to assist in archiving personal digital photograph collections. It is intended as a primer for librarians and archivists to assist their user communities in these tasks.

COMMON TERMS

JPEG (Joint Photographic Experts Group) was a file format developed in the 1980s to handle color digital images, and it is the most common format you'll encounter. *JPEG2000* (JP2, JPF, JPX) is a newer (introduced in 2000) version of JPEG which includes a lossless setting.

TIFF (Tag Image File Format) is the U.S. Library of Congress's digital preservation standard.

RAW file formats, such as CRW, CR2, .NEF and DNG, preserve the original raw sensor data captured by the camera.

Technical metadata refers to the information that is automatically recorded in the file by the camera or scanner, such as the height and width of the image, color space, and image compression. Technical metadata is recorded using the *Exchangeable Image File Format* (EXIF), which was launched to encourage interoperability between devices and is now recognized as a de facto standard for technical metadata. It is supported by the majority of leading camera manufacturers.

Descriptive metadata is information that describes the image and is used for discovery and identification. Most descriptive metadata has to be manually inputted using a photo management system. Ideally, descriptive metadata will provide a sense of context, such as who created the image, when and where it was taken, and why. It might even describe the content, like the people or subject matter represented in the image. Essentially, it's very similar to the explanatory notes we used to write on the back of photographs, and it can be useful for easily finding and retrieving specific images.

Embedded metadata refers to descriptive metadata that has been embedded using the International Press Telecommunications Council (IPTC) metadata schema and is persistently linked to an image.

Digital asset management (DAM) comprises robust image management systems that allow you to store, organize, search, view, and usually process digital photographs.

Cloud-based photo management and/or storage systems allow you to use photo management processes, such as organizing, searching, and editing photographs, through a web-based application. The files are hosted in the cloud, not stored locally. Examples include Dropbox, Google Drive, or Flickr.

HOW TO ARCHIVE DIGITAL PHOTOGRAPHS

Planning: What Are You Going to Keep?

The first step in helping someone to set up an archival process starts earlier than most people imagine—it is important to start by understanding what is going to be archived. Knowing what they are going to keep, and for what reasons, will help people to decide what the most appropriate method is for archiving their collection. With digital photographs, you will need to help people identify exactly what kinds of images are in their collections and what the patron wants to be able do with them in the future.

Questions you can ask patrons include:

- Are they pictures they took themselves?
- Are they photographs they were sent, or photographs they've digitized?
- Do they want to be able to search and find photographs from specific events?
- Are they planning on passing the photographic collection on to family or friends for safekeeping, or do they want to share them right away?
- Are they planning on leaving the collection to an institutional archive?

Starting from an understanding of each of these basic uses is important. The process of patrons thinking through what they want to do with their archive will help to create an archival process that is best suited to their needs and capabilities.

The final step in planning is to make sure patrons have the best-quality photographs possible. It is difficult to predict what uses will be made of the photographs over a fifty-year time frame, and getting the highest-quality images at the start of the process, when the picture is first taken, can only help future access and long-term preservation. This means taking photographs at the highest resolution possible and choosing the best file format.

What Is the Best File Format?

For preservation purposes, you will want to recommend the use of file formats that have the best chance of being readable in the future. To ensure this, the structure and nature of the format should be openly documented and supported by multiple applications. The three most commonly used file formats are JPEG, TIFF, and RAW, each of which has its own advantages and disadvantages.

For most personal archives, a JPEG file will be the best preservation file format. It's the most common format that is captured by cameras[4] and is openly documented. It's a relatively lightweight file size, meaning that less storage space is required for archiving images in this format. The major disadvantage to this format is that JPEG uses lossy data compression, meaning it reduces the file size of an image by merging similar or "redundant" pixels, so less information is kept overall. For most people and most uses, however, this is not a significant issue. However, JPEG2000, which is a newer version of JPEG, is not widely supported or used. This makes it a poor choice for preservation.

While TIFF is a proprietary file format, it is well documented and broadly supported. It is a lossless image format, and a good choice for people who are looking to preserve the highest possible image quality. The major disadvantage of this format is that TIFFs generally result in very large file sizes for only a small gain in image quality. It is therefore the best choice for professionals, but not necessarily for the rest of us.

RAW file formats can be compared to a digital negative, since they contain all the information used to render a digital image. Working with RAW files is more difficult—they are read-only files that require additional software to access and edit. With the exception of DNG, they are all proprietary formats that are specific to certain camera models; DNG is openly documented and supported by Adobe. In almost all cases, RAW files are not appropriate for personal photographic archives. They should only be used in the rare cases where there is a need to make substantial edits in the future that require all of the information captured in this format.

Consolidating: Where Are All the Photographs?

Before creating an archive with someone, it is important to gather all their photographs into one place. When working with people, you will likely find that this is the first big hurdle you encounter, but it can be overcome with careful planning.

First, identify all the image sources being used. This includes all the devices that both they and their families are using to take photographs, such as cell phones and cameras, and also any printed photographs that they have already or will be scanning. When it comes to cell phones, it is important to understand where photographs are stored in order to ensure they are all transferred. The camera function inside an application, such as Facebook or Instagram, for example, may not store photographs in the same place as the native camera application.

The goal at this stage is to make sure that all their photographs are stored in the same location on their computer. This principle is often referred to as the "Rule of One." This location contains the master versions of a user's photographs, and is used as the source for all backup copies.

Regularly transferring photographs to the master location is critical, given the vulnerability of portable devices such as smartphones and cameras to theft, loss, or damage. Encourage people to get into the habit of transferring photographs from portable devices to their computer on a regular basis. The simplest method is to use the default software that comes with their camera or their phone. Another option is to use photo management software, which we'll talk more about in the section on organizing photographs.

The next step is equivalent to the archival appraisal process; it involves selecting what to keep and what to discard. Although it may seem simple enough to just keep everything, *encourage people not to ignore this step*. A smaller photograph collection is significantly easier to organize and maintain, and makes it much easier to find specific photographs. If someone you are helping is hesitant to do this, you can remind them that the price of film and of having photographs printed used to limit the number of photographs we took. There used to be a selection process that happened before we even took a picture, and that helped to keep the number of photographs in our collections under control. In addition to these usability concerns, there are also technical advantages to smaller collections. The larger the collection, the greater the risk of file corruption when migrating the collection to new storage media.

FILE-NAMING BEST PRACTICES

This is also a good time to suggest thinking about the naming of files, and how this can help with preservation and access. A good file-naming system should be easy to communicate and self-evident when looking through files.

File-Naming Tips

1. Ensure that your file names are unique. Your photo or camera will typically assign file names using sequential numbering, but these will eventually be repeated. Adding something before or after the file names when transferring images to your computer will help prevent duplicate file names.

2. Adding meaningful and descriptive file names will help you browse and search for photographs. Adding a level of description in the file name also allows you to take advantage of the sorting capabilities of built-in file systems.

3. Be concise: long file names can cause issues in the future with migrations between media and computers.

4. Avoid complex or illegal characters. Avoid using blank spaces, capital letters, and special characters in your file names because certain computers have trouble reading them and they can cause problems when moving files between computing environments.

Renaming files individually isn't practical, but when transferring files to a computer, there is often an option to add a prefix to the file names of all the photographs being transferred. This can help designate an event (such as a birthday or a holiday), a location, or a date.

ORGANIZING
Putting Things in Order

Once you've helped someone gather all their photographs in the same place, they will need to have a system to organize them. There are any number of ways to organize photographs, and choosing between them comes down to what works best for the owner of the collection. Identifying what the owner wants to do with the archive will make it easier to decide how to best organize the person's collection. Like file-naming, the best organization method is one that is consistent, self-evident, and expandable. A good place to start is using the default structure that is created when photographs are downloaded from the camera to the computer. Often these programs will automagically organize photographs using embedded technical metadata, such as creation date. Using this structure as a base, you can create sub-directories based on other meaningful information, such as subject or event.

SOFTWARE

The easiest way to organize and manage a digital photograph collection is to use photo management software. Common features of these programs include generating thumbnail previews, organizing images into folders or collections, and creating basic metadata. Most of these programs also support simple editing, e-mailing, and exporting of photographs.

Photo Management

The first category of software is the built-in photo management applications that come with most computers, such as Apple's Image Capture, iPhoto/ Photos,[5] and Windows Explorer Gallery. All of these provide good, basic infrastructure to be able to browse images and add basic file-level metadata, such as descriptions and tags. In addition, Apple Photos supports the recognition of "Faces," where you can identify people appearing in your photographs, and it reads embedded GPS location data if available.

A free and popular photograph management alternative is Google Photos. This application is the replacement for their popular desktop application

One small point of concern with Apple's iPhoto/Photos application is that it automatically creates a separate file library to store all of your photographs, which makes it difficult to locate individual files on your hard drive. This makes it more complicated to create backups and migrate user data. Apple is also pushing the integration of the Photos software with iCloud photo sharing and warns about possible syncing issues if you store your library on online storage services, such as Dropbox or Google drive. This is contributing to an increasingly closed and proprietary computing environment, which makes it more difficult to implement good archival practices.

Picasa, which was officially retired in March 2016. Like iPhoto/Photos, it supports adding descriptions, tagging people in photographs, and reading embedded GPS location data. Other software options include XnView MP and FastStone.

Digital Asset Management

Digital asset management programs represent the next level up in terms of features and complexity. These are robust applications with extensive photo-editing and processing features and excellent support for standards-based descriptive metadata. There is a great deal of information available online about how to use these programs to effectively organize photography collections. They are commonly used by advanced amateurs and professional photographers. Popular examples of these programs include Adobe Bridge, Adobe Lightroom, and Extensis Portfolio.

Cloud-Based Photo Management

A new trend is to use specialized web-based applications to organize and store photographic collections. These include the previously mentioned Google Photos and iCloud photo storage. There are also photo-exclusive sites, like Shutterfly, SmugMug, Mylio, and Flickr, that let users upload and archive an unlimited number of photographs either for free or for small fees. One thing to note when using cloud-based programs to organize and store your photographs is that these require a fast and stable Internet connection in order to operate effectively.

For people who use these programs, it's strongly recommended that they maintain an additional backup of their files. A number of these companies, such as 1000memories and PictureLife, have disappeared over the past few years, taking their users' photographs with them. The sudden closure of PictureLife and the attempts of users to get their photographs back was documented in

How to Choose the Best Tools

Since software changes so rapidly, it's tricky to recommend specific software or online tools. It's better to communicate how to evaluate the tools out there. Some good questions to ask include:

Sustainability: Is the tool you are using proprietary or open source? Just like file formats, we want to encourage people to use open and well-documented tools to account for future obsolescence.

Cost: Is it free or is it a paid service? Is it a one-time payment for software or is it a subscription? Many services offer a free account with limited storage that is useful to try out software. If you pay for the service, what happens to your photographs if you miss a payment?

Security: Does the service offer secure storage and transfer? How secure? If you use cloud storage, do you know what security measures/encryption they use to keep your photographs safe?

Exporting your photographs: How easy is it to retrieve your photographs from the service? If you want to change software, can you easily migrate your photographs? What if the tool disappears; are the photographs still retrievable? If you pass away, can designated people retrieve the photographs and associated metadata?

Metadata: If you use the software to add metadata, where is it stored? If you stop using the software, will you lose all your labels or tags? When you export your photographs, is the metadata exported with them? Does the tool change the metadata in your photographs? For example, when you upload a photo to Facebook, it changes the embedded creation date to the date you uploaded the photo. Even if you are only uploading copies of your photographs, changing the metadata can create confusion later on.

an episode of the Reply All podcast.[6] These difficulties are a powerful example of some of the issues with web-based organization solutions.

DESCRIBING
Adding Context and Information

Ensuring that a photograph has accurate and thorough metadata is critical to preservation. Without good metadata, even if a photograph is saved in an archive, it may not be possible to actually find it again, and that defeats the purpose of having an archive in the first place. During the process of creation, both technical and descriptive metadata can be attached to and embedded in the photograph, and additional descriptive metadata can be added.

> *Technical metadata* refers to the information that is automatically recorded in the file by the camera, and you can see this information by clicking on the "File Information" option in most computer file-management systems.

> *Descriptive metadata* is information that describes the image and is used for discovery and identification.

While the value of metadata is high, it also takes a lot of work to create. While it's possible to be overwhelmed by the act of describing each photograph, it's important to emphasize that simple things, like adding event names at the start of file names or creating simple captions, can have a huge benefit and be of great help in finding photographs again in the future.

Embedded Metadata

Embedded metadata refers to descriptive metadata that has been embedded using the International Press Telecommunications Council (IPTC) metadata schema and is persistently linked to an image. Since its release in 1991, IPTC has been the de facto standard to transfer information, and it includes extensive fields to capture granular information such as the photographer's name, contact information, and copyright statement. Upgraded in 2011, the schema is now based on Adobe's Extensible Metadata Platform (XMP) framework[7] and is compatible with Extensible Markup Language (XML). IPTC is an open format, supported by both Adobe products and over seventy other programs.[8] An advantage of using widely available image file formats, such as JPEG and TIFF as opposed to proprietary RAW files, is that they support embedding metadata into the image file.

Adding Metadata

The simplest way to embed information into the file is to select a file on any computer (Mac or PC) and then select File > Get Info, where you will find a text field that you can write comments in, much like the back of a photograph. One thing to note is that field names and terminology, such as "caption" and "description," are sometimes different from program to program.

Photography professionals routinely use photo-editing software to add metadata to their digital photos for copyright and business reasons. Most of the photo management systems that we talked about in the "Organizing" section also have the ability to add descriptions and other information to a photograph.

Another advantage of adding descriptions that are embedded is that they can be read by websites when you want to publish and share photographs online. For example, both Flickr and Facebook read embedded descriptions and display them as captions when you post the photos. Unfortunately, this is still not very standardized. The Embedded Metadata Manifesto initiative created by the IPTC and supported by a number of other photography associations has been doing tests to determine which online services read the metadata and preserve it in the file when downloaded.

STORING
Where Should You Keep All the Files?

After helping someone to consolidate and organize all of their files, it is vitally important to then help them set up a system to back up their photographs. The reality is that computer hard disks fail, and files can be lost in natural disasters, or as a result of a power surge or theft. Without a backup, any of these scenarios would mean they would lose all of their photographs—but it would not take much effort to prevent this with backups.

How many backups should you encourage someone to have? A popular recommendation is the 3-2-1 approach. This means recommending keeping three complete copies of all files, with at least one copy at an off-site location. In my personal archive I have a system where I regularly copy my photos to my computer master folder (first copy). Once a month or so I'll make a copy of the entire photo folder from my computer onto a portable hard drive (second copy), and I use a program to run nightly cloud backups automatically (the third copy, at an off-site location). Instead of using cloud storage, you can recommend storing an external hard drive off-site, like at a relative's home or in a safety deposit box. This off-site copy is critical in the event of a catastrophe (flood, fire) that could destroy any locally stored backups. Even in that worst-case scenario, the photographic archive would survive.

HOW DO YOU CREATE A BACKUP?

Backups can be tedious and time-consuming to make. Using software to automate the process can be extremely helpful. Backup software makes it easy to synchronize selected files on a storage system separate from your main hard drive, and then replicate file changes when they occur. Most backup software can schedule regular scans of a hard drive for new and changed files on a daily, weekly, or monthly basis, or the software can continually monitor the computer for changed or new files. It is likely to take a long time to perform the first synchronization, since all the data in the archive has to be read and copied. After that first sync only the differences in the data are synchronized, which makes for a much quicker process.

While this makes backups easier, it also means that any changes made to the master files will almost immediately be made to the backup as well, since the files are mirrored. This means that the backup files are as vulnerable to accidental changes and deletions as the master files. Examples of local backup software include GoodSync and Chronosync.

You should also be able to recommend appropriate storage media. An external solid-state drive is a good option; they are easy to use, inexpensive, and provide sufficient capacity for many people. An external drive used for backup should be used exclusively for backups and stored in a safe, secure place. It should not be used to transport files. This minimizes the possibility of damage to the drive and data loss. If you need to recommend more storage than an external drive provides, consider suggesting a NAS device (network attached storage), which is a small computer with a lot of storage capacity designed to operate as an appliance for storing and sharing files over a network. It is a more advanced and more flexible option, but it is also more expensive. CD-Rs or DVD-Rs are not recommended for backing up photographic collections. The transfer time is more time-consuming and the limited capacity of these media may result in splitting data over several disks.

Cloud-Based Storage Options

There are a number of cloud-based storage options, where storage is provided by a commercial data center. The obvious advantage of storing photos in the cloud is that they are accessible from anywhere. Like all Internet services, they require a high-speed connection and a large data allotment to make them practical options. This is a real concern when thinking of the digital divide and rural communities. As with cloud-based photo management applications, you also need to be aware of security and longevity issues, and the same questions about choosing the best tool apply here. Some examples of online backup services that back up your data to the cloud include CrashPlan, Mozy, and Backblaze.

When looking at and evaluating cloud-based tools, there are differences between the ones that focus on general storage and the ones that are geared toward photography. General cloud storage sites not only offer folder and file syncing, but also media-playing and device syncing. Examples of these are Apple's iCloud, Google Drive, Microsoft OneDrive, and Dropbox. Photography-specific sites such as Flickr and Google Photo support only image and video files, but they include more storage and provide more features, such as built-in editing and management tools. For example, Flickr offers one terabyte of free storage, and SmugMug, which is aimed at professional photographers, has unlimited storage for only forty dollars a year.

Refreshing Archival Data

All current storage media (CDs, DVDs, memory keys, HDs) have a shelf life and will eventually fail due to physical degradation. In any archival system, the data must be migrated to new storage media on a regular basis. This means checking the integrity of your archival storage and replacing your archival storage media with new media at regular intervals (every 5 to 10 years). One type of archival media that should not be forgotten is printing photos. If properly produced and cared for, printed images can last for hundreds of years—much longer than contemporary digital storage media.

CONCLUSION

While this chapter presents the archival process as a neat chronology, I would argue that it doesn't all need to be done in the order presented here. If someone is overwhelmed by a hard drive that feels like it is overflowing with photographs—and anecdotal evidence suggests that many people are in this position!—then we can start by helping them get all of their photographs in the same place and then backed up. From there, encouraging them to commit to regularly transferring their photographs to their computer and then to subscribe to a cloud backup service can have a huge impact with only minimal effort. After that, the conversations about deleting photographs and planning can happen more calmly. When their collection has been slimmed down to a more manageable size, introduce the concepts behind describing key moments and identifying people, and how this can help to better organize their collection. Finally, look into current software with them and offer advice on what tools they can use to support their archiving process. If enough people adopt these best practices, it will have a profound impact on the quality and quantity of our future visual historical record.

Preserving the ever-increasing number of digital photographs that are being produced is a growing concern shared by the public, photographers, and cultural institutions alike. Recently we've started to see a paradigm shift, where preservation and archiving are being recognized as something that needs to start with the creator, at the beginning of his workflow when a photograph is first taken. Institutionally, we can take a number of useful steps: we can encourage the standardization of procedures for creating, managing, and storing born-digital images; we can support the development of image metadata to further improve existing profiles; and we can foster the development of open and nonproprietary technologies. But our work depends on creators adopting these best practices and implementing them in their own personal photograph collections. The work of preserving our prolific photographic output for the historical record depends on all of us.

FURTHER RESOURCES

The *Library of Congress website* is a good resource for accessible introductions to the topic of personal digital archiving.

> The section on archiving digital photographs gives a good simple overview that can be shared with the nonspecialist: www.digital preservation.gov/personalarchiving/photos.html

> They also have some excellent videos.

> - An overview of scanning photographs: www.digital preservation.gov/multimedia/videos/scanner.html
> - How to add descriptions to your digital photographs: www.digitalpreservation.gov/multimedia/videos/ personalarchiving-photometadata.html

> *The Signal*, the Library of Congress blog on digital preservation, has a category for personal digital archiving which is a good up-to-date source on many issues: https://blogs.loc.gov/thesignal/ category/personal-archiving/. Notable posts on archiving digital photographs include:

> - Ashenfelder, Mike. 2011. "Adding Descriptions to Digital Photos | *The Signal*." Web page. October 28. //blogs.loc.gov/ thesignal/2011/10/mission-possible-an-easy-way-to-add -descriptions-to-digital-photos/.
> - ———. 2012. "Update: Adding Descriptions to Digital Photos | *The Signal*." Web page. January 25. //blogs.loc.gov/thesignal/ 2012/01/update-adding-descriptions-to-digital-photos/.
> - Lazorchak, Butch. 2011. "Four Easy Tips for Preserving Your Digital Photographs | *The Signal*." Web page. October 24. // blogs.loc.gov/thesignal/2011/10/four-easy-tips-for-preserving -your-digital-photographs/.
> - Manus, Susan. 2011. "Photo Sharing Sites as Digital Preservation Tools | *The Signal*." Web page. November 2. //blogs .loc.gov/thesignal/2011/11/photo-sharing-sites-as-digital -preservation-tools/.

> *Perspectives on Personal Digital Archiving* is an e-book that is a compilation of some of the best posts from *The Signal* blog: www .digitalpreservation.gov/documents/ebookpdf_march18.pdf.

For a more in-depth introduction, I would recommend reading the Digital Preservation Coalition report on "Personal Digital Archiving." While there is no specific section dedicated to photographs, it has many good tips and resources that are applicable:

- Gabriela, Redwine. n.d. "Personal Digital Archiving." *DPC Technology Watch Report.* http://dx.doi.org/10.7207/twr15-01

For more in-depth information and resources on image management and metadata, the website http://controlledvocabulary.com/ is maintained by David Riecks, who has been a featured speaker at a number of image management and archiving conferences and webinars.

NOTES

1. Stephen Heyman, "Photos, Photos Everywhere," *The New York Times,* July 29, 2015, www.nytimes.com/2015/07/23/arts/international/photos-photos -everywhere.html.
2. "Internet Pioneer Warns Our Era Could Become the 'Digital Dark Ages,'" NPR.org., www.npr.org/sections/thetwo-way/2015/02/13/386000092/ internet-pioneer-warns-our-era-could-become-the-digital-dark-ages.
3. Donald T. Hawkins, 2013, *Personal Archiving: Preserving Our Digital Heritage,* http://public.eblib.com/choice/publicfullrecord.aspx?p=3316168.
4. JPEG is the most common file format identified in the "InterPARES survey of record keeping practices of photographers using digital technology" as cited in J. Bushey, "He Shoots, He Stores: New Photographic Practice in the Digital Age," *Archivaria* no. 65 (2008): 125–50.
5. iPhoto was replaced by Photos in OS X 10.10.3, on April 8, 2015. Nathan Ingraham, 2014, "Apple Stopping Development of Aperture and iPhoto for OS X," The Verge, June 27, www.theverge.com/2014/6/27/5849756/ apple-stopping-development-of-aperture-and-iphoto-for-osx.
6. "#71 The Picture Taker," 2016, Reply All: Gimlet Media, https://gimletmedia.com/ episode/71-the-picture-taker/.
7. As per the International Press Telecommunications Council, https://iptc.org/ standards/photo-metadata/iptc-standard/.
8. As per W3 Schools, www.w3schools.com/xml/xml_whatis.asp.

BIBLIOGRAPHY

"#71 The Picture Taker." 2016. Reply All: Gimlet Media. https://gimletmedia.com/ episode/71-the-picture-taker/.

Bushey, Jessica. 2008. "He Shoots, He Stores: New Photographic Practice in the Digital Age." *Archivaria* no. 65: 125–50.

———. 2016. "The Archival Trustworthiness of Digital Photographs in Social Media Platforms." Electronic Theses and Dissertations (ETDs) 2008+. University of British Columbia. doi: http://dx.doi.org/10.14288/1.0300440.

Cushing, Amber L. 2013. "'It's Stuff That Speaks to Me': Exploring the Characteristics of Digital Possessions." *Journal of the American Society for Information Science and Technology* 64, no. 8: 1723–34.

Gadoury, Nancy. 2009. "Evaluation of Photographs in Digital Format." *Archives (Quebec)* 41, no. 1: 31–43.

Hawkins, Donald T. 2013. *Personal Archiving: Preserving Our Digital Heritage.* http://public .eblib.com/choice/publicfullrecord.aspx?p=3316168.

Heyman, Stephen. 2015. "Photos, Photos Everywhere." *The New York Times,* July 29, 2015. www.nytimes.com/2015/07/23/arts/international/photos-photos-everywhere.html.

Ingraham, Nathan. 2014. "Apple Stopping Development of Aperture and iPhoto for OS X." The Verge. June 27. www.theverge.com/2014/6/27/5849756/apple-stopping -development-of-aperture-and-iphoto-for-osx.

"Internet Pioneer Warns Our Era Could Become the 'Digital Dark Ages.'" 2016. NPR.org .www.npr.org/sections/thetwo-way/2015/02/13/386000092/internet-pioneer -warns-our-era-could-become-the-digital-dark-ages.

Keough, Brian, and Mark Wolfe. 2012. "Moving the Archivist Closer to the Creator: Implementing Integrated Archival Policies for Born Digital Photography at Colleges and Universities." *Journal of Archival Organization* 10, no. 1: 69–83. doi: 10.1080/15332748.2012.681266.

Marshall, Catherine C. 2008. "Rethinking Personal Digital Archiving, Part 1." *D-Lib Magazine* 14, no. 3/4.

———. 2008. "Rethinking Personal Digital Archiving, Part 2." *D-Lib Magazine* 14, no. 3/4.

National Digital Information Infrastructure and Preservation Program (U.S.). 2013. *Perspectives on Personal Digital Archiving.*

"Personal Digital Archiving | Digital Preservation—Library of Congress." 2016. Web page. http://digitalpreservation.gov/personalarchiving/.

Redwine, Gabriela. n.d. "Personal Digital Archiving." DPC Technology Watch Report. doi: http://dx.doi.org/10.7207.

2

Archiving Social Media

WHY ARCHIVE SOCIAL MEDIA? To some this might seem either futile or unnecessary: as an individual you cannot possibly capture it all, and anyway, isn't someone probably already storing and saving everything online? After all, we hear constantly that anything put online can never truly be erased and removed from the Web. Librarians hopefully know better. Archiving and preserving something is a conscious process that needs a lot of planning. Furthermore, issues of privacy complicate the archiving of many social media platforms. Just as a library could not preserve a handwritten letter without the letter's owner allowing the library to have access to the document, this is also the case with social media behind a password wall. Privacy controls on social networks make it difficult or impossible to view much of the information without permission from the account owner. To protect themselves from privacy violations, social media companies are unlikely to archive or store any material beyond what is useful for advertising purposes. What they do choose to keep will not likely be accessible to the general public. For most social media accounts, preservation falls to the individual user or group that maintains the account. What this means for the preservation and history of today's social culture is a matter for concern—and a topic of complexity beyond the scope of this chapter. However, the implication for librarians and archivists on a day-to-day basis is clear: we should know enough about social media to assist individuals who desire to preserve all or part of their online participation on these sites.

The reasons why someone might choose to archive social media range widely. In *Social Media Mining,* Zafarani, Abbasi, and Liu explain that the Web has "hundreds of millions of people spending countless hours on social media to share, communicate, connect, interact, and create user-generated data at an unprecedented rate."[1] Though many people use Facebook and other social networks as a news source and for other purposes (such as finding a job and scheduling events), social media users are generally more interested in interacting than in learning or information-gathering.[2] Many choose to connect with people on these networks more often than they meet in person, both for convenience and as a preference over other communication types. As a result, vast stores of our social interactions are created and stored on websites that we do not own or control. To some, this is the reason to archive: to protect what is there and take ownership of the interactions and records. This is most likely a personal interest wherein individuals may want to save their own conversations with friends, colleagues, and family. However, other reasons to archive social media are as diverse as human needs. Convenience may come into play, in that an individual wants photos and posts stored to keep track of time or events. Special projects, such as celebrating anniversaries or memorials, may drive archival need. Involvement with a group, organization, social movement, or important event may also result in the desire to "capture" what is there for posterity.

Because of these diverse needs, librarians may serve both individuals seeking to archive their own personal accounts as well as those seeking to archive the social media posts of groups or other individuals. One prominent example of the latter would be the archiving of public officials' posts. President Obama's administration announced that posts to his social media accounts would be logged and stored in the National Archives, and then deleted to offer a blank-slate Twitter handle @POTUS to the next president.[3] Ironically, by deleting the posts from Twitter these messages will be less accessible to most people. However, archivists likely look at the National Archives as a more stable home for the messages than the Twitter platform, which could change or disappear. Logging the personal posts of public figures may become more common as archives seek to capture the digital dialogue that is, and should be, part of our common historic record. Capturing the posts of local organizations is also likely. Despite the probability of these cases becoming more common, most users are likely to be looking to archive the social media posts from their own pages, or the pages of loved ones. That is the primary focus of this chapter.

SIGNIFICANT ISSUES IN SOCIAL MEDIA

Privacy is one of the most important and often-discussed issues surrounding social media.[4] Many social media sites require your birth date, real name, and e-mail address, though these items may be hidden from public view. The privacy of children is a specific concern for many users and social media sites. Many sites do not allow accounts to children under age thirteen, but this is not easily policed. Privacy policies are presented to users when they create an account and are usually easily accessible from social media websites at any time, though accessibility does not always mean that these policies are easily understood. In general, most social media sites allow users to set many of their own privacy rules. For sites not intended to be public-facing, privacy controls allow users to prevent unintended third parties from accessing their posts and profile. Beyond those privacy settings, however, social media companies also participate in data mining and regularly use the posts and related data for advertising and cooperation with government entities. What they use and how they can use it vary depending on the platform and the current privacy policy. As might be imagined, this results in a wide difference between what social networks do with our information and what we *think they are allowed to do with it*.[5] While the only fail-proof privacy control would be to avoid social networks completely, users should at the very least attempt to review the privacy settings on sites they use often.

Ownership is closely related to privacy and is another key issue. Each site's terms of use will designate what is and is not owned by the account holder, though these may not be clear. Terms of use will designate what the site can claim as theirs, such as statistical use data. Other ownership issues may not be covered in terms-of-use agreements. For example, if one person posts to social media and a second person comments on the post, who owns the comment? Can either party claim ownership and archive or save the post to use later in another way? Posts made publicly on networks like Twitter are often reused and quoted in the news and archived as part of data collection projects. Some users may not be aware of this reuse and archiving. Another growing ownership issue is the life of the social media account after the death of the person. Some terms of use clearly designate what will happen to accounts after death. For example, Facebook allows users to choose whether their account will be removed or be maintained as a memorial.

Permanence is also a prominent concern across all platforms, and is the main impetus for archiving. Users and their accounts are not static. People remove posts or whole accounts over time. Users may unfriend or unfollow one another, and that changes privacy and viewing availability. For this reason, the ideal social media preservation solution captures actions automatically and in real time.[6] Alternatively, capturing the same account at set intervals will allow for changes to be recognized over time. This is not always an option. However, as a goal, the implication is that saving more often is key to creating a true record of an account, if that is the intent. Much of the risk involved with social media accounts and information is the false assumption that the sites will be around for the foreseeable future. Because of its popularity, it might be unthinkable to imagine Facebook deciding to shutter and not offering its hundreds of millions of users access to accounts. Despite this, there have been many cases of popular sites shutting down, or shifting focus. Myspace is a prominent early example of a social media website that did not so much disappear as become unpopular, and then shift in focus. During that shift, most users did not retain anything from their accounts and these have since been lost in transition of ownership; while Myspace is technically available now, all of the posts and chats that took place on the early Myspace platform are now gone and irretrievable.[7] Even popular sites shut down, as is the recent case of Twitter's short video site, Vine. In late 2016, Twitter announced plans to discontinue the site despite high use of the platform, and many users were sent scrambling to find ways to save videos. Tools immediately sprang up to allow users to save videos before the site closed or got sold to another company. However, some users may not have heard about the archival options. Many of the videos have already disappeared as people discontinue their use of the service.

ROLE OF THE INFORMATION PROFESSIONAL

Librarians have an important role in the personal archiving of social media. Whether at a public or academic institution, librarians can hopefully recognize the importance of capturing what is, in essence, our shared social culture. Just as libraries might save letters from the nineteenth century or recorded phone conversations from the 1960s, social media interactions are the digital ephemera of our lives. In many ways, social media interactions are similar to earlier forms of communication. Letters and correspondence become rarer the older they are. That is not necessarily because there were not many letters from a period, but at least in part because so few letters were kept, protected, and preserved. It would be easy to feel that social media are unimportant in the present because so much is available right now.

Librarians could have a role in assisting people with social media transitions such as the recent shutdown of Vine, both by informing patrons of the change and by assisting them in saving their media. Guidance and education could be an important part for librarians to play in their already established role as technology leaders. As they embrace new technologies, librarians should keep social media in their sights; changes occur rapidly and being a regular user of the tools (even for practice) will be a benefit to others who seek help in these areas. If the library's policy is to assist patrons with technical questions and research, then these endeavors fall solidly into this court. As with any reference question that might have personal implications (such as questions about personal medical issues, legal questions, etc.), libraries should follow the best practices of the profession to protect privacy wherever possible.

Beyond assisting researchers and the community with this work, librarians may choose to take part in archival efforts in coordination with their community or in their role as protectors of information. Librarians could further participate in the larger-scale archiving of sites that are public, as the Library of Congress and other libraries have attempted. In 2016, three universities joined together to not only preserve Twitter feeds but to create open source applications that will assist others in archiving Twitter. When it is complete, the endeavor, called DocNow, will attempt to capture the online networking and reactions to important events.[8] Special collections and libraries with local or targeted collections may identify subsets of social media that make sense as an archived digital collection.

Assistance with curation is also a likely role for librarians.[9] Like all archives and collections, perhaps not everything that can be archived on social media is desirable or needed. This is true for library collections (should they acquire social media records) as well as for individuals creating a personal collection. Individuals may no longer submit physical papers and records to libraries in the future. Instead, libraries may work with digital records and may take part in archiving social media (or specific portions of them) for posterity, perhaps as part of an overall collection containing many other formats. This is not without controversy.[10] Whether libraries and archives decide to explore this sort of archiving on their own, the issue will likely come to them in the future; researchers, writers, and historians will most definitely seek out ways to save and preserve these interactions. In this process they may (and should) be looking to librarians and archivists for help.

COMMON TERMS

Certain terms are used frequently in relation to social media and other web technologies and it is helpful to be aware of these terms. The following are a few key terms to know when discussing social media.

A *hashtag* is an alphanumeric keyword or code to signify that the post is about a specific topic or event. A hashtag starts with the hash sign # followed by a word or string of characters with no spaces, such as #StarWars or #2016Election. Hashtags are supported on most social media platforms, including Twitter, Facebook, Instagram, Google+, Pinterest, YouTube, and Flickr.

A social media *handle* is an individual's user name on the site. On Twitter and some other sites the handle is preceded by the @ symbol; for example, @YouTube is the Twitter handle for the video-sharing network. Using the handle when talking about or to the owner will include them in the conversation. Searching for a user's handle will allow people to see their posts as well as others who have mentioned them.

Wall/timeline/home screen refers to the social media website page where users can see the posts from friends or other feeds that they have subscribed to. This aggregate list of posts continuously changes and is updated based on recent posts and the site's prioritization algorithm.

A *DM (direct message)* or *PM (personal message)* is a private message directly to another user or users. DM/PM posts do not appear on either user's wall and are more private. Most social media sites allow users to have private chats like these, and sites with archival options usually include private chats in their archive tools.

HOW TO ARCHIVE SOCIAL MEDIA

The device used to archive social media is important, and archiving on a personal computer (laptop or desktop) is recommended. The directions in this chapter are for use on a computer rather than a tablet or phone. Personal computers have a number of built-in applications that allow most basic file types to be opened or viewed. Additionally, not all archiving options will work from a mobile device, including tablets or smartphones. LinkedIn's archive features, for example, will not work from a mobile device. Some archiving functions may work partially but not completely, such as cases where the account e-mails you a file for download; some mobile devices may not be able to decompress or open those archival files. For all of these reasons, computer archiving usually works better.

Archiving Facebook

Facebook is the largest social network in use today. Tens of millions of people log in to the social media giant every day, and dozens of research studies in multiple academic fields have looked at aspects of Facebook's role and use.[11] Because users can choose who to accept as a friend on the platform, many users post personal updates and photos on a regular basis. Baby announcements, job changes, wedding and vacation photos, and many day-to-day activities are all logged with dates. Other users make comments and similar posts, resulting in a rich social interaction experience—which is the reason why so many users like Facebook and return there. These personal, social interactions are also the reason why users might desire to save posts in their accounts. Facebook, in an attempt to fill this need, has provided an account archiving tool that will satisfy the needs of many users. There are also additional options from third-party vendors.

Because of how Facebook has developed and changed the privacy rules of its platform, the primary responsibility of archiving nonpublic Facebook posts is left to the individual users.[12] This means that someone who stops using their account and then looks for it in ten years should not expect that it will be "saved" out there on the Web somewhere. While there are numerous efforts to archive the open Web (for example, the Internet Archive's Wayback Machine), those efforts can only capture what is publicly available. Even things posted on Facebook with "Public" chosen as the audience are not captured by the Wayback Machine.

The built-in tool on Facebook is straightforward enough that librarians should have no trouble guiding patrons through the process. The steps are:

1. Log in to Facebook and go to Settings under the arrow menu in the upper right-hand corner.
2. Click on Download a copy of Your Facebook data on the bottom of the screen, under the General Account Setting section.
3. Click on Start My Archive.
4. For security reasons, the archive will e-mail you a link to download your archive using the e-mail address associated with the account.

The Facebook FAQ offers a full list of what is included in the download. Currently, posts and things you have shared, messages and chat conversations, check-ins, and much more are included.

Third-party options for archiving parts of Facebook will require users to log in to their account through the third-party tool. While many of these services are well-documented and safe, users should be cautious in giving access to their accounts where so much personal data can be obtained. Many reputable third-party tools can help with archiving. IFTTT (https://ifttt.com/) can assist users in pulling photos off of Facebook into e-mail or onto another platform, such as Twitter or Google Drive. Because IFTTT is set up to work automatically, it can assist users who don't want to spend a lot of time and have specific needs (such as just photos). Mozilla Firefox additionally has a web browser add-on that assists users in saving Facebook content (photos, activity stream, friends list, and more) directly onto their hard drive (search "Firefox ArchiveFacebook add-on"). These services are just a few of the current tools available to users, but more are becoming available all the time. While having multiple options is helpful, librarians and social media users should be aware that many of these services do not last because of the competitive market. Archivists should attempt to choose tools and companies that are in high use and, if possible, have a record of consistency.

New options for archiving Facebook the old-fashioned way (paper) have also sprung up. Companies including My Social Book (www.mysocialbook .com) can print out a user's entire Facebook history and commentary or just individual years and comments, binding the memories into a book. For many people, this makes sense as a replacement for scrapbooks and photo albums that are never assembled. However, as with all paper ephemera, books are not a secure way to back up these memories because they are overly susceptible to water, heat, and other environmental conditions. Ideally, companies will begin offering an e-book or PDF version of the same collected books that are available in print—something My Social Book does say is being planned.[13]

Archiving Twitter

Twitter is a social media tool where users can share media and short comments (less than 140 characters) on a public platform. Posts to twitter are called *tweets* and sending on someone else's tweet to your own followers is referred to as *retweeting*. Twitter users can also reply to tweets, creating conversation strings between related tweets. While there is an option to use private messaging through Twitter, most things posted to Twitter are public. Following a Twitter user allows someone to see that user's posts on their main Twitter Home screen, but any tweet can be viewed by any user as well as the public. Tweets show up in Google search results and are regularly quoted on news programs like CNN, usually in reference to news events. As such, they are often collected or used to capture important news moments or social events.

Twitter offers a built-in tool for users wishing to archive their own tweets. Using this tool is relatively straightforward.

1. While logged in to a Twitter account on a desktop computer, click on the avatar icon in the upper right, between the "Search Twitter" box and the Tweet icon.
2. Select Settings from the drop-down list.
3. Click the "Request your archive" button.
4. A confirmation will appear to let you know that a link will be e-mailed to the e-mail account on file when the archive is ready.
5. When the e-mail arrives, follow the link and download the Zip file containing the archive.

Currently the Twitter archive download includes an HTML file for viewing the entire archive in a browser, as well as data files for JSON and CSV. While developers may want to make use of the JSON data, most general users will be interested in the HTML or CSV files. Double-clicking the HTML file will open it in a computer's default web browser where users can view all of their tweets and retweets by scrolling or by clicking on a month in the sidebar calendar history. The CSV file can be opened by a number of programs, most commonly Microsoft Excel or Google Sheets. Once opened, the files offer a more data-intensive view of the account's tweet history including date and time stamps, twitter identification numbers for those replied to and retweeted, and a full URL to any linked items.

Some users may wish to archive Twitter posts beyond what they themselves have posted, or from one specific topic. This is normally done by using a common hashtag. For example, choosing a hashtag before a project or event allows a user to later collect all posts or information using that hashtag after the project or event is completed, or whenever collection is needed. The reasoning for this is diverse: a hashtag could represent a wedding, a concert series, a collection of cat photos, or all of the tweets documenting a writer's creative process.[14] Currently Google Sheets offers a free add-on called Twitter Archiver, which is a slightly more advanced tool. To use it, log in to a Google account and do a web search for Twitter Archiver. Once added, you will have the option to save tweets with shared search characteristics to a Google sheet. You must have a Twitter account and a Google account in order to use these tools.

Archiving Instagram

Instagram is a mobile device application used on smartphones to enhance and share photos. Instagram can be set up as a private account where you control who sees your posts (like Facebook) or it can be a public account (like Twitter). Despite being owned by Facebook—which offers robust archiving tools—Instagram does not currently offer an internal archiving tool that includes likes and comments. It does, however, offer a built-in feature that can save Instagram photos (including edits and filters) to the phone. To do this, Instagram users can navigate to the Options screen by clicking on the gear in the upper right while in the mobile app. Then, scroll down to Save Original Photos and turn the feature ON to have all edited or filtered photos saved automatically to the phone's Photos app. Instagram also has the ability to sync with a Facebook, Twitter, Tumblr, Flickr, or Swarm account. If Instagram users want to post all of their photos on Instagram as well as one of these networks, then the option is available to back up the photos as part of a secondary archive. For example, if Instagram is set up to also post photos to Facebook, then archiving Facebook will save the photos for an archive. Archivists should note that photos saved on social media are often reduced in size and quality when they are uploaded. This makes saving enhanced photos directly to the phone a good preservation option.

Beyond syncing to another network, Instagram is much more popular with third-party applications than other social media networks. Numerous phone applications and desktop computer programs are available to assist with downloading photos into a personal archive. If it is inconvenient to save photos on the phone or via a secondary network, then a third-party application may help. Many of these programs are free, but the same rules apply to these as to other tools: users must be cautious in downloading and using tools that will gain access to personal information and should consider using popular tools that have a record of consistent quality and safety. As with Facebook, My

Social Book (www.mysocialbook.com) also includes an Instagram book-building option for those who want to have a physical copy of their Instagram photos. Shutterfly (www.shutterfly.com) and other online photo-printing services also allow users to order physical photographs from their Instagram accounts.

Archiving YouTube

YouTube (www.YouTube.com) is a popular video-sharing website owned by Google. Videos can be public or private, and both professional and social videos are posted on the site regularly. YouTube users who have added their own videos to the site can easily download them as MP4 files directly from the website if they need to archive. However, they must be the owner of the video to use this feature; in general, downloading other YouTube videos is a complex issue in regard to copyright, ownership, and privacy.

To download a video from your YouTube collection:

1. Log in to YouTube and click on the user avatar/photo in the upper right to see the small pop-up menu.
2. Click the Creator Studio button.
3. Click Video Manager in the left sidebar. This will show a list of the available videos in the user's account.
4. Click on the down arrow next to Edit for the video to be downloaded and select Download MP4.

To download all of the videos at once, YouTube users will need to use Google Takeout: this is Google's tool for backing up and downloading for any of the Google tools. To do this, log in to your Google account and search for "Google Takeout." De-select all products except for YouTube and click Next. The tool will give you options to compress/zip the file, limit the archive size, and download or send the archive via e-mail link.

Cross-Platform Services and Tools

Personal digital archivists and those who wish to preserve or search across many social media platforms at once may be additionally interested in cross-platform tools. For example, Social Searcher (www.social-searcher.com) allows users to search many social media platforms at once, including Facebook, Twitter, Instagram, YouTube, and Reddit. It is similar to Tagboard (https://tagboard.com/), which can pull together all mentions of a hashtag to build an aggregated board or wall of hashtags. However, Social Searcher allows for a CSV download of results, making it a better archiving tool. Both Tagboard and Social Searcher can only include media and posts that are public and searchable. Individuals and groups that want to track certain terms or ideas that are being talked about on social media may find this tool helpful. For example, people who choose a unique hashtag for an event may find it useful to pull all Twitter, Facebook, and Instagram posts from that hashtag together in one search. While the tool only shows the top/most recent results in search results, it allows users to export full search results into a CSV file that can be opened in a spreadsheet application such as Excel or Google Sheets. Search results will include the text of each post, with additional data depending on the platform. However, photos and videos will not appear in the file. Free accounts are limited to a set number of searches per day, though users can purchase more in-depth access.

Digi.me (www.getdigime.com/) is a powerful social media application that allows users to search, sync, manage, and download their social media accounts directly to their computer. Free accounts allow up to four platforms to be included. Accounts can be searched and organized through the downloaded application tool, and account data (including photos and CSV files of text posts) can be exported and viewed outside of the proprietary tool as well. Unlike most cloud services that offer social media backup, Digi.me offers a relatively robust tool for searching and viewing social media posts. Similar tools exist from cloud storage backup services and other applications, though most either require the proprietary tool or have fewer free options.

IFTTT (https://ifttt.com/) can also assist social media archivists. IFTTT stands for "If This, Then That." IFTTT is an online service that allows users to create "recipes" or "applets" that complete basic functions. By creating an account and giving the service access to social media and other accounts, users can create their own function recipes or use some of the pre-built scenarios, such as the following: save photos you are tagged in on Facebook to a Dropbox folder; build a Twitter list from a specific hashtag; post your Tweets to Facebook when you use a specific hashtag; or sync your new Instagrams to a Pinterest board. Many more scenarios are possible, and new recipes are created regularly to fill unique needs. This is a convenient and powerful service, but there are some privacy concerns, since it does require users to allow access to all of their accounts.

CONCLUSION

Social media archiving is a challenge, but it is not unsurmountable. Social media platforms will continue to change, requiring librarians (and in fact, all users) to continually adapt. However, tools in the area of social media archiving have been building rather than changing. This means that existing tools are getting better and more extensive, and new tools are introduced regularly. This is exciting news! New and better tools will create opportunities for capturing social media and shared culture at all levels. Social media archiving is likely to be an area where continuous lifelong learning is possible as options grow and change. The best approach for an information professional is to maintain an adaptive and flexible approach—something not uncommon to many areas of librarianship.

FURTHER RESOURCES

Curation Tools—While many online tool lists highlight sites and software to assist with preservation and archiving, the "Curation Platforms" chapter of *Social Media Curation* by Valenza, Boyer, and Curtis, a volume in the ALA's Library Technology Reports series, offers an annotated list of almost seventy free and paid tools to assist specifically in the curation of digital and social media resources.[15] Since this book was published in 2014 and digital resources transform constantly, some platforms have changed. Moreover, the focus on curation is related to but not identical to the needs of archiving; some tools are focused on collecting and linking to materials rather than preserving them. Despite this, the list is most definitely of interest to those with an interest in social media archiving.

Socialbrite's Social Media Glossary—All web users may benefit from knowing more of the language of the Web. Numerous social media glossaries are available online, though some are already out of date or are very limited. Socialbrite offers a fairly comprehensive glossary of 100 terms related to social media to help people understand the lingo related to the use of these sites. It is available at www.socialbrite.org/sharing-center/glossary/. The glossary covers basics like *hashtag* and *podcast,* as well as offering brief descriptions of more in-depth topics like *open source, Creative Commons,* and *net neutrality.*

Wikipedia Lists of Social Media Sites—To understand the scale and reach of social media websites, look to the well-maintained Wikipedia pages for "List of social networking sites" and "List of defunct social networking websites." Both lists focus on well-known networks only, which still adds up to a large list. Dating sites are not included. Wikipedia is the ideal location for this constantly changing list because site editors tend to act quickly to changes in the web arena.

NOTES

1. Reza Zafarani, Mohammad Ali Abbasi, and Huan Liu, *Social Media Mining: An Introduction* (New York: Cambridge University Press, 2014), xi.

2. Oriol Miralbell, "Knowledge Exchange in Social Networking Sites," in *Perspectives on Social Media,* ed. Piet A. M. Kommers, Pedro Isaias, and Tomayess Issa (New York: Routledge, 2015), 11–18.

3. Issie Lapowsky, "White House Prepared to Hand Over @POTUS to the Next POTUS," *Wired Online,* October 31, 2016, https://www.wired.com/2016/10/white-house-prepares-hand-potus-next-potus/.

4. Donghee Sinn and Sue Yeon Syn, "Personal Documentation on a Social Network Site: Facebook, a Collection of Moments from Your Life?" *Archival Science* 14 (2013), doi: 10.1007/s10502–013–9208–7.

5. Catherine C. Marshall and Frank M. Shipman, "Who Owns Your Social Networks?" in *ACM Conference on Computer-Supported Cooperative Work & Social Computing* (Vancouver, BC, 2015).

6. R. Madhava, "10 Things to Know about Preserving Social Media," *Information Management* 45, no. 5 (2011): 33–37, 54.

7. Felix Gillette, "The Rise and Inglorious Fall of Myspace," *Bloomberg Businessweek Online,* https://www.bloomberg.com/news/articles/2011–06–22/the-rise-and-inglorious-fall-of-myspace.

8. Lisa Peet, "DocNow: Saving Social Media," *Library Journal,* May 2016, 12.

9. Marshall and Shipman, "Who Owns Your Social Networks?"

10. Catherine C. Marshall and Frank M. Shipman, "On the Institutional Archiving of Social Media," in *Joint Conference on Digital Libraries Proceedings* (Washington, DC, 2012).

11. Sinn and Syn, "Personal Documentation on a Social Network Site," 97–99.

12. Sinn and Syn, "Personal Documentation on a Social Network Site," 101.

13. "My Social Book: Support Center," https://mysocialbook.desk.com/customer/portal/articles/search?q=PDF.

14. Josie Barnard, "Live and Public: One Practitioner's Experience and Assessment of Twitter as a Tool for Archiving Creative Process," *Journal of Writing in Creative Practice* 7 (2014): 493–503.

15. Joyce Kasman Valenza, Brend L. Boyer, and Della Curtis, "Curation Platforms," in *Social Media Curation* (Chicago: ALA TechSource, 2014), 60–65.

BIBLIOGRAPHY

Barnard, Josie. "Live and Public: One Practitioner's Experience and Assessment of Twitter as a Tool for Archiving Creative Process." *Journal of Writing in Creative Practice* 7, no. 3 (2014): 493–503.

Gillette, Felix. "The Rise and Inglorious Fall of Myspace." *Bloomberg Businessweek Online.* https://www.bloomberg.com/news/articles/2011–06–22/the-rise-and-inglorious -fall-of-myspace.

Lapowsky, Issie. "White House Prepared to Hand Over @POTUS to the Next POTUS." *Wired Online.* October 31, 2016. https://www.wired.com/2016/10/white-house -prepares-hand-potus-next-potus/.

Madhava, R. "10 Things to Know about Preserving Social Media." *Information Management* 45, no. 5 (2011): 33–37, 54.

Marshall, Catherine C., and Frank M. Shipman. "On the Institutional Archiving of Social Media." In *Joint Conference on Digital Libraries Proceedings.* Washington, DC, 2012.

———. "Who Owns Your Social Networks?" In *ACM Conference on Computer-Supported Cooperative Work & Social Computing.* Vancouver, BC, 2015.

Miralbell, Oriol. "Knowledge Exchange in Social Networking Sites." *In Perspectives on Social Media,* edited by Piet A. M. Kommers, Pedro Isaias, and Tomayess Issa, 11–18. New York: Routledge, 2015.

"My Social Book: Support Center." https://mysocialbook.desk.com/customer/portal/ articles/search?q=PDF.

Peet, Lisa. "DocNow: Saving Social Media." *Library Journal,* May 2016, 12.

Sinn, Donghee, and Sue Yeon Syn. "Personal Documentation on a Social Network Site: Facebook, a Collection of Moments from Your Life?" *Archival Science* 14 (2014). doi: 10.1007/s10502–013–9208–7.

Valenza, Joyce Kasman, Brend L. Boyer, and Della Curtis. "Curation Platforms." In *Social Media Curation,* 60–65. Chicago: ALA TechSource, 2014.

Zafarani, Reza, Mohammad Ali Abbasi, and Huan Liu. *Social Media Mining: An Introduction.* New York: Cambridge University Press, 2014.

3

Archiving Web Content

WHEN CONSIDERED IN THE REALM of personal digital archiving, web archiving may seem a bit out of place. Photos and videos are tangible family histories that can be passed through loved ones' hands for decades—but why should we worry about saving someone's website? Family photo albums and digitized home movies have a precedence of archival value for our patrons, while websites often have less immediate meaning as objects of historical import or as content to be saved for others' future use. Additionally, the term *web archiving* can still come across as some vague practice done only by institutions like the Internet Archive.

In many ways, social media has had more traction in mobilizing individuals to take action. People are increasingly aware of the ephemeral nature of our online social spaces—as evidenced by a celebrity's deletion of a thoughtless tweet, activists using social platforms only to have their posts removed or banned, or patrons' own chosen erasure of their digital pasts when revisiting posts from years ago that no longer resonate. Perhaps it is the longevity of use that social platforms have had by now in people's lives; these platforms have been around for quite some time now and will likely continue to be, though the platform of choice may ebb and flow over time. As of the writing of this chapter, I just passed the ten-year anniversary of joining Facebook. Twitter and Instagram as well hold large portions of my social history, having been around for ten and six years, respectively. The age and sustained usage of these social platforms mean that many of us have quite significant portions of our life stories within their confines. But what about our personal histories outside of social media that still exist on the Internet? Should we not also be thinking of how much we have shared through websites and blogs?

I have had multiple websites of varying purposes and meaning throughout my life—a personal website for a brief moment in my undergrad years, and websites made for class projects in graduate school. I never even thought for a moment to keep them; why would I? My extended family has also documented their life in various ways on the Internet; one relative in particular has a fantastically beautiful website dedicated to their hobby. Were these websites built with long-term care and keeping in mind? Has my family ever thought about the future of their websites and blogs? The answer is probably not.

Many of us have websites for a variety of reasons—for professional engagement, for us to explore personal spaces for our art and writing, or to market and sustain our businesses. In fact, at this moment, Internet Live Stats cites over 1.1 billion total websites, meaning "unique hostname[s] (a name which can be resolved, using a name server, into an IP Address),"[1] on the Internet today. Of those 1.1 billion websites, Internet Live Stats points to Netcraft's web survey methodology and states that 75 percent are actually inactive.[2] Literature in the field cites a range of average website life spans from 44 days in 1997 per Brewster Kahle,[3] to 75 days from a 2001 study,[4] and then to 100 days in an article from 2003.[5] So while websites flicker in and out of existence, either built by human hands or automated by computers, another issue that rears its head is "link rot." Dead links are a familiar experience to all of us when browsing the Internet. Many information professionals may remember the buzz surrounding the study of the plague of dead links in Supreme Court decisions and legal literature.[6] In fact, during the writing of this chapter, the number of dead links and missing content I encountered while exploring the literature was surprising (yet it also felt absurdly appropriate). This link rot shouldn't be perceived as an indicator of inactive websites or website deletion, as Nicholas Taylor notes on his post for the Library of Congress blog *The Signal;* "websites may have been archived or simply exist at a new location (albeit, one mediated by a paywall) to which the web server was not configured to redirect page requests."[7] So though these dead links simply indicate a movement of content in some unresolvable way, the sudden inaccessibility of information and resources is indicative of the problematic transitory nature of content on the Internet.

Now, these fast facts aren't necessarily provided to suggest that we should panic over the loss of information, let alone to suggest that everything on the Internet should be saved. Taylor notes in his discussion of website life spans that "most commercial web search engines penalize listings from such domains, [and] malware distributors are incentivized to churn quickly through massive numbers of new domains." Though his discussion is pointed at the short life of these sites, I think it is also illustrative of the amount of "junk" (depending on your collection policy and what you consider "junk") that there is bound to be among the 1.1 billion websites—whether they are malware sites, scam websites, or computer-generated web pages. However, there are also bound to be many personal websites, art websites, blogs and spaces for writing, and many different implementations of our attempts at self-documentation among these defunct websites. And knowing how many websites exist at this moment, can you imagine how many other websites have disappeared since the beginning of the Internet? There are many possible reasons: someone passed away and stopped paying their domain hosting, or grew bored with their Internet presence and deleted it, or changed their website without saving its old name or content.

As information professionals, this space is ripe for us to help support our patrons. Ideally, we can help them find new perceived value within their self-created Internet projects and take some responsibility and action over the fates of their digital legacies. This chapter seeks to provide a foundation for thinking about this type of work by citing generally accepted practices and tools and extrapolating these to the ways in which we, as information professionals, can instill new ideas based on personal digital archiving. So, to get started, let's take a look at what web archiving is and what well-known web archiving programs are doing.

What is web archiving? What exactly are these institutions practicing within the bounds of this buzzword? In the most simple definition, web archiving is the process of collecting websites, storing them, providing access to them by off-line or retroactive viewing, and then preserving them for future use by others. In practice, the actual web archiving workflow follows similar workflows for both print and digital collection development and management. Web archiving at an institution will include processes like selection, collection, quality assurance, documentation, preservation, and providing access. (The Archive-It Team at the Internet Archive has developed a detailed life cycle model for web archiving from its work that may be beneficial for organizations starting out with these workflows and processes; information on this resource can be found at the end of this chapter in "Further Resources.")

The concept of web archiving may likely be familiar because of the aforementioned organization, the Internet Archive founded by Brewster Kahle, which has been working to save the histories and content of the Internet since 1996. Now many cultural heritage institutions are also working to archive varying social, political, and cultural histories on the Internet. Web archiving collection policies vary widely: the Internet Archive seeks to capture wide swaths of the Internet; some institutions only curate their web presences within or tied to their domain; some countries work to collect everything under their national domain; and some groups have very specific collection policies, such as the New York Art Resources Consortium which collects "specialist art historical resources."[8]

THE ROLE OF THE INFORMATION PROFESSIONAL

One does not have to be an expert on web archiving to help patrons begin to engage with the idea of collecting, saving, and ensuring the foreseeable future of their digital histories. Though it may seem intimidating at first and difficult to know where to start, the key role for us is to act as facilitators of exploration and to serve as a bridge from information sources to practice. The way you approach web archiving in your community will differ depending on the people you are working with and the resources available to you.

Prior to beginning a web archiving project or program, there are questions that can help you start to think about your community and current resources in order to shape the ways you engage your patrons. To start, what would web archiving mean for your patrons? Do you have key communities with online presences within your libraries that may benefit from this work? Identifying groups that have a demonstrated or potential need to preserve their Internet presence will be critical to helping you shape your services and outreach. These groups may be local organizations interested in documenting their history in the community, activists or social justice groups whose histories might be overlooked by larger cultural heritage institutions, community members with important town or city ties, patrons interested in digital estate planning, or teens who have online presences and an interest in gaining new technical skills. Some of these communities may lend themselves more readily than others to learning about web archiving. For example, if your library space already has teen or adult programming built around technical topics, you will have a preexisting audience. Or if your library has a digital archiving lab or digital resource center, you may be able to attract interest from users who heavily utilize that resource. However, even if the target group doesn't lend itself easily to an introduction to the topic, even one step toward the idea that their lives on the Web can be saved is a great first step in helping them understand their ability to take agency over their personal digital identities and histories.

After you have identified your target community, think through what their personal digital archiving needs may be. Do you know what their digital literacy skills are? Do you know what they are trying to achieve by saving their website? Have you thought about how you may need to translate certain concepts or technologies in order to make them accessible to the group? In this situation, sitting down for a consultation or developing a user persona will help you gain an understanding of the community's background and needs.

The more you understand, the better situated you will be to start building a service, curriculum, or event that's accessible and engaging.

Next, you'll want to start to identify the appropriate tools and gather the necessary resources or support for preserving your patrons' web presence. What is available to you within your library, and what can you provide for patrons to use? Do your patrons already have access to or use certain hardware and software? While institutions that have personal digital archiving labs or community-based resources will have a head start on developing a curriculum or advertising their web archiving help, these resources aren't a necessity. Because web archiving is largely a software-focused activity, it could be adapted to libraries that find themselves limited in resources. A class or workshop session could easily be covered in a computer lab or with a cart of laptops as long as you ensure preparation time to download all the appropriate software and test that everything functions as expected. One could even offer the service one-on-one with specific patrons, though this would require more personal comfort with the potentially different computing environments you may encounter, as well as comfort with diagnosing and troubleshooting common computer problems.

Another vital piece of the information professional's role as facilitator is the array of teachable moments that web archiving presents, which may over time deepen patrons' technical literacy. It is also a potential angle one could use to drum up interest from patrons or use to support a request for financial or technical resources. Web archiving provides a great platform for introducing potentially new concepts: how information on the Web is indexed and retrieved, what transfer protocols are, what HTML is and does, the difference between file formats, migrating your media, and more.

It can be difficult to know how to standardize a workshop curriculum or service, because all patrons will come to web archiving with different technical experience and knowledge. Practicing explaining technical concepts and building exercises in small, approachable chunks will be helpful. There will likely also be a curve in learning how to break down patrons' questions in order to identify the gaps in their understanding or the technical issues they're experiencing. Learning how to ask pointed questions in a nonjudgmental and unassuming manner will be critical in helping patrons to understand the tools and technologies of web archiving. Using web archiving as an opportunity to teach technical literacy concepts is a way to not only facilitate patrons' stewardship of their digital histories, but also aid them in engaging more critically with the technologies they use daily.

Once you understand your users and your resources, you can start to figure out how to approach the topic of web archiving. Don't be afraid to try something new, since there's no set best practice for teaching the topic to your various potential audiences. If you want to use web archiving as a bridge for teaching technical literacy skills, you could try holding a set of classes or workshops that scaffold the desired concepts and skills through web archiving projects. For example, the first class or workshop could start with a discussion on how the Internet works and how we interact with it, then move into easy ways to save single pages, build up to using a tool like Webrecorder to show saving multiple pages and media, and finally progress to using a tool like WAIL to obtain a sense of what Webrecorder was doing (all of these tools are discussed in some detail further in this chapter). You could even have people build basic websites that they could then crawl in order to fully connect the information life cycle. While this approach would need to be pared down and the personal digital archiving focus adapted to the specific skills one is hoping to convey to the users, it could be an exciting way to try engaging with these topics.

Another approach one could take is advertising the consultation services or drop-in hours at your computer labs or personal digital archiving labs. Drop-in hours could have great potential if you had the ability to be present at the lab during that time. Though advertising may be slow to arouse interest from visiting patrons, it keeps you and your service visible to the community you are striving to build a relationship with. You could also advertise your web archiving classes on your institution's website or blog, or build a LibGuide—giving the topic a permanent space gives patrons a chance to engage on their own terms while allowing you to ease into web archiving as a service.

Lastly, there is also the possibility of offering yourself as a continuing resource to the communities that could benefit the most. Is there a group of activists or artists or a community organization that you could help through a web archiving project? Of course, this approach would require investment by you and your organization to support a continued relationship and help ensure the project's sustainability over time.

Of these ideas I've presented, some would be more time-intensive than others, and the option you choose to pursue should depend on the needs of your users and the resources of your organization. Hopefully, however, these ideas will provide a starting point for ways to introduce web archiving alongside other personal digital archiving programming to your patrons.

Finally, I want to reiterate that information professionals don't need to be experts on this topic. Rather, being an enthusiastic facilitator for the user's web archiving needs is what's important: this requires a willingness to help patrons understand the importance of web archiving, wade through learning new technical skills and software, and help sort through error messages, for example. It may also mean helping patrons narrow in on what it is they want to save, while also instructing them in the responsible use of their newfound web-crawling knowledge, and emphasizing the need to be careful stewards of their saved web captures after they're finished crawling. These are only a few of the things to expect, but they are all pieces of the same puzzle of channeling needs into solutions, questions into resources, and concepts into practice. As long as you are willing to learn new things and want to help users gain the skills to take agency over their digital past, present, and future, you'll have a great time.

COMMON TERMS

To set the stage for the introduction to the tools and technologies of web archiving for personal digital archiving, let's start with the important terms to know.

To start, a web crawler needs a *seed,* or a URL, for it to crawl. A *web crawler* refers to the software used to retrieve information and content from web pages. There are a wide number of crawlers available to use, many of which will be discussed briefly later in this chapter. Crawlers range from tools built for large-scale web archiving like that done at larger institutional levels to small, easy-to-use tools packaged in an appealing graphical user interface. These tools "crawl" by following links within a website as far as the user has specified or as far as they can go, following the links to subpages and retrieving copies of the website content. This content can be static or dynamic. *Dynamic* content refers to content that is not fixed in the website's structure, but instead is requested and displayed as the user accesses the website; it can often be difficult for crawlers to capture. Adrian Brown provides four examples of this content:

Databases: The content used to create web pages is often stored in a database, such as a content management system, and is dynamically assembled into web pages.

Syndicated content: A website may include content which is drawn from external sources, such as RSS feeds and advertising pop-ups, and then is dynamically inserted into the web page.

Scripts: Scripts may be used to generate dynamic content, responding differently depending on the values of certain variables, such as the date, the type of browser making the request, or the identity of the user.

Personalization: Many websites make increasing use of personalization to deliver content which is customized to an individual user. For example, cookies may be used to store information about users and their previous visits to a website. These cookies are stored on the user's computer, and are returned by the user's browser whenever the user makes a request to that website.[9]

The opposite of dynamic content is *static* content or websites, with the best definition again coming from Brown: "the structure and textual elements will typically be contained within an HTML document, which contains hyperlinks to other elements, such as images, and to other pages. All of the elements of the website are stored in a hierarchical folder structure on the web server, and the URL of each element describes the location within that structure."[10] Another term that will be seen in tandem with crawlers is *harvesting.* This term refers to the retrieval and collection of information and content from the selected websites.

Using a crawler to archive websites is also called *client-side archiving*. The term *client side* describes the user's side of a client-server relationship. The client, or the user's computer, requests information from a server on which the web content resides, which is then provided to and displayed on the client computer. A 2013 Digital Preservation Coalition *Technology Watch Report* written by Maureen Pennock states that this is the most common type of web archiving,[11] and this is probably due to the fact that, as the National Archives points out, it "can be carried out remotely and on a large scale."[12] Crawlers can be relatively easily deployed on a user's personal hardware and do not require access or permission to the server's local content.

On the other side of the client-server relationship, there is *server-side archiving,* or "direct transfer," as Brown calls it. This type of archiving is done as it sounds, on the server side by copying the locally held files that comprise the website. This type of archiving "requires direct access to the web host server, and therefore the cooperation of the website owner,"[13] making it less readily implemented than client-side archiving. Brown states that this form of archiving is "most suited to the acquisition of static websites,"[14] since the dynamic content is difficult to capture with this form. Pennock also notes that "issues are often encountered when generating a working version of the content, particularly when absolute links have been employed, when content is database driven, or when creating a similar hosting environment to that of the original live website."[15]

Another form of web archiving is *transactional archiving*. This form of web archiving is also carried out on the server side, but is "event- rather than content-driven"[16] and captures user requests to the server and the responses from it, thus recording "the content that was presented to a user on a given date and time."[17] Transactional archiving, because it captures the user's requests, does not capture all the content of a website because "content that is never viewed will never be archived."[18] Due to the specific type of information it captures and its need to access the server, this type of web archiving may be "particularly attractive as a method for internal corporate and institutional archiving, where legal accountability or compliance is important."[19]

Domain is another term that may be encountered when working with web archiving. Domain simply refers to the address of a website. More specifically, in a web archiving collection policy sense, it is referring to the "labels" in the address:

> The rightmost label is the top-level domain, which specifies either a country code (such as "uk" for the United Kingdom) or a generic domain (such as ".com" for a commercial organization). The label to the left of this defines the second-level domain, which will generally either describe the hosting organization (e.g., "microsoft.com") or define a generic domain to qualify a

country code (e.g., ".gov.uk"). Labels to the left of this may be used to define further domain and subdomain levels.[20]

Some institutions' collection policy for their web archiving program may seek to collect all web pages under a certain domain that is in line with the archive's purpose. Examples of this may be an institution collecting all web pages under the university's domain (e.g., wisc.edu) or a national archive collecting all web pages under the country's domain (e.g., .uk, .nz, and so on).

One of the final terms that a beginning web archivist will run into is *WARC file*. The WARC file format, or ISO 28500, is the generally accepted standard format for harvested web resources. The format and contents of a WARC file are as follows:

> A WARC format file is the concatenation of one or more WARC records. A WARC record consists of a record header followed by a record content block and two newlines; the header has mandatory named fields that document the date, type, and length of the record and support the convenient retrieval of each harvested resource (file). There are eight types of WARC record: "warcinfo," "response," "resource," "request," "metadata," "revisit," "conversion," and "continuation." The content blocks in a WARC file may contain resources in any format; examples include the binary image or audiovisual files that may be embedded or linked to in HTML pages.[21]

Depending on the user's purpose in archiving a website and her personal comfort with learning new file formats, the WARC format may or may not be the ideal choice for harvesting. However, it is good to be aware of this standard because there are now many easy-to-use tools through which users can create WARC files. It is also important to note that for a user to be able to open and browse a WARC file, she will need software to do so. There are multiple options available for users to explore such as WebArchivePlayer, OpenWayback, or Pywb.[22]

HOW TO ARCHIVE A WEBSITE

There are many potential ways to go about archiving a website, especially considering the potential diversity of the users you may be working with. However, one thing you can bet on is that personal digital archiving will most likely take the form of *client-side archiving* through easy-to-use, pre-built tools or web crawling. While there are best practices to follow, the choices you and your users make depend on the situation because they all come down to the community, the need, and the available resources. This next section will attempt to provide a basis for the two key components for personal web archiving:

an introduction to best practices and an introduction to web archiving technologies.

Best Practices

When sitting down to help a patron archive a website, there are some critical questions that will help you accommodate users' needs while still identifying the best solutions for them. I'll introduce a few best practices here that I consider critical for beginners in a personal digital archiving context, and I will move through them in a way that somewhat mirrors the content life cycle.

Selection

Selection here means understanding the why, how, and purpose of the user's content selection. The foremost question is: why does the patron want to save this website? Is it the written content on the website? Is it the images and embedded media? Or is it to capture the feel of the website as it stands right now? Depending on the answer, you'll be guided to tools that show deference to specific content. On top of why, how does the patron want to interact with the saved version of the website? Is the site largely shallow and static, with little content change over time? Does the user want to be able to follow all the links? If she is interested in one page that has not changed over time and can be saved once, the tool solution may be different than the solution for something like a blog that has many pages and will continue to be updated for years.

A further question to consider here is the purpose of collection. Do the patrons just want to ensure that they have documentation of how their website has grown with them over time, potentially as something to show their kids one day? Or do they think their web content may have community or historical significance and they may want to donate it to a local archive in the future? These questions will help you consider whether to save the captured website in easy-to-use formats that benefit the patron, or whether you'll need to consider web archival standards like WARC files that would benefit future archivists and information professionals. This will also help you start thinking about a preservation plan. For a personal archive, you may be able to just focus on migrating files every few years and implement strong file-naming and folder structures. An interest in sharing in the long term for historical purposes may mean that you'll want to consider bagging the captured content to help ensure fixity of the item.

Thinking about Rights

Is this the patron's website? If that's the case, go ahead and jump in! Patrons have rights over the content on their own websites, and ideally they should only be crawling content to which they hold the rights. If the website isn't theirs, is it a family member's? Is the website owner aware of the impending archiving of the website content, and has she given explicit permission to do so? If the owner of the website doesn't want the content archived, the patron who does the archiving will incur legal risk. Jinfang Niu states that for institutions, "the decision of whether to seek permission from copyright owners depends on the legal environment of the web archive, the scale of the web archive, and the nature of archived content and the archiving organization."[23] Niu also briefly discusses the risk management realities of web archives, noting that some web archives may be covered by legal deposit, some small archives may seek permission, or some larger archives may use an opt-out method for their collections.[24] However, when dealing with personal digital archiving, even though the collecting user may never share, make public, or repurpose an archived version of a website, institutions are just better suited to dealing with risk than are individual users. So when working with patrons, you should try to instill a sense of the legal reality of web archiving in order to proactively protect your patrons as well as yourself and your institution.

Collection

When using web crawlers for collection, patrons can configure the parameters of their crawls. These choices can be explored as you become more comfortable with the tools; however, there is one practice I want to be sure to note here. Patrons should crawl "politely" and obey the robots.txt, also referred to in some literature as robots exclusion, when crawling websites. Brown explains that "web crawlers belong to a broad family of software collectively referred to as 'robots' or 'spiders.'"[25] Website owners can ask to restrict these "robots" with robots.txt. The National Digital Stewardship Alliance survey explains further that "robots.txt is a machine-readable protocol used typically by website owners to request that search engine crawlers ignore certain content so that it does not appear in search results. Robots.txt is often used to mitigate traffic overload from crawling, or for other editorial reasons."[26] Among the settings for web crawlers, ignoring robots.txt is one of the options, but it is best practice for our users to follow the protocol, and this is something we should be sure to instill when teaching or using these tools.

Quality Assurance

Once the website is harvested, the next step is to ask whether the archived version captures what the patron wanted, both in appearance and content. Does it display all of the media that the user was hoping to capture? Of all the links and subsequent pages that were important during selection, can they be accessed in the archived version or do they force you to the live version of that page within a browser? It would be beneficial here to return to the questions considered during the selection phase and carefully review how the answers compare to the archived website. As Maureen Pennock notes, quality assurance "ensures that not only have the target files been captured, but also that they render acceptably and in accordance with the preservation intent."[27] Taking the time to ensure that the archived version looks and behaves as expected is not only an important component of web archiving, but will also stress the importance of careful stewardship necessary to ensure that our archived version is useful to future users in the manner their selection criteria indicated.

Documentation

After careful selection, collection, and quality assurance, users have a final archived version that they can keep, share with future generations, or potentially pass on to archives and cultural heritage institutions. However, as all information professionals know, documentation is what provides context and makes resources useful. Just like our other collections, metadata for our web archives is critical to facilitating not only others' potential future use of the archived websites, but the ability of the user to understand their crawl years down the road. It is important to note here that some tools do incorporate varying degrees of metadata in the process, which may be helpful in ensuring that you have documented as much information as possible. However, be sure that you thoroughly understand what is and isn't being captured so that you can fill in the gaps. In general, though, I would suggest getting into the habit of documenting the process as you work through it and stressing that to the user. Making documentation part of the workflow is much easier than trying to have a user or yourself document everything retroactively. The most straightforward way to teach this, and perhaps the most effective way to do this, is to create a README file in a plain text document. Keep the document up alongside the software to log all the technical and descriptive metadata during the process. This metadata may include things like the name and a description of the tools, settings for those tools, workflows used, date and time stamps, archivist's name, purpose of the collection, the seed URL, and any selection choices made or missed content. If you're capturing the website more than once, be sure to include a list of all captures with their file names and relations to one another and all pertinent descriptive information, as well as anything else that may be pertinent to someone needing to understand the archived website.

Management, Obsolescence, and Preservation

In the preceding paragraph, I provide instructions on how to document the web archiving process in a plain text document. This act also provide a potential segue for discussing ideas of continued management, obsolescence, and preservation. Saving the documentation in a plain text, nonproprietary file format will help ensure that a future user can open the file regardless of the platforms or software on her computer. It also helps to safeguard the documentation against the potential future obsolescence of software or proprietary file formats that with their disappearance could render the file unopenable. These will be key ideas to introduce to the patron at the close of a web archiving project, when you can encourage your patrons to begin thinking about the preservation of their archived websites in an active and involved role of continued management. However, I want to give fair warning that it will likely be the least exciting portion of the process and the hardest sell to make to patrons. It may be difficult to get patrons to really commit to these practices, but if you are at the very least able to impress upon them the importance of continued stewardship of their archived website, the better you are preparing their archives to be accessible and useful for a long time to come.

Technologies

There are an abundance of tools available for web archiving that span a range of technical complexity. Rather than cover every tool in depth, this section should be thought of as providing a basis for the available technologies and a starting point for comparison when considering tools for specific projects or users. As always, the purpose of collections and the needs of the users should be considered when selecting appropriate tools. This section will start with an introduction to best practice considerations, and then move on to simple tools that are easy to implement. From there it will move into an introduction of specific web crawlers and wrap up with a brief note on other tools of which to be aware.

Starting Out Simple

Submitting a personal web page to be saved on the Internet Archive's Wayback Machine website is one low barrier to entry for web archiving. Once a URL is submitted, if that page is able to be crawled it will be available for the user to view through the Wayback Machine. It is important to note here that the Wayback Machine will only capture the single landing page from the submitted URL and will not crawl any further links, so it will not capture the full website and does not guarantee any other future captures of the page.[28] Another potential downside of this option is that the captured crawl of the page does not end up in users' physical possession on their local computer or hardware, so the care and keeping of the archived page are out of their personal control. While it seems unlikely that the Internet Archive will change or dissolve, it is important to be aware that organizations, companies, and technologies are subject to change quickly. Any potential change at the Internet Archive imposes a degree of risk for the patron's archived copy of her web page.

If the patron is interested in maintaining control over her web archive and captured crawls but would still prefer a straightforward tool, the "Save as" feature can be found on the toolbar within most browsers. This is an option that patrons may already be familiar with if they have ever used this option to save a web page to read off-line. It is also a good option for patrons who, again, are interested in saving a single web page rather than a full website, since this option will only save that single, selected page. It is most appropriate for users who are more invested in saving the content within the page rather than retaining the use and "feel" of the page. This is also an option that provides satisfaction due to the ease of capture and immediate availability of the web page.

An important note to make when deciding to use this method is that the output file formats created from the "Save as" options will vary by the browser being used. For example, as of the publication of this chapter, under the "Save as" feature in Firefox three options will be found—to save the complete page, the text files, or the HTML files only. The Google Chrome browser currently offers two options: saving the complete page, or saving the HTML files only. The Safari browser offers two options as well—to save the "Page source" (HTML) or a "Web Archive" file, a Safari-specific file format for saving web pages (though the file extension name may harken back to WARC, it is not the same file format). Due to the variety of options offered by browsers, the user may want to download the same web page through different browsers or via the separate save options and then compare the resulting off-line experience to see which option best saved the key components of the page the user was hoping to capture.

Some Internet browsers also have extensions or add-ons built by users that can be utilized to save off-line versions of web pages. These extensions come in a variety of flavors and offer to save selected web pages in a variety of file formats, from PDF to Mozilla Archive Format. Some offer a button that will be placed in your browser toolbar and will push the selected web page to archiving services like Internet Archive's Chrome extension.[29] Again, these extensions are likely most suited for capturing the content rather than the interactivity or feel of the page, and in the case of a button to push page information, they should be evaluated for what service that information is being sent to. One tool to note of the many extension options is WARCreate, a Google Chrome extension and a forebear to WAIL, a tool that will be discussed a little later in this chapter.[30] WARCreate, created by Matt Kelly, will place a button in the browser toolbar much like Internet Archive's extension, but WARCreate will save the single selected web page into a WARC file on the user's local computer.[31] Due to a step up in file format technicality and the necessity for software to replay the WARC file, this option is likely best suited for patrons with greater technical comfort or literacy.

Another tool with a low barrier to entry for many potential users is Webrecorder.io, a tool that comes from Rhizome, an organization that "commissions, exhibits, preserves, and creates critical discussion around art engaged with digital culture."[32] Webrecorder is notable for its connection to Documenting the Now, a joint project of the Maryland Institute for Technology in the Humanities, Washington University in St. Louis, and the University of California, Riverside to build a web application for social media and web archiving as well as create a platform for discussion of the ethics surrounding social media archiving.[33] Documenting the Now cites its interest in the Webrecorder tool because "unlike more traditional automated approaches to Web archiving it uses the attention of the curator to guide preservation, and the curator's browser as an intrinsic part of the process."[34] This free, elegant tool is used in a browser on the Webrecorder website to "record" a website. The user selects a website and pastes the URL into the Webrecorder front page, then selects "record." From there, users are taken to the URL and are able to click links, play streaming media, and interact with the page(s) as they so choose. Every link clicked, page visited, or media interaction is captured by Webrecorder and is saved to a collection. Users can make temporary collections for free or download their captured page(s) into a WARC file on their local computer, or they can make an account and save collections to revisit.[35]

The ease of use of this tool provides instant gratification to new users and could provide a stepping-stone for moving from saving a single page to engaging with WARC files for users. There are some notes to make about this tool, however. Webrecorder still produces WARC files for the user's local computer, which necessitates having a tool to play back the WARC files. If users do not download their WARC files, they exist on Webrecorder's platform and are subject to the life span, funding, or preservation of Rhizome. Finally, this tool only captures the links and items explored by the patron, so reviewing captured pages is important to ensure that important content was successfully saved.

The options listed above are easy-to-use, quick solutions that require little preexisting technical literacy and could be beneficial tools for introducing the concept of web archiving to patrons or users. If you are not teaching users but instead are part of an organization looking to start a web archiving program, you may also be looking for tools that have more control and are suited to larger, scalable crawls. In this case, web crawlers would be the next step. However, web crawlers can have a learning curve because their hardware or software requirements, number of configuration options, and less-friendly user interfaces can ramp up quite quickly. Many of these crawlers have wide use and sufficient documentation to help make the transition to using these tools easier. Again, there are many tools out there, but I will cover only a few here to give an idea of the landscape available.

Crawlers to Know

Perhaps the easiest crawler to begin using for new web archivists or those looking to explore this type of tool is Web Archiving Integration Layer (WAIL). As of 2017, there are two versions of WAIL available: WAIL and WAIL-Electron, both of which will be discussed below.

WAIL is a free, open source tool developed in 2013. Available for both Mac and Windows, WAIL "seeks to address the disparity between institutional and individual archiving tools by providing one-click configuration and utilization of both Heritrix and Wayback from a user's personal computer."[36] Through WAIL's simplified graphical user interface, a user can interact with the web crawler and open source Wayback Machine, a tool to view WARC files in "Basic" and "Advanced" views, which allows users to crawl at the push of a button or have access to more advanced options as they so choose.[37] This streamlines the web page retrieval and viewing process for those new to web crawlers. It should be noted, though, that the documentation for WAIL is a little sparse.

The new version, WAIL-Electron, has an attractively updated user interface, runs a newer version of Heritrix (described below), has a different playback software, and is now available on Linux systems as well. At first glance, the user interface may seem a little more complicated to use because it does away with the "Basic" and "Advanced" views of the original WAIL. However, the interface is simple, clearly labeled, and helps self-direct the user with pop-up communications. It is also more clearly documented with a wiki to help guide new users. Another important update with WAIL-Electron is the ability to save crawls in collections that help organize and describe your crawls, something that was previously unavailable with the tool. The final major update to WAIL-Electron is its ability to now archive tweets from specific Twitter users or tweets that feature specific keywords. This update would be beneficial for a user interested in exploring how to capture both the Web and social media.

Heritrix is another example of a web crawler. Created by the Internet Archive, Heritrix is free and open source. It requires a Linux distribution to run[38] and is designed for flexible, large-scale, and broader crawling.[39] Heritrix can produce both ARC and WARC files and can "be adapted to collect streamed content including YouTube videos. Heritrix can also be configured to de-duplicate data harvested in previous crawls."[40] An example of a project built using this crawler is the End of Term Archive, a partnership between the Internet Archive, the California Digital Library, the Library of Congress, the University of North Texas Libraries, and the U.S. Government Publishing office. The project, founded in 2008, harvests governmental domain websites and documents the changes in those websites during the transfer of power to a new presidential administration.[41] Organizations also frequently use this tool: in 2013 a survey by the National Digital Stewardship Alliance reported that 29 percent of institutions capturing content in-house used the Heritrix crawler.[42] Due to its advanced requirements and ability to crawl at large scale, Heritrix is likely not the first choice for a patron interested in personal digital archiving, and is better suited for organizational use.

Another tool that can be used to capture websites and requires a little more technical proficiency is HTTrack. HTTrack is a free, open source tool that calls itself an "offline browser utility"; it can download a website and "mirror" it, meaning that it will reflect the original link structure in the downloaded version. This allows the user to browse from link to link on the captured website, much like the user can do using other tools.[43] HTTrack opens captured websites in the user's browser and allows the user to update previously mirrored sites with new content.[44] Though HTTrack is an older tool, it still has an active user community and forum that could be beneficial to new users. It is also important to note that HTTrack does not output WARC files, though this may not be an issue for a personal archivist who is not concerned about using an accepted standard format. As of 2013, organizations that were collecting websites in-house were still using HTTrack.[45] However, Maureen Pennock notes that the tool "re-writes links so that they point to the local HTTrack copy of the files, rather than to the live website,"[46] consequently overwriting the file names and original information about the website. Pennock contends that this has prompted some institutions to prefer Heritrix.[47]

Two final tools to mention that can be used to crawl websites are the free, open source command line tools Wget and Wpull. These tools are similar, though the Wpull documentation notes that "Wpull is designed to be (almost) a drop-in replacement for Wget with minimal changes to options. It is designed to run on much larger crawls rather than speedily downloading a single file."[48] Because Wpull was built with larger crawls in mind and with version 1.14 of Wget,[49] both tools enable users to save their files in the WARC file format, making both Wpull and Wget potential tools for users who are interested in following accepted web archiving standards. Since these tools are used in the command line, they may not be suitable for users who are unfamiliar with using their computers and file systems in this manner. However, the tools may be appropriate for users who have programming experience, are comfortable with reading technical documentation, or enjoy more detailed and hands-on control over their crawls.

Beyond the Crawl

As noted previously, if the crawler or capturing tool that a user has selected does not have a playback feature for WARC files, a viewer or playback software will be needed. There are many options available, but there are a few to note that are used by other integrated tools or are often mentioned. These include OpenWayback from the International Internet Preservation Consortium; Pywb, a Python-based software; and WebArchivePlayer—all of which are freely available on their respective GitHub pages. Information professionals should read the accompanying documentation to decide on the most appropriate tool because the tools have varying levels of technical complexity. WebArchivePlayer has a fairly direct download and use process, while Pywb requires comfort with Python and the command line, and OpenWayback will require a Linux system and building from the source code.[50]

To round out this section, I want to be sure to briefly mention a few tools that may not be immediately pertinent to web archiving in a personal digital archiving context, but may still be of interest. For those interested in how to best store files, there is Bagger, a tool from the Library of Congress built on the BagIt specification, which is best described as "a hierarchical file packaging format for the creation of standardized digital containers called 'bags,' which are used for storing and transferring digital content."[51] The Bagger tool provides an interface for users that "allows creators and recipients of BagIt packages to verify that the files in the bag are complete and valid. This is done by creating manifests of the files that exist in the bag and their corresponding checksum values."[52] Finally, I want to note that there are also two free curation tools available for web archiving that may be of interest to organizations: Web Curator Tool and NetarchiveSuite. Subscription services such as Archive-It from the Internet Archive as well as multiple commercial solutions are also available for institutions to use for web archiving programs.

There is a bevy of tools that exist, and new projects are continually undertaken in the web archiving space, more than I could possibly cover in this chapter. I encourage you to explore all that's available to you. Be sure to think critically about how tools and resources may impact the work of web archiving in personal digital archiving spaces, but you should above all enjoy engaging with them and learn to appreciate the exciting ways that they spark creation and innovation.

CONCLUSION

How you choose to approach web archiving as a personal digital archiving resource for your patrons is up to you. As has been made clear in this chapter, there are many potential paths one could take to reach out to community members, build out programming, or undertake any other form of resource sharing.

Web archiving is currently an incredibly timely topic, so much so that we may see greater engagement with it as a potential practice for our users. In 2016 we saw the rise of discussion about the documentation of social justice and activist movements through social media; this was focused on saving content that was easily removed by users and platform owners. In the wake of the 2016 United States presidential election and continuing on after the inauguration, the End of Term Archive called for help identifying at-risk web pages. Many scientists, programmers, information professionals, and others also went to work to identify, harvest, and preserve public data sets that were disappearing as governmental websites changed with the incoming presidential administration. Though these occurrences have many implications for society as a whole and may seem far removed from personal digital archiving, they are a reminder that we too should be looking at our own web content and presences as precious personal histories to be saved.

FURTHER RESOURCES

The following list contains websites that may prove useful for information professionals who are interested in practical resources for discussing, organizing, developing, or implementing personal digital archiving programs or web archiving programs at their own libraries or other institutions. These resources are just the tip of the iceberg, but hopefully they provide a launching point for further exploration.

"Web Archiving"—International Internet Preservation Consortium. This website provides myriad resources for learning about and putting into practice web archiving, including a detailed list of tools for different portions of the web archiving life cycle. (www.netpreserve.org/web-archiving/overview)

"Web Archiving"—Library of Congress. A look at the Library of Congress Web Archives. (https://www.loc.gov/webarchiving/)

Web Archiving Roundtable—A group under the Society of American Archivists for those who may want to get further involved with discussions concerning the web archiving life cycle. (www2.archivists.org/groups/web-archiving-roundtable)

The Web Archiving Life Cycle Model, Archive-It Team. The Archive-It team at the Internet Archive developed a life cycle model from its work with member institutions which may be of interest to professionals who are interested in best practices, workflow models, or approaches at a larger institutional level. (http://ait.blog.archive.org/files/2014/04/archiveit_life_cycle_model.pdf)

NOTES

1. "Total Number of Websites—Internet Live Stats," www.internetlivestats.com/total-number-of-websites/#sources.
2. "Total Number of Websites—Internet Live Stats."
3. Brewster Kahle, "Scientific American: Article—Special Report," May 4, 1997, http://web.archive.org/web/19970504212157/www.sciam.com/0397issue/0397kahle.html as cited by Nicholas Taylor, "Average Lifespan of a Webpage," *The Signal*, November 8, 2011, http://blogs.loc.gov/thesignal/2011/11/the-average-lifespan-of-a-webpage/; and by Maureen Pennock, "Web-Archiving," Digital Preservation Coalition, 2013, http://dx.doi.org/10.7207/twr13-01,7, page 3.

4. Steve Lawrence et al., "Persistence of Web References in Scientific Research," *Computer* 34, no. 2 (2001): 26–31, as cited by Nicholas Taylor, "Average Lifespan of a Webpage," and Maureen Pennock, "Web-Archiving," 3.

5. Rick Weiss, "On the Web, Research Work Proves Ephemeral," *Washington Post,* November 24, 2003, https://www.washingtonpost.com/archive/politics/ 2003/11/24/on-the-web-research-work-proves-ephemeral/959c882f-9ad0–4b36 –88cd-fb7411db118d/?utm_term=.51601ac4e2ce, as cited by Nicholas Taylor, "Average Lifespan of a Webpage," and Maureen Pennock, "Web-Archiving," 3.

6. See Jonathan L. Zittrain, Kendra Albert, and Lawrence Lessig, "Perma: Scoping and Addressing the Problem of Link and Reference Rot in Legal Citations," SSRN Scholarly Paper (Rochester, NY: Social Science Research Network, October 1, 2013), https://papers.ssrn.com/abstract=2329161.

7. Taylor, "Average Lifespan of a Webpage."

8. New York Art Resources Consortium, "Web Archiving," www.nyarc.org/content/ web-archiving.

9. Adrian Brown, *Archiving Websites: A Practical Guide for Information Management Professionals* (London: Facet, 2006), 45.

10. Brown, *Archiving Websites,* 44.

11. Pennock, "Web-Archiving," 7.

12. National Archives, "Web Archiving Guidance" (Crown, 2011), https:// nationalarchives.gov.uk/documents/information-management/web-archiving -guidance.pdf, 5.

13. Brown, *Archiving Websites,* 46.

14. Brown, *Archiving Websites,* 46.

15. Pennock, "Web-Archiving," 7.

16. Brown, *Archiving Websites,* 61.

17. Pennock, "Web-Archiving," 7.

18. National Archives, "Web Archiving Guidance," 15.

19. Ibid.

20. Brown, *Archiving Websites,* 36.

21. "WARC, Web ARChive File Format," August 31, 2009, www.digitalpreservation .gov/formats/fdd/fdd000236.shtml.

22. For a great explanation of the WARC file format, see Nicholas Taylor, "Anatomy of a Web Archive | *The Signal,*" web page (November 5, 2013), //blogs.loc.gov/ thesignal/2013/11/anatomy-of-a-web-archive/.

23. Jinfang Niu, "An Overview of Web Archiving," *D-Lib Magazine* 18, no. 3/4 (March 2012), doi: 10.1045/march2012-niu1.

24. Niu, "An Overview of Web Archiving."

25. Brown, *Archiving Websites,* 50.

26. Jefferson Bailey et al., "Web Archiving in the United States: A 2013 Survey," National Digital Stewardship Alliance, September 2014, http://hdl.loc.gov/loc .gdc/lcpub.2013655118.1, page 14.

27. Pennock, "Web-Archiving," 12.

28. Internet Archive, https://archive.org/about/faqs.php#The_Wayback_Machine.

29. Alexis Rossi, "If You See Something, Save Something—6 Ways to Save Pages in the Wayback Machine | Internet Archive Blogs," January 25, 2017, http://blog .archive.org/2017/01/25/see-something-save-something/.

30. Mat Kelly, WARCreate, version 0.2016.12.15 build 1720, 2016, http://warcreate .com.

31. Kelly, WARCreate, http://warcreate.com.

32. "Rhizome," Rhizome, http://rhizome.org/.

33. Ed Summers, "Introducing Documenting the Now," Maryland Institute for Technology in the Humanities, February 16, 2016, http://mith.umd.edu/ introducing-documenting-the-now/.

34. Summers, "Introducing Documenting the Now."

35. Dragan Espenschied, "Introduction to Webrecorder," https://www.youtube.com/ watch?time_continue=466&v=n3SqusABXEk.

36. John Berlin, "Electric WAILs and Ham," Web Science and Digital Libraries Research Group, February 13, 2017, http://ws-dl.blogspot.com/2017/02/ 2017–02–13-electric-wails-and-ham.html.

37. "Web Archiving Integration Layer," http://machawk1.github.io/wail/.

38. Hunter Stern, "System Requirements," Heritrix 3.0 and 3.1 User Guide, June 23, 2011, https://webarchive.jira.com/wiki/display/Heritrix/ System+Requirements.

39. Gordon Mohr et al., "An Introduction to Heritrix: An Open Source Archival Quality Web Crawler," International Web Archiving Workshop, 2004.

40. Pennock, "Web-Archiving," 22.

41. "Project Background," End of Term Archive, http://eotarchive.cdlib.org/ background.html.

42. Bailey et al., "Web Archiving in the United States: A 2013 Survey," 18.

43. Xavier Roche et al., "Overview," HTTrack, 2007, https://www.httrack.com/html/ overview.html.

44. HTTtrack, https://www.httrack.com.

45. Bailey et al., "Web Archiving in the United States: A 2013 Survey," 18.

46. Pennock, "Web-Archiving," 22.

47. Pennock, "Web-Archiving," 22.

48. Christopher Foo et al., "Wpull," version 2.0.1, n.d., https://wpull.readthedocs.io/ en/master/intro.html.

49. Pennock, "Web-Archiving," 23.

50. "How to Install," OpenWayback, n.d., https://github.com/iipc/openwayback/wiki/ How-to-install.

51. "The BagIt Library," Digital Curation Centre, n.d., www.dcc.ac.uk/resources/ external/bagit-library.

52. John Scancella, "Bagger's Enhancements for Digital Accessions | The Signal," web page (April 26, 2016), //blogs.loc.gov/thesignal/2016/04/ baggers-enhancements-for-digital-accessions/.

BIBLIOGRAPHY

"The BagIt Library." Digital Curation Centre, n.d. www.dcc.ac.uk/resources/external/bagit -library.

Bailey, Jefferson, et al. "Web Archiving in the United States: A 2013 Survey." National Digital Stewardship Alliance. September 2014. http://hdl.loc.gov/loc.gdc/ lcpub.2013655118.1.

Berlin, John. "Electric WAILs and Ham." Web Science and Digital Libraries Research Group. February 13, 2017. http://ws-dl.blogspot.com/2017/02/2017–02–13 -electric-wails-and-ham.html.

Brown, Adrian. *Archiving Websites: A Practical Guide for Information Management Professionals.* London: Facet, 2006.

"End of Term 2016." End of Term Archive. http://eotarchive.cdlib.org/2016.html.

Espenschied, Dragan. "Introduction to Webrecorder." https://www.youtube.com/ watch?time_continue=466&v=n3SqusABXEk.

Foo, Christopher, et al. "Wpull," version 2.0.1. https://wpull.readthedocs.io/en/master/ intro.html.

"How to Install." OpenWayback, n.d., https://github.com/iipc/openwayback/wiki/How -to-install.

Kahle, Brewster. "Scientific American: Article—Special Report." May 4, 1997. http://web .archive.org/web/19970504212157/www.sciam.com/0397issue/0397kahle.html as cited by Nicholas Taylor, "Average Lifespan of a Webpage," and Maureen Pennock, "Web-Archiving," 3.

Kelly, Mat. WAIL. "Web Archiving Integration Layer," MacOS X, version 0.2016.07.09, Windows 7+, version 0.2013.2.19. http://machawk1.github.io/wail/.

———. WARCreate, version 0.2016.12.15 build 1720, 2016. http://warcreate.com.

Lawrence, Steve, et al. "Persistence of Web References in Scientific Research." *Computer* 34, no. 2 (2001): 26–31, as cited by Nicholas Taylor, "Average Lifespan of a Webpage," and Maureen Pennock, "Web-Archiving," 3.

Library of Congress. "WARC, Web ARChive File Format." Web page, August 31, 2009. www.digitalpreservation.gov/formats/fdd/fdd000236.shtml.

McCain, Edward. "2016 Ndsa Web Archiving Survey Report Highlights." DLF Forum, Milwaukee, WI, November 10, 2016. https://osf.io/gh2ve/.

Mohr, Gordon, et al. "An Introduction to Heritrix: An Open Source Archival Quality Web Crawler," International Web Archiving Workshop. 2004.

The National Archives. "Web Archiving Guidance." Crown, 2011. https://nationalarchives .gov.uk/documents/information-management/web-archiving-guidance.pdf.

New York Art Resources Consortium. "Web Archiving." www.nyarc.org/content/ web-archiving.

Niu, Jinfang. "An Overview of Web Archiving." *D-Lib Magazine* 18, no. 3/4 (March 2012). doi: 10.1045/march2012-niu1.

Pennock, Maureen. "Web-Archiving." Digital Preservation Coalition, 2013. http://dx.doi .org/10.7207/twr13–01.

"Project Background." End of Term Archive. http://eotarchive.cdlib.org/background.html.

"Rhizome." Rhizome. http://rhizome.org/.

Roche, Xavier, et al. HTTrack, version Version 3.48–22 (04/26/2016), n.d. https://www
.httrack.com.

———. "Overview." HTTrack. 2007. https://www.httrack.com/html/overview.html.

Rossi, Alexis. "If You See Something, Save Something—6 Ways to Save Pages in the
Wayback Machine | Internet Archive Blogs." January 25, 2017. http://blog.archive
.org/2017/01/25/see-something-save-something/.

Scancella, John. "Bagger's Enhancements for Digital Accessions | *The Signal*." Web page.
April 26, 2016. //blogs.loc.gov/thesignal/2016/04/baggers-enhancements-for
-digital-accessions/.

Stern, Hunter. "System Requirements." In Heritrix 3.0 and 3.1 User Guide. June 23, 2011.
https://webarchive.jira.com/wiki/display/Heritrix/System+Requirements.

Summers, Ed. "Introducing Documenting the Now." Maryland Institute for Technology in
the Humanities. February 16, 2016. http://mith.umd.edu/introducing-documenting
-the-now/.

Taylor, Nicholas. "Anatomy of a Web Archive | *The Signal*." Web page. November 5, 2013.
//blogs.loc.gov/thesignal/2013/11/anatomy-of-a-web-archive/.

———. "Average Lifespan of a Webpage." *The Signal*. November 8, 2011. http://blogs.loc
.gov/thesignal/2011/11/the-average-lifespan-of-a-webpage/.

"Total Number of Websites—Internet Live Stats." www.internetlivestats.com/total
-number-of-websites/#sources.

Weiss, Rick. "On the Web, Research Work Proves Ephemeral." *Washington Post*. November
24, 2003. https://www.washingtonpost.com/archive/politics/2003/11/24/on
-the-web-research-work-proves-ephemeral/959c882f-9ad0–4b36–88cd
-fb7411db118d/?utm_term=.51601ac4e2ce, as cited by Nicholas Taylor, "Average
Lifespan of a Webpage," and Maureen Pennock, "Web-Archiving," 3.

Zittrain, Jonathan L., Kendra Albert, and Lawrence Lessig. "Perma: Scoping and
Addressing the Problem of Link and Reference Rot in Legal Citations." SSRN
Scholarly Paper. Rochester, NY: Social Science Research Network, October 1, 2013.
https://papers.ssrn.com/abstract=2329161.

YVONNE NG

4
Archiving Audiovisual Materials

DUE TO ITS TECHNOLOGICAL COMPLEXITY, the diversity of formats over time, and a short list of user-friendly archiving tools, video can be a challenging medium to preserve. In many instances, individuals with audiovisual collections will not know where to start, and may find the archiving process too cost-prohibitive to do on their own. However, with shared information and resources, audiovisual archiving and preservation becomes much easier and less intimidating.

Librarians and libraries are well-placed to provide the kind of support that is needed to help individuals and communities digitize, manage, and preserve their personal video collections. This support could take many forms, both informational and material, including workshops, guides and toolkits, community archiving events, access to digitization equipment and assistance, and digital tools and storage.

This chapter seeks to provide librarians and information professionals with an introduction to digital audiovisual media and approaches to archiving it. It cites current professional standards as a point of reference, but discusses how these standards may be modified to fit a personal archiving context realistically. Finally, it suggests various ways that librarians and information professionals might help fill existing gaps in knowledge, skills, and resources to best support their communities.

ROLE OF THE INFORMATION PROFESSIONAL

People interested in and motivated to preserve their videos will vary in their needs and level of experience working with the media. Some will be professional or semiprofessional video makers with sizable collections, while others may not be video creators themselves, but have a few recordings of high value that they want to save. An individual who finds a few videotapes from her childhood in the attic may just want help, for example, making high-quality digital masters to put on a hard drive. Meanwhile, an activist recording oral histories and documenting her community may have a strong interest in learning how to preserve current born-digital formats, but less interest in digitizing old videotapes. Alternately, an established artist or filmmaker with years of raw footage, elements, and masters may have a solid technical grounding in the medium, but be more concerned about how to organize and identify pieces of a vast collection in a sensible way.

There are many possible approaches to video archiving, and each librarian or library will need to identify the specific needs of the communities they are trying to serve and meet them accordingly. What is important to remember in a personal digital archiving context is that individuals and communities will most likely need to preserve their content themselves long after the information professionals are gone, so the approaches need to result in content and methods that are easily sustainable and that people are motivated to maintain.

As an example, the current professional specifications for preserving analog videotape call for a 10-bit uncompressed digital preservation master. These files are large (approximately 102GB/hour) and will not play well on everyone's video players. A library providing community-based digitization services would need to consider its users, and whether they are likely to be motivated and able to keep masters like this, or whether a friendlier-access copy is more likely to be appreciated and cared for over time. Alternately or additionally, the library may also find ways to make sustaining the large master files easier for users, for example by providing free managed storage.

VIDEO ARCHIVING CHALLENGES

While some of the challenges of digital audiovisual archiving are common to other kinds of personal digital archiving, there are a few factors that make video especially vexing.

Proprietary formats. There are dozens of digital video formats, and many of the popular ones are proprietary, meaning their documentation is not publicly available or that they require specific hardware to play or license to decode. This increases the likelihood that they will become obsolete and that the media on them will become difficult to access. Unfortunately, the open formats that are used in institutional and professional preservation contexts are not particularly marketed and promoted by the video industry, and so are not commonly encountered by ordinary people.

Readability. Because of format issues, but also because it is a time-based audiovisual medium, video is less transparent than other media. That is, it is harder to read and analyze the content of a video than text or still images. A video cannot be easily parsed or viewed as a whole in an instant, so creating descriptive metadata for it is time-consuming and labor-intensive.

Evolving standards and practices. Professional audiovisual archiving standards and practices are still relatively new, so there are not always ready answers that can be passed down to the personal archiving realm. Where approaches and tools do exist, they often lack user-friendliness for nonspecialist audiences.

File size. As an information-rich medium, video requires a lot of bits to represent. This means larger file sizes and greater demands on storage and bandwidth than other media like text or still images.

Lack of accessible and reliable information. There are some, but not many freely available resources about audiovisual preservation aimed at nonprofessional archivists. What one finds from a quick Google search comes from websites offering the conversion of home movies to DVDs or streaming video files. While many customers are probably happy with these services, the information about the digitization process and digital audiovisual files on these websites can be imprecise, obfuscating, or inaccurate.

COMMON TERMS

Before discussing best practices and tools, this section outlines some basics of digital video. While it is not possible to explore these topics in depth in this chapter, these fundamentals can at least aid in comprehending the specifications cited in standards or in other descriptions, and help in the application of best practices. This is especially useful when working in personal digital archiving contexts, when modifications to standards and best practices may be called for, or when choices need to be made between tools.

Let's look at an example of specifications for digitizing analog video in a professional or institutional preservation setting to see some of the properties that are most often used to describe the technical aspects of video:[1]

File Wrapper: .mov

Video Stream: Uncompressed, 10-bit 4:2:2 YUV

Audio Stream: 48Khz/24-bit PCM

Master files should retain the source formatting, including interlacing, frame rate, aspect ratio, audio levels, and recording standard (NTSC, PAL, SECAM)

File wrapper: When talking about video "format," people often get confused between the *wrapper or container format* versus the *encoding.* Multimedia wrappers include formats like Quicktime (.mov), Audio Video Interleave (.avi), MPEG-4 Part 14 (.mp4), and Matroska (.mkv). Wrappers hold the multiple bitstreams that make up a video, such as video, audio, and subtitles. These bitstreams can be encoded and compressed in different ways, so the container format in itself does not always tell one much about the video quality or usage (although some containers specify certain encodings).

Video stream encoding: The way a video stream is encoded is called a codec (a portmanteau for *compress/decompress* or *code/decode*). Some common video codecs include H.264 (also known as MPEG-4 AVC, used for streaming video), Apple ProRes (used in video editing), and MPEG-2 Part 2 (also known as H.262, used for DVD video). When working with video, it is important to be aware of how it is encoded. Changing a video's encoding can affect its quality as well as its functionality. However, it may be necessary to reformat or re-encode a video for preservation purposes—for example, if the original format becomes obsolete. V210 is the uncompressed 10-bit 4:2:2 YUV (these terms are explained further below) encoding used often in professional or institutional settings for analog video digitization. It is a preferred encoding because it is of high quality, accommodates a range of video properties, and is well documented, widely adopted, and relatively transparent.

Chroma subsampling: The ratio at which brightness (called "luma" or indicated by the letter "Y") is digitally sampled versus two measurements of blue and red color (called "chroma," or indicated by the letters "U" or "Cb" and "V" or "Cr") in a video. Common color sampling ratios are 4:2:2, 4:1:1, and 4:2:0. The first digit is almost always a "4," which represents the luma. So 4:2:2 chroma subsampling means that for every 4 luma samples, 2 blue samples and 2 red samples are taken. (Since the human eye notices brightness much more than color, not much is lost by sampling color at half the frequency as brightness.)

Without going into more detail, the main point to note is that different codecs have different chroma subsampling (sometimes it is stated in the name, like ProRes 422). Re-encoding a video with one chroma subsampling scheme to another involves re-sampling and can affect visual quality.

Video bit depth: The number of bits used to store each luma/chroma sample's information. The more bits in a sample, the more precise the information, and the more variation in brightness and color is possible. If a sample is only

1 bit deep, for example, it can only have values of 1 or 0 (i.e., black or white). A sample that is 2 bits deep can have values of 00, 01, 10, and 11 (i.e., four colors), and so on. Most digital video will use at least 8 bits per channel (i.e., per Y, Cb, and Cr). As mentioned above, the standard for preservation-quality analog video digitization is 10 bits per channel.

Audio sampling rate: The number of digital audio samples that are taken per second, measured in kilohertz (kHz). 48 kHz is the audio sampling rate used in almost all professional and consumer video formats and equipment. For preservation digitization, sampling rates of 48 kHz or 96 kHz are generally used.

Audio bit depth: Similar to video bit depth, audio bit depth is the number of bits in each audio sample. The higher the bit depth, the more precise the sample can be. Bit depth only applies to pulse-code modulated (PCM) audio, which is the standard way of representing audio waveforms digitally. Many digital video formats use 16-bit or 20-bit audio. For preservation digitization, 24-bit audio is generally used.

Interlaced or progressive scanning: Video frames are either *interlaced* or *progressive*, often just referred to by their initials "i" and "p." Interlaced scanning is an older system used in analog videos and early digital videos. An interlaced frame is made up of two alternating *fields*, which each only show every other horizontal line of the image. The two fields' purpose was to enable the frame rate to be doubled—thus improving the appearance of motion—without increasing the bandwidth required to transmit it. Newer formats and displays all use progressive scan, in which each frame contains all of the horizontal lines.

For preservation, the original scan mode should be maintained. For presentation, however, interlaced video may appear to have jagged edges when played on computer monitors, which are all progressive and are not designed to play interlaced materials. It is useful to *deinterlace* access copies in order to display them properly on modern screens.

Frame rate: The number of frames per second that make up the video. "Frames per second" is usually written as "fps." The number of frames per second greatly affects how a video looks—compare, for example, the "filmlike" motion-blur appearance of video at 24 fps, and the hyperreal "choppy" look of video at 60 fps. Changing the original frame rate of a video requires deleting or synthesizing new frames, and should be avoided for preservation.

Display aspect ratio (DAR): The ratio of the visual image's width to its height when displayed on a screen. Common display aspect ratios are 4:3 (older, SD television) and 16:9 (wide-screen SD and HD television). The display aspect ratio is determined by *frame size* dimensions and *pixel aspect ratio*.

Frame size: The width and height of the video image, measured in pixels. The frame size of miniDV video, for example, is 720 × 480 pixels. This is considered SD, or standard definition. HD, or high definition, is usually defined as having frame heights of 720 pixels and higher (e.g., 1280 × 720 and 1920 × 1080). While it is possible to "upconvert" or scale an SD video to HD, say, for production purposes, this should not be done for preservation. Scaling an SD video to HD just adds pixels that did not originally exist in the recording; it does not improve the quality of the image and can introduce artifacts.

Pixel aspect ratio (PAR): The ratio of an individual pixel's width to its height. This can vary by format and settings. The relevant point to note here is that digital imaging and newer digital formats typically use square pixels, while older video formats typically use non-square rectangular pixels. This is why older videos shown on newer displays, or stills from older videos exported to imaging software, can appear stretched or squished. It is necessary to correct any software misinterpretations of the pixel aspect ratio when working with older video formats.

Recording standard: The standardized specification for frame size, frame rate, and color that a video adheres to, such as NTSC, PAL, and SECAM. These recording standards date back to analog television and are less relevant to current digital video, which can vary in specifications. For preservation, it is important to maintain the original recording standard. Changing the recording standard can affect image quality and introduce artifacts.

HOW TO ARCHIVE ANALOG VIDEO

Digitization is considered the only way to preserve content captured on analog videotape, since videotape formats themselves are all obsolete now. Many audiovisual archivists have rung the alarm on what they call a "magnetic media crisis," estimating that we have only 10–15 years until tape degradation and the lack of usable equipment make the video digitization of analog videotape impossible, or at least too expensive to realistically entertain.

The preceding section cited the digitization specifications used in a professional or institutional archive setting as an example. However, as mentioned, it is not always possible (or even desirable) to follow a standard like this in a personal digital archiving context. Given the shortage of time remaining to preserve the content held on videotape, it is more important that it gets transferred *at all.* The goal should be to create a usable and sustainable digital surrogate that preserves as many of the qualities of the original (see properties in the section above) as possible, given the resources at one's disposal.

Digitization Equipment

Digitization involves specialized equipment and software. While individuals can acquire components themselves or pay a vendor to do the digitization, there is also an opportunity for libraries and other organizations to collaborate and help people with this process (as the case studies in this book demonstrate).

Setting up a digitization station requires some planning, and usually some troubleshooting along the way. It is important to understand who the users of the digitization station will be, and what their needs are in terms of format and specifications. It is also important to plan to make sure that different components of the digitization station will work together, and that there is a sensible signal path.

At a minimum, a digitization station must include:

- A playback deck (or camera) for each videotape format to be digitized
- An analog-to-digital converter or capture card
- A computer with capture software
- Sufficient internal hard-drive storage for the captured media (capturing to an external drive may cause sync errors)
- Cables that meet the input/output requirements of all of the equipment in the setup

Playback decks range widely from consumer to professional decks and will vary in quality, durability, recording mode support, and number and types of inputs/outputs. Analog-to-digital converters also vary widely in quality and cost, depending on what digital formats/specifications they support and their inputs/outputs. Some consumer playback decks may even come with their own built-in analog-to-digital converter. Some analog-to-digital converters come with capture software, while some people can use the capture functionality in their video-editing software.

Beyond the minimum setup, the following components are usually included in professional digitization workflows:

- Time base corrector (TBC) to stabilize the signal from the playback deck and to allow the adjustment of luminance and chrominance
- CRT monitor to monitor the video pre-digitization
- Waveform monitor and vectorscope for measuring luminance and chrominance
- Black Burst sync generator to synchronize the equipment in the workflow
- Machines using higher-end inputs/outputs (e.g., BNC, SDI, balanced audio)

It is possible to digitize videotape without a TBC, monitors, sync generator, and higher-end connectors, but it is likely that there will be errors and distortions in the analog video signal that will be captured in the digitized copy.

Depending on how closely the digitizer wants to adhere to professional preservation workflows and how many formats the digitization station needs to support, it can be a complicated undertaking to build a smoothly functioning station. You should also be aware that the playback equipment will inevitably be older and used, and may require maintenance; there is an ever-shrinking pool of experts who are able to fix analog video equipment.

Digitization Workflow

Assuming one has access to the appropriate functioning digitization equipment, the steps to digitization can be summarized as follows:

Pre-playback inspection: Inspect the tape and tape case for physical damage, biological contamination, and chemical deterioration. If the tape or case is broken, is covered in either powdery or thread-like growths, smells waxy or like dirty socks, has flaky bits of oxide coming off, or is badly warped, it should not be put in a machine. Badly damaged or deteriorated videotape should be digitized by a vendor that specializes in this work. Activate the record safety (either by removing the plastic tab/button or moving the slider to "save") before loading the tape in a playback deck.

Pre-transfer preparation: If possible, calibrate any monitors using standard SMPTE color bars. If necessary, clean the heads on the playback deck with tape-cleaning swabs and 99 percent isopropyl alcohol (take care to avoid rubber parts). Deck cleaning is especially necessary after playing back a deteriorated tape. With a clean deck, insert the tape, fast-forward all the way to the end, and then rewind to the beginning to ensure smooth playback.

Before capture, play the tape and make any necessary adjustments to the luminance and chrominance using the time base corrector. Along with a CRT monitor, a waveform monitor/vectorscope is helpful for objectively seeing whether the brightness is within proper limits, and if the color saturation and hue are accurate. If the tape has color bars, this can be used as a basis for making adjustments; otherwise, it may be necessary to find parts of the recording that contain whites, blacks, and skin tone (any color skin) and adjust on the basis of those.

Finally, set up or check the settings on the capture software to ensure proper specifications and capture destination. Ensure that there is sufficient storage capacity for the file that will be created.

Monitoring digitization: Ideally, someone should be monitoring the digitization as it takes place. On a practical level, this ensures a proper transfer and protects the tape against damage. At the same time, in a personal archiving context, it can be a wonderful opportunity for an individual to view the contents of her videotape, often for the first time in years, while also witnessing the digitization process.

During a transfer, many types of audiovisual errors can occur. While some cannot be fixed, some can be addressed easily and the tape recaptured. BAVC's AV Artifact Atlas[2] is an excellent resource for diagnosing audiovisual errors.

Quality assurance: After the transfer is complete, it is essential to check the digital file for completeness and quality. A simple method is to play a few minutes from the beginning, middle, and end of the recording. Pay attention to the aspect ratio, audio, brightness/image details, and color, and check for dropout or other artifacts.

HOW TO ARCHIVE DIGITAL VIDEO

Capturing Digital Media from Physical Carriers

Though distinct from digitization, which is the conversion of analog video to digital video, born-digital video also sometimes needs to be captured off of obsolete or unstable physical carriers. For example, MiniDV is a fragile and obsolete digital tape format, and DVD is a fragile and increasingly obsolete digital optical disk format.

Now-obsolete digital videotape formats commonly used in a personal context include miniDV, DVCPro, HDV, and Digita18. The process for capturing these formats in the "DV" family is similar to the analog digitization process in that real-time playback is required, but the process is simpler because no analog adjustments to the signal are necessary.

Playback decks (or cameras) for miniDV, DVCPro, HDV, and Digita18 have FireWire (aka DV) outputs that connect directly to a computer. Unfortunately, FireWire is an obsolete interface, so it is necessary to use older computers that have these ports; for computers with Thunderbolt ports, FireWire-to-Thunderbolt adapters are available.

To capture the streams from the tape, some kind of capture software is needed. MiniDV, DVCPro, and Digita18 videos are encoded with the DV codec, while HDV is encoded as MPEG-2 Part 2 (H.262). Many people use the capture functionality in editing software, like Premiere Pro and Final Cut Pro 7 and older. This is a good option, since many who work with video already have it installed on their computers. For those who do not have editing software, there is also software specifically for capturing DV formats called LiveCapturePlus, which is available for around $100. It is only officially supported up to OS 10.6 and Windows 7, but may work on later operating systems. Dvgrab[3] is a free capture tool that only runs on Linux. It has not been actively maintained in many years, but is purported to still work.

Meanwhile, there are two approaches to capturing DVD-Video (i.e., the kind of DVDs that can play on traditional DVD players, rather than DVD-Rs that can be used as a generic computer storage medium for any kind of file). DVD-Video uses a Universal Disk Format file system with a standardized directory and file structure: a VIDEO_TS folder that contains MPEG-2 video streams (inside .VOB wrappers) and metadata files (.IFO and .BUP).

Individuals can either create a disk image, or just copy the contained folder and files. A disk image is a complete copy of the disk, including its files and structure, and can be mounted and played like an authored DVD on a computer. Disk imaging can be done with many tools like DVD Decrypter (Windows),[4] ISO Buster (Windows),[5] and Disk Utility (Mac). Disk imaging is considered a preservation standard since it is a faithful and complete reproduction of the disk. With a disk image, however, it is not as easy to access the individual files on the disk. In cases where the access to the files is more valuable than the preservation of the disk as a disk, copying the files and folders might be a preferable method. This can be done in the Explorer/Finder or with a tool like Duke University's Data Accessioner,[6] which can also export valuable preservation metadata.

A complication with some DVDs is digital rights management systems such as Content Scramble System, which is used to protect commercial DVDs from copying. In a personal digital archiving context, however, this will likely be less of an issue. Individuals should be discouraged from copying copyrighted commercial materials, not only for legal reasons, but also because that content is likely available elsewhere.

Importing from Phones, Camcorders, SD Cards, and Other Physical Devices

Audiovisual media recorded on mobile phones, camcorders, and SD cards are digital files that can be simply imported, or copied, from the device/card to more permanent storage. The most straightforward way is to just copy and paste, or drag files over in Finder or Explorer. Individuals can also offload files to online platforms like Google Photos or use applications like Apple Photos. When using platforms or applications, it is advisable to import the original files and not transform them during import. Google Photos, for example, asks users to choose between "original" and "high-quality" imports. Be aware that choosing anything other than the original involves transcoding or recompression, and will likely result in a loss of audiovisual quality and metadata.

Organizing Digital Video Files

Some people will prefer the ease of using media platforms and applications like Apple Photos, which allow them to import, organize, edit, and share photos and videos all within the platform/application. These tools provide intuitive and visual interfaces for sorting, searching, and viewing media. All of the organization of the files in storage is done automatically by the application, and is hidden from the user. The user does not need to worry about naming files or putting them into directories, or in some cases, even storage backup.

Other people, especially those who use video for production more professionally or semiprofessionally, will want to be able to organize and manage their files more directly. There are many different ways to effectively organize one's media, and the best way will depend on the individual user and her needs. Each situation is different, and librarians can work with individuals to identify and develop appraisal and organizing strategies that work best for them. The following are some general guidelines.

"Packaging" files: This concept borrows from the Open Archival Information System (OAIS) Reference Model[7] idea of the Archival Information Package (AIP) and is useful for organizing larger video collections. A "package" can be considered the basic unit of a collection. It is essentially a file directory that contains video files that belong together, and possibly metadata about those video files and package information. For example, an hour-long family history interview might be made up of multiple video files, created each time the camera was stopped and started. If a DSLR camera was used, there might also be audio files that were recorded separately. Additionally, the filmer may have transcribed the interview and noted other important metadata, like the family member's name and the date in a text document. All of this media could be placed in a computer folder, or "package." The package could also include information about the package itself, such as a list of files (like a packing list). Exactly,[8] built on the Library of Congress Bag It protocol,[9] is a tool that can help people make their own self-describing packages.

It is important to note that some native camera formats, like AVCHD or XDCAM, have their own file/folder structure. To maintain the usability of these formats, the original structure and file names should be maintained within the package.

Organizing packages into other directories: Once packaged, the AIPs can be organized into directories according to the needs and workflows of the individual. A video editor, for example, may want to organize her packages into directories by project. A video blogger may wish to organize his packages into directories by date.

Naming files and packages: When creating folders/packages and new files, individuals will need to assign file/folder names. File names should generally be kept short: use only alphanumeric characters or underscores or hyphens, and avoid spaces. Individuals should devise a system for naming their files that enables them to uniquely identify the files in their collection, and they should use that system consistently. For example, a file name might include a title, date, and generation/version:

Video-PDA_20170306_Master.mov

Video-PDA_20160306_YouTube.mov

A package or folder name might include an ID, title, or date:

001_YvonneInterview_20170306

Regarding raw footage from cameras, there is not a consensus about whether files need to be, or should be, renamed with more meaningful names. In situations where an individual creates and works with many video files, it is arguably best to leave file names assigned by the camera alone. Camera-assigned file names help keep raw footage in the correct original order—this is valuable in situations when a single filming event may yield dozens of individual files. Keeping camera file names is also less work (since if one is going to rename files, one should be consistent and rename all the files), and mitigates against user-created file names that are too long or that use reserved characters. In a production context, avoiding renaming files as a general practice ensures that raw media does not become disconnected from projects.

Storing Video Files

Other than file size, the storage of video files does not differ much from other kinds of digital media. Video files do tend to be much larger than other types of media, however, so storage capacity (and cost) are a consideration. As these examples demonstrate, file sizes will vary widely according to the encoding and specifications of the video:

- Typical 720p H.264/MP4 YouTube upload: ~2.2 GB/hour
- MiniDV captured from tape: ~12 GB/hour
- Typical 1080p ProRes 422 video: ~53 GB/hour

Portable hard drives and networked attached storage devices are the most common storage media for video. Some small organizations also use LTO data tape for backup. Because of file size, cloud storage may not always be viable for individuals with higher-quality video or larger collections. However, this may change in the future as storage costs continue to drop.

As with all digital files, it is ideal to have two backups—one local, and if possible, one off-site. At minimum, a local backup is highly recommended. Off-site backup can be more challenging, but some realistic options include dropping off a drive at a relative's house or at one's self-storage space, or uploading to a cloud account.

Providing Access to Video

There are many ways that individuals can make their videos accessible to friends, family, or the public. Virtually every social media platform supports video uploads. Individuals can also build their own websites or blogs to feature their videos.

While an individual should archive the full or highest-quality copies of their videos, these formats are not always ideal for uploading or sharing. Some file formats are not supported on certain platforms, and large files can be difficult to transmit electronically. Individuals may need to transcode their videos to other formats and encodings, or compress them to make the file sizes smaller. Some free and useful tools for transcoding include Handbrake,[10] FFmpeg[11] (command line interface), MPEG Streamclip,[12] and VLC.[13]

The specifications that the individual should follow will depend on the needs of the user or platform. Some of the tools mentioned above include common presets, which can make the choices easier. Platforms may also provide guidelines on ideal settings.

CONCLUSION

Libraries and librarians are in unique positions to support individuals, families, and communities to archive and preserve their personal audiovisual collections. While individual needs and interests will differ, as a medium video presents some challenges common to all. By helping to develop new solutions for archiving video in personal contexts, and sharing their knowledge, skills, and resources with the public, libraries and librarians can make a seemingly daunting undertaking achievable.

FURTHER RESOURCES

Ashley Blewer, *Minimum Viable Station Documentation,* http://ablwr.github .io/blog/2016/12/02/minimum-viable-transfer-station-documentation/.

> A blog post and ongoing collaborative Google Doc created by the developer/archivist Ashley Blewer to provide concrete recommendations for setting up a viable audiovisual digitization station.

Bay Area Video Coalition, AV Compass, www.avcompass.bavc.org/.

> An accessible (and humorous) online resource with videos, written guides, and an inventory tool for organizing, preserving, viewing, and appreciating personal audiovisual collections.

Kara Van Malssen, *"Digital Video Preservation and Oral History," Oral History in the Digital Age,* http://ohda.matrix.msu.edu/2012/06/digital-video -preservation-and-oral-history/.

> A practical primer on preserving oral history video recordings, aimed at record creators.

WITNESS, *Video Archiving*, https://archiving.witness.org/.

> A website that includes videos and the written "Activists' Guide to Archiving Video," aimed at providing video archiving guidance for activists and small groups.

NOTES

1. Paula De Stefano et al., *Digitizing Video for Long-Term Preservation: An RFP Guide and Template* (New York: Barbara Goldsmith Preservation & Conservation Department, New York University Libraries, 2013).
2. Bay Area Video Coalition, "AV Artifact Atlas," https://bavc.github.io/avaa/.
3. Kino Video Editor, www.kinodv.org/.
4. DVD Decrypter File Mirror, www.dvddecrypter.org.uk/.
5. Isobuster, https://www.isobuster.com/.
6. DataAccessioner, http://dataaccessioner.org/.
7. Consultative Committee for Space Data Systems, *Reference Model for an Open Archival Information System (OAIS)* (Washington, DC: CCSDS Secretariat, 2012), http://public.ccsds.org/publications/archive/650x0m2.pdf.
8. AVPreserve, "Exactly," https://www.avpreserve.com/tools/exactly/.
9. J. Kunze et al., "The BagIt File Packaging Format (V0.97)," IETF Trust, 2016, https://tools.ietf.org/html/draft-kunze-bagit-14.
10. Handbrake, https://handbrake.fr/.
11. FFmpeg, https://ffmpeg.org/.
12. Squared 5, www.squared5.com/.
13. VideoLAN Organization, "VLC Media Player." www.videolan.org/vlc/index.html.

BIBLIOGRAPHY

Bay Area Video Coalition. "AV Artifact Atlas." https://bavc.github.io/avaa/.

Consultative Committee for Space Data Systems. *Reference Model for an Open Archival Information System (OAIS)*. Washington, DC: CCSDS Secretariat, 2012. http://public.ccsds.org/publications/archive/650x0m2.pdf.

De Stefano, Paula, and Kimberly Tarr, Melitte Buchman, Peter Oleksik, Alice Moscoso, and Ben Moskowitz. *Digitizing Video for Long-Term Preservation: An RFP Guide and Template*. New York: Barbara Goldsmith Preservation & Conservation Department, New York University Libraries, 2013. http://guides.nyu.edu/ld.php?content_id=24817650.

Kunze, J., J. Littman, L. Madden, E. Summers, A. Boyko, and B. Vargas. "The BagIt File Packaging Format (V0.97)." IETF Trust. 2016. https://tools.ietf.org/html/draft-kunze-bagit-14.

JAMIE WITTENBERG
AND CELIA EMMELHAINZ

5

Assess, Annotate, Export

Quick Recipes for Archiving
Your Personal Digital Life

THIS CHAPTER OFFERS STEP-BY-STEP INSTRUCTIONS, or "recipes," for archiving different kinds of digital objects. Because other chapters in this volume offer approaches for preservation, these recipes focus on extracting digital objects from platforms in a state that facilitates preservation. The goal of our PDA recipes is to provide practical, immediate guidance that will be applicable to a broad range of archiving circumstances. The recipes do not require extensive technical knowledge or a strong theoretical understanding of digital archiving. This makes them very useful as templates to pass on to patrons who have immediate archival needs.

Many of these recipes target cloud or web-based applications because these tools can require less conventional methods of extracting digital objects. Furthermore, it is increasingly common for digital items to live online, rather than on internal and external hard drives or storage devices like CDs. While each recipe addresses a specific category of digital object, there are general principles that apply across these categories. The three steps of "assess, annotate, export" are broadly applicable and represent core practices of preparing materials for archiving: assessing the current environment, capturing and/or adding metadata, and retrieving the digital object in an appropriate format.

These recipes often reference both "proprietary" and "open" tools. This language refers to the accessibility of the software's source code and the user's ability to examine or adapt the tools. There are many software distribution models, and proprietary/open does not necessarily correlate to whether the software publisher is commercial or nonprofit. Both models have advantages and disadvantages. These include:

Proprietary (software with its copyright and/or patent rights retained)

Pros: This software often has support staff, bug fixes are developed by the same organization that created the software, a larger development budget sometimes means the software has more advanced features, in some cases the software has a larger user community, and documentation is often user-oriented.

Cons: If the company fails, the software is unsupported and no one can fix problems, some software companies make exporting content difficult in order to "lock" users into the software package, the company usually requires that a license be bought in order to use the software, and terms may change unexpectedly (i.e., you used to be able to use these features for free, now you have to pay).

Open (software whose source code is accessible to users)

Pros: A community of users contributes to the code, there are often many more eyes on bug fixes, the mechanics are transparent, if the community falters, standards will still be available, and there is no incentive to prevent users from moving content between platforms.

Cons: The software is sometimes not as widely used, bugs may not be fixed as quickly because there is less incentive to do so among a small community, a smaller development budget may mean less advanced features, and the documentation may be highly technical.

When evaluating the platform you are currently using, you'll want to consider first how to archive what you've put into that website, including captions, views, and other contextual information. You'll also want to consider whether you're better off moving to another platform because it lets you more fully preserve and share. The following questions should be considered:

1. Can you easily review and assess everything on the platform? Is there an overall view of how many posts, notes, or videos you have? Can you filter and see which content may be most useful to save? Although many websites let you do a bulk download, you may be better off being more selective in what you archive for the future.
2. Can you annotate your files easily while online, or will you need to go back and merge information about your files with your files manually once they're stored on your computer? If you export, will it include everything, such as captions or comments? Is there a way you could document your files before uploading to the cloud, so you don't have an enormous job later?
3. When you export your files or online presence, can you easily get them into an open format, one that you or your loved ones may be able to open, print, or reuse long into the future? Will you be able to export in bulk, or will you have to do it one by one? Is the website committed to allowing you to fully export your files, or are you obliged to use an external application to pull out your data, one that's possibly a risky website to your computer?

There is no easy answer to the question of tradeoffs between using proprietary but popular websites, or using more open formats that are probably less likely to be used by other people in your social circle. However, we hope to give you some guidelines to get you thinking about what you currently use in your online life, as well as whether it will be something that you can store or reuse in the long run. New online tools will always come along, and these may be very useful for your social, business, and personal life. We won't cover everything in these recipes, but we'll give you a place to start.

Archiving Web-Hosted Video

Web-hosted video includes moving images and associated audio that are hosted by a streaming service. Much of this guidance will also apply to born-digital video more generally.

Instructions	Context
Assess: Before archiving video, determine who holds the copyright for the video and determine whether you are licensed to archive it. Once you determine that you may legally archive the video, identify whether you can download directly from the hosting site or whether you will need to use a third-party application to download it. Identify the highest-quality version of the video that you can find.	The consequences for violating copyright law can be severe. It is not recommended to archive video if you do not have a license to do so. Typically, commercial hosting sites like YouTube will allow you to download your own videos in the video manager. If you are unable to access the account, a third-party application may be effective. These applications are ubiquitous and some may contain malware. Be cautious.
Annotate: Document the original format of the video, any migration or conversion you do, the date of download, and the date of creation in a text file. Describe the content of the video, the creator, and the subject. Include contact information for the copyright holder. If you are the copyright holder, consider applying a Creative Commons license.	Because video files are often large and can be time- or resource-intensive to play back, written descriptions of videos will help future viewers find the video they are looking for, or they can potentially make a case for allocating resources to recover a corrupted file so that it can be played back. A Creative Commons license will allow others to legally save and share your video.
Export: Download the video that you wish to archive. If your video is in a format that is not widely supported or difficult to play back, like the Flash container format FLV, use a converter to migrate the video to a widely used format with well-supported playback software and open standards. Ensure that documentation is stored with the video files.	The Library of Congress recommends the following formats, in order of preference, for personal digital video archiving:[1] - MPEG-2 - MPEG-4_AVC - MPEG-4_V - MPEG-1 - Compressed in wrappers like AVI, QuickTime, WMV, and so on

Archiving Notes

There are many flavors of note-taking applications that can be used in a browser, off-line, or on mobile devices. Notes are usually organized into one or more notebooks and are automatically saved locally and to the cloud.

Instructions	Context
Assess: Take inventory. How are your notes currently organized, and what kinds of media do they contain? Text? Photos? Audio recordings? If you have separate notebooks for various purposes, like work and personal, consider archiving these separately.	Taking inventory, or assessing your content, helps you make decisions about what you want to keep and what you don't. It also gives you important information about how much you have and what kinds of items you have. This kind of information will inform your preservation decisions.
Annotate: If you have photos, audio, drawings, or other media, ensure that they have descriptive names, ideally using a consistent naming convention. Be sure to put the creation date of a note into its text or title, because it will otherwise be stripped away when you export.	Descriptive file names are crucial during this process because programs like Evernote will automatically group all of the media from a single note together and move it into a separate folder. During this process, the media may lose some of its context.
Export: To export one or more notes, select the notes that you wish to export. Then, navigate to "Export" (usually in the File menu). Choose a text-based format like HTML or TXT. You will then have an opportunity to choose a descriptive name for your folder. All of the notes you selected will be files in this folder. Usually the media embedded in the note will be in a subdirectory in this folder.	When selecting a format for your notes, consider how you would like to access them or how you would like others to access them. If there are important formatting considerations, HTML or even PDF-A may be preferable to TXT. However, if you are only interested in the content itself, a TXT file is much more expedient and inexpensive to preserve.

Archiving from Photo Platforms

Flickr is a major photo-sharing site; patrons may also be storing photos in iCloud, Facebook, or Instagram—or on their mobile device. Apple devices may be set up to back up photos to iCloud.

Instructions	Context
Assess: Take inventory in Flickr. Are your photos currently organized in sets or by the batch uploaded? Do they have descriptive captions? Your primary option for sorting Flickr photos is "date taken" or "date uploaded," although a Magic View (!!) attempts to automatically identify birds, dogs, architecture, and other photo features.	Assessing your photos helps you decide which need to be downloaded, and what caption editing you may want to do before you back them up to your computer. In the future, it would be wise to add captions on your computer before uploading, and back up the photos to an external hard drive.
Annotate: Make sure that your photos on Flickr have descriptive captions, including the date, name, and place. The sub-caption description will not be downloaded with the file, nor does a caption seem to be retained from your original upload. The date of the original photo will remain available in file information under "modified" or "date taken," but after downloading the file, it will be listed as "created" on today's date.	To have photos with sortable file names, make up a system to list dates first, location first, person first, or some other method of sorting. Unless you download each batch separately and save to a separate folder (recommended), all of your photos will be in one .zip file.
Export: In the past, Flickr users ran third-party programs like Bulkr or Flickr Downloadr. As of 2015, Flickr offers native support for batch downloading. To download and back up your files, log in and click Camera Roll, and select either by individually tapping on photos or choosing Select All above all uploads on a given date. A download icon will appear at the bottom. Click "download" to save a .zip file to your hard drive containing all the photos. Files are named according to your caption in Flickr (but not the description), so make sure that photos are properly captioned (above) before downloading.	Photos can be downloaded from Flickr as .JPEG files, which are the most popular standard for personal archiving (see Severson's "Digital Photos" chapter). This will be adequate for most users, but .TIFF provides archival quality for professionals.

Archiving Social Media

We increasingly conduct our social relationships online, and social media sites such as Instagram, Facebook, and Twitter document our family and friend relationships. These won't be saved for the future, unless you follow this handful of steps to download.

Instructions	Context
Assess: What social media accounts are you currently using? How full of data are they likely to be? Do you keep regular backups, or could you set up a schedule to do so?	Because social media accounts go in and out of fashion, it's good practice to keep track of the ones you use most frequently, and assess the kinds of information that would be helpful to export. If the site itself doesn't allow a full export, sometimes third-party sites or browser add-ons may be able to access the data and provide you with an alternate view.
Annotate: Social media accounts like Instagram will export (through Instaport.me) a folder of jpg images. However, they include no captions, and re-creating those manually could be difficult.	Social media sites vary on how much information they export, and how well linked that information is. When a site includes only partial contextual images or captions, you can go back and add that information to a file manually. Other sites include full metadata in their export. In that case, do your best to describe the photos and the people therein when first posting.
Export: In Facebook, go to Settings and download a copy of your Facebook data. Open the .html file in a browser to see your photos by album, with comments; messages; timeline posts (but without links!); a plain-text list of friends, and more. In Twitter, go to the bottom of your Settings page and request your archive. It will include a .csv file for analysis in a spreadsheet, as well as an .html file for viewing in a browser.	Social media sites come and go, so it is good to make a backup (if available) at least once a year. You won't be able to do this for all accounts, but put exports of your data on your calendar so that you're preserving your digital record. You may even want to open exports (e.g., html files) and save the images to a new format like PDF.

Archiving Documents

Microsoft Word dominates the market, followed by Office for Mac and Google Docs. All are in proprietary formats and should be moved to .rtf for long-term storage.

Instructions	Context
Assess: Open a folder of files to see what format they currently use: doc, docx, or pages? Check the file size, and look inside a few files to see if they have a header with more information on the purpose of that file. You may also check for descriptive file names that will allow people to easily sort and find what they want.	Word-processing programs go out of style, and you don't want to always be monitoring your file formats. Open Document Text (.odt) or Rich Text Format (.rtf) are formats likely to survive into the future. The odt format is more fully open but not as widely used as rtf, which is produced by Microsoft. Beware that complex features like comments and track changes may not be supported in open formats, so save those to PDF.
Annotate: Before or after saving to an open format, make sure your file is named descriptively so you know what's inside without having to open every file. You might also add a paragraph at the top of each document explaining its purpose and any necessary contextual information.	While you want to keep file names brief, you also want them descriptive: "2017–10–21_widget_inventory _CE_v1.rtf" will tell you when a file was created, what it's about, the author, and the version.
Export: In Google Docs, select File → "Download as" and select rtf (Rich Text Format) or odt (Open Document Text). In a desktop program like Microsoft Word, select File → "Save as" rtf format, an open file type that preserves both formatting and accessibility. If you don't need to save highlights, boldface, and the like, .txt is an option and is easier to analyze in large batches.	In the future, you can change the options in any word-processing program (in MS Word it's File → Options → Save → Save file in format). Saving automatically to rtf will save you time later. Also remember that no hard disk or flash drive lasts forever; make sure to copy and back up your files every 3–5 years.

Archiving E-Mails

You likely use Mail on an iOS device, Microsoft Outlook, or Google Mail to manage your e-mails. These e-mails can be exported in bulk bundles, or individually as text documents.

Instructions	Context
Assess: How many e-mails are in your in-box, and are they all useful? Have you organized them into folders or labeled them? Do you know which ones are most important for you to save—and are they individual e-mails or whole groups?	You may not want to export all e-mails in one huge cluster, since that makes them difficult to view and organize later. Before annotating, you might search and delete unneeded advertisements or topics by sender or subject. You'll also want to think about which parts of your e-mail archive you need and why.
Annotate: Search for e-mails by subject, content, or sender and add the results to folders or labels. Going forward, you can set up certain topics to be automatically labeled as they come into your in-box. Organizing in this way makes it much easier to pull an export of only the e-mails you want.	Your e-mail comes with built-in annotation in the form of to, from, subject, and date, so there's not much to do on the annotation front. Although you can export all e-mails, adding annotation to folders or labels makes it easier to selectively export your e-mails. You can also save them to txt or PDF in most programs—make sure to name files descriptively.
Export: In Outlook, look for File → Options → Advanced → Export and export all mail or one folder to a .pst file. This is not an open format. To save one e-mail, use File → Save as. Google Takeout lets you bulk export mail, calendars, and contacts to open formats. You can export all mail or only certain labeled messages. On iOS, select all messages and save as "raw message source" to get an mbox file.	Most e-mail programs can export all mail to mbox, an open file format that can be viewed in open source programs like Thunderbird. Use the ImportExportTools add-on to export a folder of messages to text or PDF format. Note that Microsoft's .pst format needs to be converted to .mbox to be used in this way. Individual e-mails can also usually be saved to text or eml, or printed to PDF.

Archiving Spreadsheets

A spreadsheet is a document that contains data structured in a grid or matrix.

Instructions	Context
Assess: Determine what software was used to create the spreadsheet(s). Identify whether the workbook (collection of sheets) contains data, graphs, images, functions, or other material. Identify whether formatting in the spreadsheet is meaningful—for example, cells with background colors or bold font.	Spreadsheets may be generated using statistical software like R, Stata, and SPSS, or by using word-processing software like Excel or Google Sheets. Often, documentation will be embedded within the spreadsheet, hyperlinks will be embedded, or cells will be highlighted.
Annotate: Create a copy of the original workbook and alter it so that it is as platform-independent as possible. If formatting has meaning, create another column to indicate the meaning with text. If functions are used in cells to calculate value, create a column for calculated value and function used. Cells should contain only unformatted numbers and text. Repeat for each sheet in the workbook.	It is important to preserve the file in its original state before taking steps to create a clean version. All major spreadsheet-generating software will allow for export to a Comma Separated Value (CSV) file, but only plain text will be preserved. Embedded hyperlinks, formatting, and figures will all be lost if the spreadsheet is not cleaned.
Export: If the spreadsheet contains any charts or images, export them in a widely accessible image format like JPEG. Export your altered version of the spreadsheet to create one CSV file for each sheet in the workbook. Put the .csv files, the original spreadsheet file, all images, and a text file describing the contents of the spreadsheet(s) and the version of the software in a folder.	CSV files are flat; they do not have an internal hierarchy. This means that sheets within a workbook cannot be sufficiently represented within a single CSV file, and instead, the relationship between sheets must be created externally and documented. Each sheet can be represented as a single CSV file, and a combination of file names and documentation can describe the relationship.

Archiving Websites

Web archiving is the process of saving content that has been published to the Web—often using programs known as "crawlers" that automatically "crawl" from site to site, downloading content.

Instructions	Context
Assess: Determine what is within your scope to archive based on the collection guidelines and the mission of your organization. Evaluate how much you expect to acquire and what resources you have to dedicate to web archiving. If you expect to archive sites intermittently or manually, evaluate your needs for storage and access.	Institutions frequently choose to archive all content within a domain—for example, Indiana University archives all web content published in the "indiana.edu" domain. Some web archives are event-specific; for example, the September 11 digital archive collects resources from a variety of content producers.
Annotate: When a website is downloaded, the source code will contain important embedded metadata, but it is also important to include contextual metadata, ideally in a "readme" stored with the website. Include information about the date and time accessed, the archiving institution, and any media missing from the site.	Even highly sophisticated crawlers cannot capture all of the content available from websites. Sites that are database-backed, dynamic, have embedded media, gated content, or are protected by robots.txt[2] may not render in a web archive. It is important to document what is missing so that users are aware they are not accessing a complete record.
Export: The format of archived web content will depend upon your users' needs. For small, manual collections with a limited number of users, HTML or PDF are acceptable. For larger collections with broader user bases, the WARC (Web ARChive) file format is standard.	There are several widely used web archiving services available from the nonprofit Internet Archive. Heritrix is a free, reliable Java-based tool, while Archive-it is a fee-based, user-friendly service. For intermittent or manual archiving, the Wayback Machine allows users to submit a single page to be archived.

NOTES

1. "Sustainability of Digital Formats," last updated 2014, http://digitalpreservation.gov/formats/content/video_preferences.shtml.
2. The robots exclusion protocol, or robots.txt, is a standard that allows site owners to "tell" crawlers that they do not wish to have their content accessed. Reputable web archiving services will honor a robots.txt file.

PART II

Personal Digital Archives and Public and Community Audiences

JAIME MEARS

6

The Washington, DC, Public Library's Memory Lab

A Case Study

The Memory Lab was launched in February 2016 at the Martin Luther King Jr. Memorial Library, the DC Public Library system's central branch in Washington, DC. The Memory Lab was the first permanent, public-facing transfer lab opened at a U.S. public library with resources and programming to support personal archiving best practices. In addition to serving as a unique case study, the lab was developed to serve as a model for other organizations interested in supporting their communities with this emerging need. Though the project has been documented through blog posts and professional presentations, this is the first cohesive account of the lab's development, implementation, and impact.

THE ORIGINS OF THE MEMORY LAB

While working for the DC Public Library's Special Collections, the digital curation librarian Lauren Algee recognized an increase in patrons who were seeking advice on personal archiving and requesting access to the archive's

DISCLAIMER: The views in this chapter are my own and do not represent those of the Library of Congress.

professional scanning equipment. Meanwhile, personal audiocassettes, video-tapes, and other at-risk magnetic media accessioned by the archive steadily increased in number. The DC Punk Archive, a popular collection tracking the history of DC's vibrant punk rock scene from 1976 on, also grew rapidly with musicians' and fans' personal collections, including videos and audiotapes of shows and concerts. These obsolete formats were cumbersome for the archivists to select and review, serve in the reading room, or share online or during public programming, unless digitized by a vendor. Most importantly, with the increased scale of created content and formats, the problem was sure to grow.

DC Public Library (DCPL) staff asked themselves: what if a lab existed to help patrons archive for themselves? It would meet patrons' immediate need to transfer their home movies and photographs into easily shared, viewed, and mixed digital files. The lab could also be an entry point to raise awareness and educate patrons on personal archiving, including preserving digital files and the growing number of born-digital records on personal computers, electronic media, and the Web. In the long term this education, combined with the increased availability of what otherwise would be transfer services at cost, could have a trickle-up effect on the condition of the personal collections donated to the DCPL's Special Collections. It would ensure that a diverse cross section of DC's history could be saved through years of rapidly changing technology and an exploding and increasingly unmanageable scale of distributed personal records.

DCPL Innovation Manager Nick Kerelchuk is responsible for the build-out of the Labs at the DCPL (maker spaces connecting patrons to equipment and providing training for creative projects). He saw a personal archiving space as an opportunity to further the Labs' commitment to connecting people to technology and lifelong learning. Users would not only be able to access and share memories trapped within obsolete formats; they could also learn how to transfer media and take care of their digital files, supporting the library's efforts to democratize digital literacy in Washington, DC.

The direct relationship between Special Collections and this personal archiving lab was discussed in detail. Like many library systems, the DC Public Library is strongly committed to patron privacy, and the staff agreed that they would not require any copies of digital files created in the lab to go to the archive. A hands-off, advisory-only approach would create a culture of community archiving without violating privacy or inundating the staff with material that falls outside of the library's collection development policies. The importance of this decision cannot be understated. Allowing communities to archive themselves—especially those that have been left out of traditional archives or, worse yet, whose stories and songs have been taken and/or exploited for scholarship—shifts the traditional relationship paradigm between archivists and community members from protectors to enablers of cultural stewardship.

In spring 2015 the National Digital Stewardship Residency (NDSR) Program, funded by the Institute of Museum and Library Services (IMLS) and administered by the Library of Congress, selected Algee and Kerelchuk's proposal, "Digital Preservation Access and Education through the Public Library,"[1] as a host project. It is at this point that I come into the story as the National Digital Stewardship Resident paired with the project. Along with four other members of the 2015 DC NDSR cohort, I had applied for residency positions just as we finished our MLS degrees in order to gain hands-on, practical experience with a DC cultural heritage organization facing a digital preservation problem. Of the five host proposals, which included submissions by the U.S. Senate and the American Institute of Architects, I was matched with the DC Public Library, and would spend the majority of the next twelve months implementing what we now refer to as the Memory Lab. My charge was to research, develop, and implement the Memory Lab, as well as serve as its primary ambassador to the larger library community through conference presentations and publications. Just as importantly, my job, as you'll read more about as the chapter continues, was to be able to walk away from it at the end of twelve months and leave a sustainable, functional service in my wake.

The NDSR award—and the reality of having a resident committed to the project for a year—convinced library staff to allocate $12,000 in LSTA funding for its build-out. A dedicated space was selected: a 12 × 4-foot cubicle in the corner of the central branch's public computing space, the Digital Commons. The thirteen librarians, library assistants, and manager running the Labs would train and eventually take over daily operations of the nascent personal archiving lab. A Labs librarian would become the Memory Lab librarian and take over direct supervisory responsibilities of the transfer station, programming, and resources. The personal archiving lab, named the Memory Lab, would not have expensive, potentially hazardous, and sophisticated equipment like in the Fabrication and Studio Lab spaces, making it a great candidate to test a do-it-yourself operation model that would lessen the inevitable strain on staff time.

RESEARCH AND DEVELOPMENT

Other chapters in this book delve into the current literature on personal archiving, so I will only discuss the work that most influenced the Memory Lab's design. Although the resources and classes created during the project addressed physical and born-digital archives, digital material is more difficult to preserve and was therefore my research focus. Catherine Marshall's identification of user behavior as the most pernicious threat to the personal archiving of digital material accurately reflects what I experienced as an archivist and a producer of digitally recorded life: "The study participants had lost their online content largely by losing track of it, by not understanding the terms and conditions of the storage they used, and by storing it in proximity to illegally stored stuff, but not by what we generally think of as the most immediate path to loss: hardware failure."[2]

Benign neglect, or the idea of hoping for the best but not actively working to preserve personal records, has many causes: the scale of our stuff; the inability to decide what's worth saving; money; time; and above all, motivation.[3] So what will make someone archive? Kirk and Sellen suggest that defining the self, framing the family, fulfilling one's duty, connecting with the past, honoring those we care about, and preventing forgetting are key motivations for archiving,[4] and Cushing points to periods of life transition as times when we may find archiving valuable.[5] Noah Lenstra witnessed during his work with Illinois Public Library patrons that the ability to connect with others' lives and histories was a primary motivator for archiving, citing the popularity of sharing sites such as Facebook.[6] In her presentation during the Personal Digital Archiving conference in 2015, Jessica Bushey shared findings from an international survey showing that the connotation of the photograph was changing with technology.[7] Where analog personal photographs were associated with permanence, digital photos were associated with sharing, performance, and consumption.[8] She also found there was a lot of confusion about digital preservation, and many producers had high (and unrealistic) expectations that social media sites and photo-sharing sites would provide digital preservation and long-term access to their material.[9]

This research grounded my expectations as a professional archivist. Many archival workflows were not going to translate, and motivating the public would be a central challenge. Because photographs are some of the most meaningful memory objects in personal archives, they can be used as an entry point for learning about preserving other digital files. Because social media are often a default storage medium, resources and programming must be developed to address these media head-on, giving people a rubric to measure whether a new platform is preservation-friendly. Because many retirees in life transitions are interested in archiving projects, classes catering to these types of users, such as digital estate planning, should also be available.

RESOURCES

Personal archiving resources created by organizations, including the Library of Congress, WITNESS, Culture in Transit, POWRR, and indiepreserves.info, represent a rich array of engaging and accessible efforts aimed at personal archiving education. But their distribution across the Web made them difficult to find—unless you happened to be a practitioner. Inspired by the Vancouver

Public Library's Inspiration Lab, I used the DC Public Library's existing Lib-Guide platform to centralize and create public web access to these resources, as well as those created by DCPL staff. The platform also serves as a reservation portal and central guide for the Memory Lab's transfer workflows and program information.[10]

The zine *Maximum Preservation 2: Electronic Boogaloo,* a collaboration between myself and the Special Collections librarian Michele Casto, is one of the site's most popular resources.[11] Its success is a testament to the importance of design when appealing to the archiving motivations of the public, as well as the need to balance specificity with the resource's longevity. The best approach to creating resources and classes is to focus on best practices and not tools because they change too often. Teaching how to evaluate files, software, cloud platforms, devices, and so on with preservation in mind has the most impact.

A final section of the LibGuide, "Build Your Own Memory Lab," was later added to support other libraries, organizations, and patrons interested in creating transfer stations of their own. Nine institutions reached out to the DCPL directly with questions about adopting a memory lab. The most common questions involved the equipment purchased, budget, and scalability. In that final section, I shared wiring diagrams, an equipment list, a budget, an FAQ, and a list of other institutions with public transfer labs or related public programs.[12]

PROGRAMMING

Webinars and lesson resources for librarians and archivists wanting to teach personal archive classes have been published by the Library of Congress, the American Library Association, the Society of Georgia Archivists, the Atlanta Chapter of ARMA International, and the Georgia Library Association. I also found personal archive programming on the calendars of public libraries such as the San Francisco Public Library and Madison Public Library, and by groups such as the LA Archivists Collective. In summary, interviews with these teachers revealed that attendees had mixed digital literacies, found tool demos very valuable, and came with very different motivations—to save their archive, to delete it out of privacy concerns, or to learn how to teach others. One librarian told me that he had even had requests for home visits.

Through my work with the Memory Lab, I taught or cohosted twelve programs in DCPL branches and around the city. Many programs included the same content, which was just repackaged for targeted audiences or built around existing branch program themes. I created reproducible info "packets," including a presentation with notes and handouts for the programs Personal Archiving with Facebook,[13] Personal Archiving 101, and Digital Estate Planning.[14] These packets were shared with DCPL staff through Google Drive, and I reviewed some programs on my blog.[15]

On average, attendance at my programs ranged between five and fifteen people with varying technical ability. Classes were usually emotional; patrons expressed high interest and anxiety, but found the information extremely valuable. Some attended multiple sessions for reinforcement. It became clear that many digital preservation best practices—consistent file-naming and folder structures, creating stable PDF surrogates, and understanding terms of use when signing up for cloud services—were relevant in all library digital literacy classes.

Several program attendees asked if they could check out personal archiving books. Finding that there were none, I selected several that are now in circulation: *Your Digital Afterlife: When Facebook, Flickr and Twitter Are Your Estate, What's Your Legacy?* by Evan Carroll and John Romano (an excellent resource for digital estate planning); *Personal Archiving: Preserving Our Digital Heritage*, edited by Donald T. Hawkins; and *How to Archive Family Keepsakes*, by Denise May Levenick. Many continue to be published (such as this one!), and should be a part of the public library collection scope.

Training is equally important for the sustainability of personal archive programming. Each year, DC Public Library public service staff members must complete SMART goals, training, and projects that are focused on professional development and are factored into annual reviews. For a digital preservation SMART goal, 50 DCPL staff attended two to three digital preservation classes and taught patrons or created a resource for their branch or for the Memory Lab LibGuide. The staff's first class focused on best practices for digital preservation. The second class discussed the LibGuide's content, including transfer workflows and tools to recommend to patrons for digital preservation. The third class, required for librarians, shared how to develop, market, and run a personal archive program at a branch library; students learned about two classes I created, with public lesson plans and slides.

Librarians were required to run a personal archiving program at their branch. Library assistants were required to assist in a librarian's program or produce a brochure, handout, blog post, or resource for the Memory Lab LibGuide on a personal archiving topic. Some staff work can be found on the LibGuide, including an inventory template, an infographic on preserving archival paper materials, and a guide comparing digital storage options. One librarian wrote a series of blog posts on digitizing family photographs at the transfer station.

A librarian who ran a program at her local branch felt that a digital estate planning class was most needed for her community members: "I considered the significant amount of retirement-age and older patrons we serve here and, especially, my experiences in assisting such individuals with technological resources . . . The Digital Estate Planning program . . . seemed to me a way to introduce the community to an element of digital life of which they might not be aware, but which would be relevant to them and best discovered in an environment in which they could ask questions and express concerns."[16] In her

SMART goal report, she found her suspicions were confirmed. The class drew eight attendees who were "engaged" and "expressed gratitude" for this type of program. Attendees reported that they had not previously thought about the topic, or they had considered it but thought the prospect was too daunting. Terms of service were an especially difficult issue for many, and a comment was made about the relevance of this type of program for those who run small businesses and nonprofits.

When asked how they could be supported post-residency, staff requested a digital location to share resources and information, a central leader, a dedicated online method of communication (such as a discussion list), and a personal archiving event tag that they could use when submitting events on the library's online calendar. I transferred ownership of the resources on Google Drive to the Memory Lab librarian. I also encouraged staff to reference and contribute to the Drive folder as they work on personal archiving programming. As initially imagined, I designated the Memory Lab librarian as the central leader to encourage, support, and cross-promote personal archive programming at the neighborhood branches and monitor the Drive folder for additional resources to add to the LibGuide. The Memory Lab librarian also disseminates transfer lab information to neighborhood branches.

TRANSFER STATION

As archive programming built momentum, I simultaneously conducted research on the transfer station, which was for me (and perhaps for many of you) the most intimidating aspect of the project. Before this residency, I had no formal preservation training with audiovisual materials in an archives setting. Benefiting from the DC metro region's concentration of some of the best archives and audiovisual experts in the United States, I conducted a series of site visits to learn about preservation-quality transfers, preferred software and hardware, workflows, and common challenges.

I never presumed that Memory Lab patrons would use the exact same workflows as professional archivists, due to the expertise required to use the equipment and the resulting large files, which are more expensive to store and maintain over time. But because preservation was a focus, I made these options available, if storage capacity and time allowed. Including reel-to-reel transfers or a scope in our workflow would be too operationally difficult, but I learned the importance of selecting professional equipment in ensuring transfer quality.[17] Staff at the National Museum for African American History and Culture recommended our current workflow, which incorporates the software Handbrake for encoding and MetaZ for description.

After an extensive search, I found six free, public-facing transfer labs and/or programs: Vancouver Public Library's Inspiration Lab; Kalamazoo Public

Library's The Hub; Brooklyn Public Library's Info Commons; Indiana University at Bloomington's Scholars Commons Digitization Lab; XFR Collective, a nonprofit in New York City that provides low-cost digitization for artists, activists, and other groups; and Culture-in-Transit, "a partnership between the Metropolitan New York Library Council (METRO), the Brooklyn Public Library and Queens Library to bring mobile scanning equipment to smaller libraries, archives, museums, and the communities they serve."[18] Staff interviews led me to some important takeaways for the Memory Lab's implementation. First, most transfer labs were highly valued and very popular. In addition to transferring VHS tapes, scanning photos and slides was the most desired service. Storage on USB or burning to a disk were the preferred storage formats. Machine failure was not a prevalent challenge, but gaps in user expectations were, including underestimating transfer time commitment (which happens in real time), the relationship between file sizes and transfer settings, and the level of staff support (ranging from users wanting no support to their wanting full intervention). Though format transfer capabilities varied, the most popular ones were reflective photographs and negatives, VHS, VHS-C, DV, audiocassettes, 3.5-inch floppy disks, Hi8, and Betamax. Storing files on USB and CD was most desired, but transfers to cloud accounts, e-mail, and external hard drives were also available. Most labs required patrons to provide their own storage (on cloud accounts, hard drives, flash drives, and CDs), though some had USBs available for purchase or would offer temporary storage if a patron forgot his preferred storage environment. Digital preservation usually was not within the scope of service. Only two programs, XFR Collective and Culture-in-Transit, included the life span of the created digital files as a part of their service mission. This is not at all surprising, considering that many librarians and library assistants have no formal archives training and are instead responsibly reacting to an immediate need for free access to transfer equipment.

Procurement of equipment was based on these interviews, a literature review that pointed to the most popular magnetic media formats found in personal collections, equipment listings online for other in-house digitization labs, and reviews on audiovisual discussion lists, such as digitalfaq.com.

I tested workflows using magnetic media from my personal archive and those of brave Special Collections staff members, transferring around fifty hours of audiocassettes, VHS, VHS-C, DV, and several 3.5-inch floppies. I used a Trello board to track testing, capturing usability and functionality problems, actions taken, and a final analysis on most of the equipment and software now live in the lab. During this phase, I discovered that the consumer-level converter we purchased was not reliable or preservation-friendly. If you haven't recognized this already from this chapter, the audiovisual preservation community is an incredibly valuable support system. The Dance Heritage Coalition, a national network of institutions dedicated to the preservation and access of materials that document dance, heard about the lab and generously loaned us more professional-grade equipment during the temporary closing of their DC hub.

In addition to archival best practices, ten of twelve Labs staff members had to be trained to run the Memory Lab. Training before the lab opened included hands-on practice with transfer workflows, troubleshooting, before-and-after processing of patrons, and wiring. A second, more in-depth training that included deck and scanner maintenance was held for the five Memory Lab working group members during the lab's second month of operation. The Memory Lab is closed to the public on Fridays and Sundays so staff members can do necessary maintenance and transfer their own items to become more familiar with the workflows.

A Labs librarian was assigned to lead the Memory Lab; I worked with him more extensively than with any other staff member. He shadowed me in the lab, at trainings, at conference presentations, and at meetings. After the Memory Lab had been open for a month, under the supervision of the Labs manager and with the consultation of the Special Collections digital curation librarian, the Memory Lab librarian took over customer and staff issues, as well as the daily managerial duties of the lab, including requests.

USING THE MEMORY LAB

Customers encounter DCPL's transfer lab, or the Memory Lab, primarily through word of mouth or from library communications. They may book a one-hour "drop-in" session to get a hands-on orientation of the space, or they can book a three-hour session directly. The lab is available for booking Monday through Thursday, and Saturday during library hours. Customers can reserve time in the lab online through the library's Memory Lab web page. A Labs staff member can also book the reservation for a patron in person or over the phone. When the project began, Labs staff were managing all programs and equipment reservations through Excel spreadsheets and a central Google calendar. The addition of the Memory Lab bolstered the case for purchasing scheduling software to manage daily bookings in the Labs. We picked Acuity software to manage reservations and patron information. It reduced hours of staff labor, and the easy report functionalities offer quantitative data that inform decisions and support the argument for more resources.

The booking form requires a library ID number or patrons to identify what format(s) they are transferring and what storage environment they will provide (the library does not store any files, even temporarily, that are created in the lab). To help them with their decision, customers are given a rubric to estimate how much storage space they will need. Figure 6.1 describes the current formats and storage environments accepted.

FORMATS ACCEPTED	FORMATS SAVED ON (Customer Provided)
• VHS • VHS-C • DV • MiniDV • Audiocassette • 3.5" floppy • Photos/slides/negatives	• External hard drive • USB • Cloud storage • CD • DVD

SOURCE: DC Public Library, "The Memory Lab," www.dclibrary.org/labs/memorylab.

FIGURE 6.1
Formats accepted at the Memory Lab

Most importantly, users must assert that they can follow directions independently and have basic computer skills, defined as the ability to type, search, and save independently. If a customer does not meet these requirements, they are referred to the library's basic computer classes.

During their first visit to the Memory Lab, customers are required to sign a liability waiver protecting the library from legal action if material is damaged. They are then led back to the space, where a Labs staff member has turned on the equipment they will be using and opened the LibGuide to the appropriate workflow. The staff member asks if the patron has any questions, then the patron is left on her own. If at any time patrons need assistance with their transfer, they return to the staff desk and an employee helps troubleshoot. This is not a seamless operation, since the Digital Commons reference desk is the busiest in the entire system. We learned that a do-it-yourself space like this would likely be more successful in a quieter library space with more staff availability.

At the Digital Commons reference desk, Labs staff are responsible for setting up and closing down the Memory Lab for customers. This process includes checking booking information; turning on necessary equipment before sessions; testing machines; deleting files and browser history from the lab's computers; tidying the space and cleaning the equipment; turning off machines throughout the day; and assisting customers as needed.

We established a Memory Lab working group, composed of the Memory Lab librarian, three Labs staff members, and a Special Collections representative who serves as an advisor. The working group meets monthly to discuss the transfer lab and personal archive programming. The four Labs staff members also are responsible for checking the Memory Lab's e-mail, supporting other staff in the lab, planning personal archive programming, cleaning decks regularly, calibrating the scanner, and updating the computers. The Memory Lab librarian is responsible for staff supervision, personal archive programming, updates to the LibGuide, deck maintenance, procurement orders for the lab, following trends in digital preservation and personal archiving, maintaining relationships with Special Collections and external stakeholders, and serving as the point of contact and representative for all personal archiving and Memory Lab–related issues for the DCPL system.

HOW IT'S BEEN GOING

Based on reports from Acuity Scheduling Software, in its first eight months the Memory Lab LibGuide had more than 8,000 views, and 428 three-hour transfer sessions were booked in the lab, totaling over 1,000 hours. Of these 428 bookings, only 176 were unique users. Single appointments were booked by 105 patrons, 37 booked two times, and 34 booked three or more times. There are currently no limits to the number of appointments a user can make, and the most frequent user registered for 48 sessions for scanning. It has been difficult to keep up with the demand for service, and patrons have to wait as long as two months for an appointment. VHS and photo scanning are the most popular formats transferred, with floppies being the least popular. Not including our most frequent user, 233 of the appointments used USB drives. Ripping JPEGs of family photos from CDs to a thumb drive and patrons using their own camcorders are examples of unpredicted uses.

Users who booked a Memory Lab appointment received a survey to gauge customer satisfaction and their personal archiving knowledge before and after their visit. Twenty-one patrons responded. The majority of respondents reported that their knowledge of personal archiving increased after using the Memory Lab. In the "other" category, two users replied that they knew more about digital photo preservation specifically, one had not been to his appointment yet, and one said it was too difficult to use. Eleven respondents confirmed that they had used the LibGuide to look at personal archiving resources, and six reported taking preservation actions on files they created in the lab, such as adding metadata or storing a backup in a different location. Ten reported sharing the files with family and friends; creating a physical or digital photo album was the most popular creative repurposing cited. (See figure 6.2.)

When asked to describe their experience using the lab, ten respondents confirmed a learning curve ranging from "slight" to "difficult," three reported that they had needed staff assistance, and two experienced technical difficulties. Six respondents used the word "easy" to describe their experience, three requested better instructions for plugging in equipment (some had brought their own), one was unable to do a transfer because of technical failure, and one had not been to her appointment yet. Seventeen of our survey respondents replied that they have recommended the lab to others, and several used

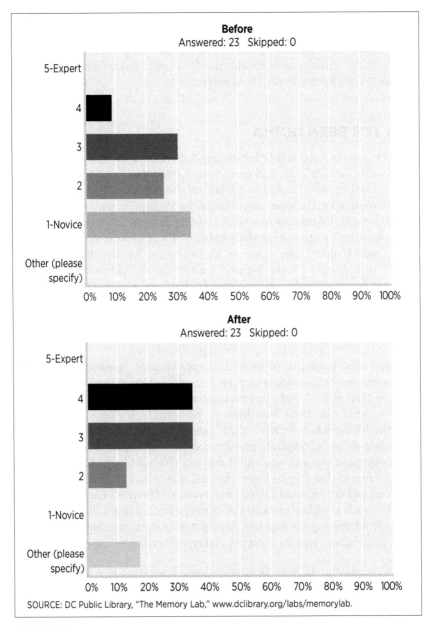

Before
Answered: 23   Skipped: 0

After
Answered: 23   Skipped: 0

SOURCE: DC Public Library, "The Memory Lab," www.dclibrary.org/labs/memorylab.

FIGURE 6.2

"How much did you know about personal archiving/digital preservation before and after using the Memory Lab?" survey responses

QUESTION: Is there anything else you'd like to say about the Memory Lab?
Thank you for providing this for the public!
I appreciate Memory Lab's efforts to encourage people to digitize and preserve their home movies and photographs.
It is a great resource! I couldn't imagine a better use of library resources. I've recently moved out of DC and I'm disappointed my current library doesn't have a similar facility.
I am happy about how the library is adapting to technology and making itself relevant to many people.
It's nice that this service exists at the library at no cost.
THANK YOU. Also, I would love it if there was a way to transfer Super 8 and other old film reels. I have a lot of them.
SOURCE: Memory Lab Survey by Jaime Mears, September 29, 2016

FIGURE 6.3
"Is there anything else you'd like to say about the Memory Lab?"
survey responses.

the word "relevant" to describe its value. When asked for further comment, four of the fifteen who responded gave suggestions for increasing the lab's availability and accessibility. Eleven of the fifteen used the survey as a place to say thank you. (See figure 6.3.)

The heavy use of obsolete hardware is a constant challenge for the lab. Procuring duplicates is essential because equipment can, will, and has broken. In these cases, easily swappable equipment is a lifesaver. An established maintenance time line helps staff keep an eye on the wear and tear of the machines before a major problem occurs, and it provides an opportunity for staff to learn how to clean decks and troubleshoot. Cultivating and enriching relationships with archivists, enthusiasts, and repair experts not only pays off when items break, but also acts as a preventive measure. For example, when a component in the Memory Lab's VCR malfunctioned, the repair vendor was not only able to detail why the component likely stuck (buildup from moldy tapes and/or tapes with "sticky shed"), but also what staff could do to maintain the machines and prevent or delay buildup in the future. This correspondence helped to modify workflows and educate staff.

Continuing professional development on personal archiving, digital preservation, and audiovisual transfer for all members of the working group, but especially the Memory Lab librarian, is needed to support programming and an up-to-date LibGuide. Besides continued support from Special Collections staff, resources should be allocated for staff to attend archiving conferences and workshops, as well as increase their site visits to local audiovisual archives.

Overall, the DCPL counts the Memory Lab as a success, and it is committed to its ongoing development and expansion. Personal archive programming continues throughout the library system, and new programming that pairs preservation best practices with creative projects, such as a class on transferring and making mixtapes, is springing up. While this chapter was being written, the staff at the Martin Luther King Library hosted DC Home Movie Day for a second year in a row, partnering with local audiovisual archivists to teach community members about film preservation.

Due to high demand and the relocation of central library services for the library's renovation, the DCPL plans to place Memory Lab stations in three library branches. The goal is to expand to branches within established neighborhoods that serve residents who hit the key demographics of common users. It is imperative to have these sites well distributed across the city. Staff at these branches have ideally already been trained through the Digital Preservation SMART goal.

A CASE FOR MEMORY LABS

There is an overwhelming need for free personal archive programming and transfer services in every community around the country. Libraries are best poised to take on this responsibility because they have dedicated spaces, a history of public education, and a commitment to accessibility. Subjects such as file naming, file description, understanding terms of use, and creating an inventory could be integrated easily into existing community history and creative programming series, as well as digital literacy efforts. Engagement with this topic will not only attract audiences that normally do not visit the library, but will also create opportunities for new cooperative partnerships with community organizations. The lab staff also expressed an appreciation for the professional development opportunity this project provided:

> As a public librarian I am particularly in tune with how best to promote programs to my community, and what groups or organizations are best to partner with. I don't have to think like an expertly trained archivist to know I am sharing helpful information and tools with my community. I think having continued education with archivists who can train the trainers/public librarians is important. I might not be able to stay up on trends and changes as this topic isn't the focus of my day-to-day job, but I would love to keep learning and teaching about it. I am confident these topics will only become more interesting to library patrons and community members, and the public library has an obligation to program to the needs and desires of its community.[19]

As this librarian points out, a common challenge is finding ongoing support from the archivist community as new obstacles, tools, and workflows arise. We are lucky at the DCPL because we have our own Special Collections, but many public library systems do not, and it's important that local archives support these efforts and for those in the library community to document and share personal archiving resources. As I discovered during the research phase of this project, publishing what you create at every opportunity will be useful to someone, or it might even serve as a helpful reference point for your own projects moving forward.

Although the purpose of this chapter is to serve as a case study, there are endless implementation options. From designing a single class about personal archiving to building a transfer lab, any effort is valuable and will impact the community you serve. In fact, slow-growth implementation can be a successful strategy in this space, ensuring an iterative, user-focused design process that empowers people as they preserve their personal, family, and community histories.

NOTES

1. DC Public Library, "Digital Preservation Access and Education through the Public Library," Library of Congress, www.digitalpreservation.gov/ndsr/DCPL%20 Summary.pdf.

2. Catherine C. Marshall, "Social Media, Personal Data, and Reusing Our Digital Legacy," in *Personal Archiving: Preserving Our Digital Heritage,* edited by Donald T. Hawkins, chapter 6 (Medford, NJ: Information Today, 2013).

3. Catherine C. Marshall, "Re-thinking Personal Digital Archiving, Part 1: Four Challenges from the Field," *D-Lib Magazine* 14, no. 3/4 (March-April 2008), www .dlib.org/dlib/march08/marshall/03marshall-pt1.html.

4. David S. Kirk and Abigail Sellen, "On Human Remains: Values and Practice in the Home Archiving of Cherished Objects," *ACM Transactions on Computer-Human Interaction* 17, no. 3, article 10 (July 2010): 10:16, https://www.microsoft.com/ en-us/research/wp-content/uploads/2016/02/a10-kirk.pdf.

5. Amber L. Cushing, "A Balance of Primary and Secondary Values: Exploring a Digital Legacy," *International Journal of Knowledge Content Development & Technology* 1.3, no. 2 (December 2013): 67–94, https://core.ac.uk/download/ pdf/25824919.pdf.

6. Mike Ashenfelder, "Reality Check: What Most People Do with Their Personal Digital Archives," *The Signal,* May 15, 2013, https://blogs.loc.gov/thesignal/ 2013/ 05/ reality-check-what-most-people-actually-do-with-their-personal-digital-archives/.

7. Jessica Bushey, "How Online Sociality and Free Terabytes Are Shaping Personal Digital Archives," presentation, Personal Digital Archiving (PDA) Conference, New York, 2015.

8. Bushey, "How Online Sociality and Free Terabytes Are Shaping Personal Digital Archives."

9. Bushey, "How Online Sociality and Free Terabytes Are Shaping Personal Digital Archives."

10. Vancouver Public Library, "Inspiration Lab," www.vpl.ca/programs/cat/C1051.

11. Michele Casto and Jaime Mears, *Maximum Preservation 2: Electronic Boogaloo* (Washington, DC: Issuu, 2015), http://issuu.com/dcp19/docs/maximumpreservation2.ebook/1?e=23093933/32765994.

12. DC Public Library, "Build Your Own Memory Lab," in Memory Lab LibGuide, http://libguides.dclibrary.org/build.

13. Jaime Mears, "Class: Personal Archiving with Facebook," *Notes from a Nascent Archivist* blog, October 16, 2015, https://jaimemears.wordpress.com/2015/10/16/class-personal-archiving-with-facebook/.

14. Jaime Mears, "Class: Digital Estate Planning," *Notes from a Nascent Archivist* blog, April 20, 2016, https://jaimemears.wordpress.com/2016/04/20/class-digital-estate-planning/.

15. Jaime Mears, *Notes from a Nascent Archivist* blog, https://jaimemears.wordpress.com/.

16. Julia Strusienski, "Digital Estate Planning at Georgetown: A Digital Preservation I FY16 SMART Goal Report," DC Public Library, 2016.

17. Jaime Mears, "Getting the Public to Archive," Council on Library and Information Resources, *Re:Thinking* blog, April 7, 2016, http://connect.clir.org/blogs/jaime-mears/2016/04/07/getting-the-public-to-archive.

18. Culture in Transit, "About," www.mnylc.org/cit/?page_id=43.

19. Bobbie Dougherty, e-mail message to author, October 10, 2016.

BIBLIOGRAPHY

Ashenfelder, Mike. "Reality Check: What Most People Do with Their Personal Digital Archives." *The Signal.* May 15, 2013. https://blogs.loc.gov/thesignal/2013/05/reality-check-what-most-people-actually-do-with-their-personal-digital-archives/.

Carroll, Evan, and John Romano. "Your Digital Afterlife: When Facebook, Flickr and Twitter Are Your Estate." In *What's Your Legacy? (Voices That Matter).* San Francisco: New Riders, 2010.

Casto, Michele, and Jaime Mears. *Maximum Preservation 2: Electronic Boogaloo.* Washington, DC: Issuu, 2015. http://issuu.com/dcp19/docs/maximumpreservation2.ebook/1?e=23093933/32765994.

Cushing, Amber L. "A Balance of Primary and Secondary Values: Exploring a Digital Legacy." *International Journal of Knowledge Content Development & Technology* 1.3, no. 2 (December 2013): 67–94. https://core.ac.uk/download/pdf/25824919.pdf.

DC Public Library. "Build Your Own Memory Lab." In *Memory Lab LibGuide.* http://libguides.dclibrary.org/build.

———. "Digital Preservation Access and Education through the Public Library." Library of Congress. www.digitalpreservation.gov/ndsr/DCPL%20Summary.pdf.

———. "The Memory Lab." www.dclibrary.org/labs/memorylab.

———. Memory Lab LibGuide. http://libguides.dclibrary.org/memorylab.

Dougherty, Bobbie. E-mail message to author, October 10, 2016.

Hawkins, Donald T., ed. *Preserving Our Digital Heritage.* Medford, NJ: Information Today, 2013.

Kirk, David S., and Abigail Sellen. "On Human Remains: Values and Practice in the Home Archiving of Cherished Objects." *ACM Transactions on Computer-Human Interaction* 17, no. 3, article 10 (July 2010): 10:16. https://www.microsoft.com/en-us/research/wp-content/uploads/2016/02/a10-kirk.pdf.

Levenick, Denise May. *How to Archive Family Keepsakes: Learn How to Preserve Family Photos, Memorabilia and Genealogy Records.* Family Tree Books, 2012.

Marshall, Catherine C. "Re-thinking Personal Digital Archiving, Part 1: Four Challenges from the Field." *D-Lib Magazine* 14, no. 3/4 (March-April 2008). www.dlib.org/dlib/march08/marshall/03marshall-pt1.html.

———. "Social Media, Personal Data, and Reusing Our Digital Legacy." In *Personal Archiving: Preserving Our Digital Heritage*, edited by Donald T. Hawkins, chapter 6. Medford, NJ: Information Today, 2013.

Mears, Jaime. "Class: Digital Estate Planning." *Notes from a Nascent Archivist* blog. April 20. 2016. https://jaimemears.wordpress.com/2016/04/20/class-digital-estate-planning/.

———. "Class: Personal Archiving with Facebook." *Notes from a Nascent Archivist* blog. October 16, 2015. https://jaimemears.wordpress.com/2015/10/16/class-personal-archiving-with-facebook/.

———. "Getting the Public to Archive." Council on Library and Information Resources. *Re:Thinking* blog. April 7, 2016. http://connect.clir.org/blogs/jaime-mears/2016/04/07/getting-the-public-to-archive.

Strusienski, Julia. "Digital Estate Planning at Georgetown: A Digital Preservation I FY16 SMART Goal Report." DC Public Library. 2016.

Vancouver Public Library. "Inspiration Lab." www.vpl.ca/programs/cat/C1051.

NATALIE MILBRODT
AND MAGGIE SCHREINER

7

Digitizing Memories and Teaching Digital Literacy in Queens, NY

QUEENS MEMORY IS AN OUTREACH-BASED community archiving program of the Queens Library that collects and makes accessible oral histories, photographs, and other personal records documenting contemporary life in the borough of Queens in New York City. The program's website features curated content from local institutional archives as well as personal and family collections and recorded memories. Queens Memory hosts public scanning events where community members can have their photographs, documents, and memorabilia digitized and added to the Queens Memory digital collections. Over time, the community scanning event format has expanded to include education about local history and personal digital archiving. This chapter will discuss the development of the Queens Memory program and community scanning model, as well as the specific tools and methodologies used to teach personal digital archiving in a public library setting.

ENVIRONMENTAL SCAN

Community archiving efforts such as these have been evolving and growing in number over the past decade. An early artist-led project, Graeme Miller's 2003

Linked project, created a soundscape on a four-mile motorway in East London featuring excerpts of oral histories with former residents. The Museum of London provides long-term preservation for the Linked interviews.[1] Museums continue to play an important role in supporting such projects. The Museum of Chinese in America (MoCA) in New York City hosts Family Treasure information fairs in which museum visitors can bring questions about the preservation of personal artifacts in a variety of formats (photographs, textiles, born-digital files, etc.) to preservation experts who are available to provide consultations.

The Digital Public Library of America (dp.la) has also been an important agent in facilitating institutional efforts to digitize and preserve local history records for a national and international audience. Projects like Scan PA and Minnesota Reflections have state and municipal libraries, institutions of higher learning, and historical societies working together to provide a level of preservation and access that was previously unimaginable for local history collections.

Archival and library science scholars have helped to reframe the role of the archivists and librarians who are working with communities to document their own cultural heritage. Patricia Galloway of the University of Texas's School of Information recommends three courses of action for archivists working with communities. The first is assembling a "longitudinal documentation of a changing tradition," in which upcoming generations are recorded as they learn, carry, and pass on traditional knowledge.[2] The second involves an archivist becoming a "tradition-bearer by apprenticing" with a community member who passes the knowledge directly to the archivist as if training a member of the community. The third of Galloway's suggestions is for archivists to advise and supervise community members creating their own records. This involves and empowers members of the community toward self-documentation. In this way, an archivist is an activist, instilling archival values in a community.[3] Similarly, the Knowledge River initiative at the University of Arizona's School of Information is dedicated to "educating information professionals who have experience with and who are committed to Latino and Native American populations."[4] Graduate students in the Knowledge River program engage in service learning projects to document community histories. Their work is chronicled on the Knowledge River Mukurtu website (https://knowledge-river.mukurtu.net/).

Examples of efforts led or facilitated by academic institutions to capture public contributions include event-based efforts such as the American University in Cairo's University on the Square project (2011) on Facebook, whose stated mission was "preserving the January 25th Revolution in Egypt." The project crowdsourced first-person accounts from an extraordinary social and political moment in Egypt's history in real time.[5] There are also ongoing efforts organized around serving specific self-identified groups such as the

South Asian American Digital Archive (SAADA), which was founded in 2008 by Michelle Caswell and Samip Mallick, who worked at the University of Chicago at that time as assistant bibliographer for Southern Asia and South Asia outreach coordinator, respectively. They established SAADA out of a combination of personal and professional interest in order to counteract the "archival absences" that exclude the history of South Asian peoples in the United States.[6]

In the public library sector, efforts such as the Washington, DC Public Library's Memory Lab have begun to address the preservation of privately held family records without an expectation of serving as a repository for the materials. (See chapter 6 in this book.) The equipment made freely available in the Memory Lab addresses both the crisis of unstable formats common in family collections and the challenge of acquiring the digital literacy needed to successfully migrate and preserve these records for future generations. Queens Memory supports the digitization and preservation of both privately held materials and those contributed through the program to Queens Library by individuals and community organizations for long-term preservation and public access. This work fits well into the library's larger mission to preserve and make accessible the cultural heritage of one of the most ethnically diverse and populous counties in the United States.

QUEENS MEMORY

The Queens Memory program began in summer 2010 as part of project director Natalie Milbrodt's independent study while she was an archives fellow in Queens College's Graduate School of Library and Information Studies. She conducted thirteen oral history interviews with her own neighbors living in the rapidly changing, 100-year-old Waldheim neighborhood in Flushing, Queens. Interviews, photos, and other records donated by residents provide accounts of (a) change over time in the neighborhood, (b) personal histories, and (c) a "snapshot" of the community in 2010. This pilot effort established the project's standard procedure of interviewers working within their own communities to document the borough. Seeing the potential for the project to develop into a collaborative digital archive, Milbrodt sought support from Queens College and the Archives at Queens Library. Together, the team submitted a successful collaborative digitization grant proposal for $25,000 to the New York Metropolitan Library Council (METRO). These funds supported what has become the Queens Memory program. The founding team who established Queens Memory had a strong desire to engage the public in innovative ways, but neither Queens College nor the Queens Library had, prior to this project, a well-developed digital presence for archival materials.

The grant supported the development of a shared workflow between partner institutions and established a foundation for the project's digital presence.

A core project team emerged through the grant, which included archivists, digital librarians, archival educators, and software developers, including the founder of Whirl-i-Gig, the company that developed the open source digital asset management software CollectiveAccess. The Whirl-i-Gig team configured and modified CollectiveAccess software to enable the creation of MARC and VRA Core records that could be ingested for long-term preservation in the Queens Library's Vital DAMS.

By the end of the METRO grant cycle in the fall of 2011, the project site went live. It featured about 300 audio and visual records. For the next twelve months, the team focused on training and supervising volunteers, developing workshops for participants, and drafting strategic documents for the development of the project. In October 2012 the Queens Library committed to becoming the lead partner in the Queens Memory program, hiring Milbrodt as the library's first digital content and strategy coordinator, and later as head of Metadata Services, a new division combining the cataloging and archives digitization teams. This role allowed her to expand the Queens Memory program within the library's regular operations and foster the continued involvement of Queens College and other key partners.

Queens Memory began holding "community scanning days" after Hurricane Sandy in early 2013 to assist residents in Queens neighborhoods that were severely impacted by storm damage to digitize and preserve their rescued family records. These events expanded to other interested neighborhoods as the small team of Queens Memory staff, interns, and volunteers were available. A significant expansion of this work came in 2014 with the Culture in Transit project, funded by a Knight Foundation Library Challenge grant. The Queens Library joined with the Brooklyn Public Library and its lead partner, METRO, to expand the concept of digitization events across New York City and Westchester County. Best practices and workflows established by the Queens Memory program were adapted for use by Culture in Transit partner institutions. After a year of experimentation in the field, the Culture in Transit team of project archivists—Maggie Schreiner, Caroline Catchpole, and Sarah Quick—published a toolkit with tested workflows for processing community contributions, tips for planning and hosting successful events, and equipment reviews for mobile digitization kits.[7]

The primary goals of Queens Memory are first to increase the use and awareness of archival collections; and second, to democratize the archives with the records of residents who, for reasons of race, ethnicity, religion, immigration status, socioeconomic status, age, or gender, might otherwise not be featured in the historic record. One strategy the team used to achieve this goal was to mobilize students to document their own lives and family histories in an effort to connect personal histories with the broader historical context of the students' communities, the region, and the nation. In the process of creating oral histories and photo documentation of their families and communities, the students gained digital literacy skills that were transferable to a variety of professional contexts.

Curricular initiatives that incorporate graduate library and information studies students seeking their archival certification at Queens College have been essential to the project from the outset. The Graduate School of Library and Information Studies is a reliable source for talented students who come to work on the Queens Memory program through a competitive application process to join a fellows program facilitated and funded in a partnership with the Citi Center for Culture. Each cohort of fellows learns research, cataloging, and social media and Wikipedia editing skills that are helpful in making archival collections more accessible to the public.

Other curricular initiatives at Queens College involve oral history training in classrooms that result in semester-end record submissions to the Queens Memory collections. The first such effort in the 2012 spring semester was the English professor Bette Weidman and library studies professor Benjamin Alexander's co-taught course on oral history literature and methods, which was designed especially to facilitate contributions to the Queens Memory project. In a second classroom-based collaboration, the sociology professor Anahi Viladrich invited Milbrodt to co-teach six sessions of her undergraduate research methods course. The sessions prepared students to conduct interviews that were focused on food and healing traditions in immigrant communities. These curricular initiatives continued in Viladrich's spring 2013 Immigrant Research course.

UNIQUELY SUCCESSFUL

Institutional digitization efforts are underway at both the Queens Library and Queens College that provide "more product" with less processing. These larger-scale efforts have afforded Queens Memory the luxury of remaining a laboratory for content curation and experimentation with new delivery methods. The flexibility of a laboratory environment has made it possible to pursue grant-funded development opportunities and the partnerships with external organizations that have driven the project's public success and maintained its internal support from Queens Library and Queens College.

Since the program's inception, organizational partnerships have resulted in the addition of rich and varied content to the collections. Queens Memory's early partners included StoryCorps, the Queens Historical Society, the office of the Queens Borough president, St. John's University, and Historypin. Individual journalists and artists who produce blogs and other original content about their communities have also been sources of born-digital collections.

The library's preservation storage and free public access for their content offer an appealing afterlife for content produced by creative people who are interested in pursuing other projects, but who wish to sustain public access after they no longer pay for a web-hosting plan for their online content. Joining the Queens Memory collections also places crowdsourced donations into the larger context of materials from the Archives at Queens Library. The library's archival collections consist almost entirely of materials connected to local history. This consistency in subject matter makes Queens Memory donations an excellent fit in terms of aligning with institutional collecting policy. This alignment creates a consistent ecosystem for materials donated by the public and reinforces the existing mission of the library.

Having an adequate number of full-time staff to support the work of Queens Memory is largely due to the program's institutional orientation as part of the Queens Library's 32-person Metadata Services division. The library maintains a small staff operating the system's Archives division, with only two full-time archivists to provide public service and collection processing. With the decrease in the acquisition of print materials in the library's circulating collections, staff in the Metadata Services division have time to engage in digitization, description, and preservation activities for archival materials. This transition has meant the preservation of Technical Services jobs within the institution and the availability of highly skilled full-time staff members for Queens Memory events and materials processing.

COMMUNITY SCANNING PROCESS

Community scanning events are held in branch libraries and other community spaces, including seniors' centers, churches, schools, and bars. Queens Memory staff work closely with branch librarians and local community organizations to conduct outreach to neighborhood residents, build interest in the scanning event, and spread knowledge of the Queens Memory program more broadly. On the day of the event, the mobile scanning equipment is set up in an accessible, visible space and community members are invited to bring in their family photographs, documents, or other mementos and have them digitized and then returned.

The donation and digitization process takes place in a small group setting. Staff members and volunteers work with each donor individually to sign a consent form granting Creative Commons licensing to the digital surrogates, and to collect as much metadata as possible about each item being digitized. Staff aim to record the date, location, and the names of any people depicted in a photograph, and any other contextual information the donor wants to share. The material is then digitized while the donor waits, and the original items are returned to the donor immediately after they are scanned. Participants receive a flash drive containing digital files of the items they shared, saved as TIFF and JPEG files, as well as a scanned version of the signed consent form. The participants leave the event with their original material, a flash drive containing the digital surrogates and consent form, a brochure about the Queens Memory program, and a brochure about personal digital archiving.

After a community scanning event, the Queens Memory team catalogs each item in the project's digital asset management software, CollectiveAccess, using the descriptive keywords provided by the donors. Once material is cataloged and visible on our website, staff notify the donor, and make revisions to the description if requested. The library serves as the long-term custodian for these materials, which are maintained through the preservation workflows of its Metadata Services division. The records are also harvested by the Empire State Digital Network for inclusion in the Digital Public Library of America (DPLA). The library's digital archives and Queens Memory websites provide a local platform and context for the materials, while DPLA gives national visibility to these records and contextualizes the material alongside similar records from a wide variety of institutions. The flow chart of figure 7.1 depicts the full workflow process.

The program's pop-up model of community scanning events is dependent on mobile equipment kits. The Culture in Transit grant from the Knight Foundation provided the opportunity to research and purchase new equipment, with a focus on choices that were affordable and lightweight. The scanning station is based on the Epson scanner; for mobile purposes the Queens Memory team uses and would recommend either the V600 or V800 models. Laptops have SilverFast scanning software installed, which in addition to having better color management and more granular options than the default Epson software, also allows for a faster workflow due to the pre-scan and selection functions. Culture in Transit project staff also experimented with using a mobile copy stand at community events in order to photograph larger and 3-D material, but found that it was too difficult to reliably capture high-quality images during unpredictable and fast-paced community events.

The scanning station is augmented by an outreach kit, which allows staff to incorporate education about local history and archives into the scanning events. The outreach materials include a large-screen tablet that is used to display captioned historic photos from our collections, a smaller tablet and over-ear headphones which serve as an oral history listening station, and a large, laminated map of the neighborhood for community mapping activities. Slideshow selections and oral history clips are curated to reflect specific neighborhoods or themed events. These tools give library patrons and community members a point of entry into Queens Memory and the community scanning event. The oral history clips teach that the lives and stories of "regular"

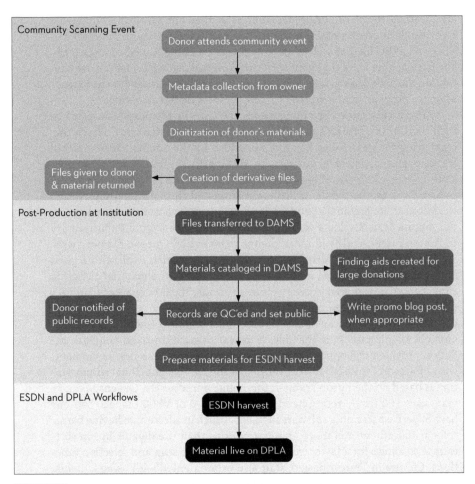

FIGURE 7.1
Overview of the Queens Memory community scanning workflow

individuals can be historically interesting and personally meaningful. Photographs can be used to demonstrate the types of material that traditional archives collect, and what Queens Memory might be interested in collecting at a community scanning event. If a slideshow for a particular neighborhood does not contain a lot of photographs, it can become a great opportunity to talk about archival absence, as well as a way to encourage community members to donate and fill in these gaps. This locally focused outreach and engagement develops an understanding of the project, how people can participate, and why their participation is important.

CHALLENGES

The biggest challenge in conducting community scanning events has been find-ing reliable ways to turn out an ideal number of event participants. Ideally, a community history event would have a large enough turnout (5–15 attendees) to motivate conversation and exchange among the participants, but not so many participants that it becomes impossible to scan the materials they bring within the time constraints of the event. In most cases, the team has strug-gled to get a big enough turnout to events. The most effective solution for getting an active core group of people who bring interesting materials to share has been involving existing, cohesive community groups, such as the Forest Hills Asian Association (FHAA). The FHAA self-organizes and sees community history events as an opportunity for their membership to access valuable free resources and to get their community's history into the archives. Leading up to an event, FHAA leadership specifically requests those members with valu-able personal materials to attend the scanning event and bring their family treasures for digitization. Because the group's leadership trusts the Queens Memory program staff, that trust extends to the membership. The FHAA also contributes resources such as refreshments and guest speakers who enliven the proceedings and tailor them to the interests of the group.

Another challenge comes after events, when many donors who have con-tributed materials require individualized follow-up from staff. The team work-ing at an event has to communicate to the processing team back at the office about any donors who asked for specific follow-up. Since events are staffed by a combination of interns, volunteers, and project and full-time staff, this communication can be challenging to execute in a timely and consistent man-ner. Even maintaining consistent communications with the pool of Queens Memory volunteers is challenging. Volunteers do a wide variety of tasks, from conducting interviews to cataloging and helping to process donated materi-als during public events. Keeping their skills sharp and properly appreciating their efforts are a significant time commitment. The core Queens Memory team is moving toward more standardized roles that volunteers can assume, with training modules offered regularly to make sure they are comfortable doing the work needed. This kind of codified volunteering protocol is still in development.

There is a similar challenge around issues of obtaining truly informed consent in regard to copyright and online access from donors. Care must be taken to explain to donors who are unfamiliar with the Internet that their per-sonal images will be shared freely on such a platform. As much as possible, the team demonstrates the visibility and discoverability of other donated mate-rials through a web browser if a donor is unfamiliar with web technologies. Donors are also asked to grant a Creative Commons license for the materials they donate. Since participants often donate materials contained in decades-old family photo albums, precise information about copyright ownership is frequently unknown to the donor. The Queens Memory team makes an effort to explain the terms of a Creative Commons license and then posts a take-down notice on the program's website so that interested parties can easily submit questions and requests about content on the site.

The Queens Memory team has found that both volunteers and donors come with a wide range of digital literacy skill levels. At the high end of technological competency are the graduate students and professional librarians, journalists, and artists who often bring their own high-end equipment to the tasks of recording interviews, digitizing historic artifacts for donation, and editing time-based media. At the low end of digital literacy, the Queens Memory team helps donors and volunteers to operate digital cameras, draft and edit documents in Microsoft Word, and use a smartphone or digital recorder to record an interview.

Queens Memory participants leave the community scanning events with both their original material and a flash drive of digital surrogates created during the event. The flash drive is the most tangible outcome of their participation in Queens Memory. However, many donors do not have the necessary digital literacy skills for the flash drive to be a meaningful takeaway from the event. In fact, some donors do not know what a flash drive is, or how to connect it to a computer. This issue reflects current research findings into public library patrons' digital preservation knowledge: individuals are either not aware of the impermanent state of digital possessions, or they do not have sufficient knowledge to mediate this impermanence.[8] Participants in the study lacked knowledge about the storage formats and devices that are appropriate for long-term preservation and access to digital content, and, as researcher Andrea Copeland states, "as a result, valuable representations of personal memories intended for future generations will be lost through ignorance and/or benign neglect."[9]

TEACHING PARTICIPANTS PERSONAL DIGITAL ARCHIVING

It was evident that it was necessary for Queens Memory to incorporate digital literacy education into its activities, and personal digital archiving was a natural fit for the community scanning events, which are simultaneously framed by both local and digital history. For librarians and archivists who work in a public library setting, creating opportunities to teach patrons about digital literacy broadly, and personal digital archiving specifically, is part of the service mission of the Queens Library.[10] The Library of Congress has also noted that public libraries "are increasingly involved in spreading digital literacy—facility with the internet and developing technology skills—into the communities they serve, and the knowledge of digital preservation and personal digital archiving is certainly part of digital literacy."[11] Queens Memory community scanning events provide the opportunity to integrate PDA education into a structured, history-focused event. Studies of information literacy training have demonstrated that "linking adult learners' prior and authentic experiences to practice new skills and knowledge helps them construct meaning and promote reflective thinking in the learning process."[12] Over the course of several months in late 2015, the Queens Memory team developed several teaching tools, iterating from a simple handout, to a brochure, and then a two-hour digitization training.

THE "WHAT'S ON MY THUMB DRIVE?" HANDOUT

The first tool Queens Memory developed to integrate PDA education into its community scanning events was a simple brochure explaining what files are on the flash drives that donors receive. The Queens Memory team provides donors with both TIFF and JPEG versions of each digital surrogate they create. The robust TIFF files can be used to print or enlarge images; the smaller JPEG files can be e-mailed to the donors' family members or friends, or posted to social media. The Queens Memory team recognized that donors might not be able to create their own JPEG files, and in fact might not even know the differences between the two file types. The small handout, given with the flash drive, explains what types of files are on the flash drive, and suggests how each file type is best used. Although this information is very simple, it gives participants a starting place for understanding the digital material on their flash drives, and potentially also on their home computers. Queens Memory staff and volunteers also frequently have one-on-one conversations with donors, discussing the file types and their different uses, and demonstrating how to plug the flash drive into the computer and open the file folders.

THE "PRESERVING YOUR DIGITAL MEMORIES" BROCHURE

Building on this simple handout, Queens Memory staff created a brochure to give participants a more comprehensive resource explaining how to care for the digital surrogates created during the community scanning events, as well as any digital files that donors may already have. The brochure attempts to balance accessibility with robust information and professional standards. In creating the text for the brochure, unnecessary technical language was avoided,

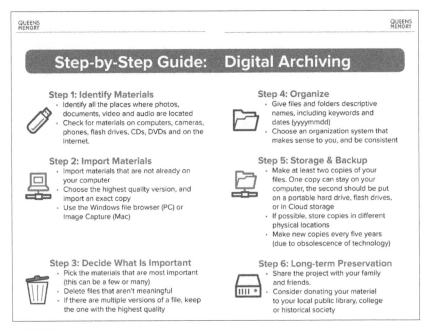

FIGURE 7.2

Centerfold from Queens Memory brochure "Preserving Your Digital Memories"

since this consists of "speed bumps for the general public that only disrupt the flow of explanation."[13] In retrospect, accessible language could have been emphasized even more. Photographs donated during past community scanning events were included to make the brochure more attractive and relevant to donors' lives and personal collections.

The brochure begins with an overview of the types of digital content that people might have, and how that material is uniquely fragile. The main threats to the longevity of digital material are outlined, including format obsolescence and the failure of computers and hard drives. The brochure then introduces the idea that digital content requires care, and the brochure provides a step-by-step guide for digital archiving (see figure 7.2).

As shown in figure 7.2, the brochure provides simple instructions for identifying material stored on multiple devices, importing it, deciding what materials are important, and organizing files as well as storage options and backing up. The last step in the guide includes options for long-term preservation, such as sharing the project with family members or donating to a local archival institution. In researching and developing these guidelines, Queens Memory staff relied heavily on the recommendations of the Library of Congress, which are simplified versions of the steps that organization uses for its own digital collections,[14] and the "Activists' Guide to Archiving Video," produced by WITNESS.[15]

The brochure also includes tips for digitizing photos and documents. This is a frequently asked question when staff and volunteers encounter donors at community events where their personal mementoes are being digitized. Donors often have scanners at home, or have family members with scanners, but they don't know how to get started. Although the information included in the brochure is very brief, it provides basic standards for digitizing photos and documents. Finally, the brochure includes a description of the Queens Memory project, as well as contact information. This provides another opportunity to educate donors about the program, and make the connection between Queens Memory's local history and community archive missions and the field of personal digital archiving.

DIGITIZATION TRAINING SESSIONS

Another way that Queens Memory shares this information with community members is through more in-depth digitization trainings. Over the course of the yearlong Culture in Transit grant, Queens Memory staff worked with community partners to develop and conduct two trainings that taught the principles, best practices, and workflows for digitizing photographs and documents. The first training was with a local historical society in Breezy Point, a small community that experienced extensive flooding during Hurricane Sandy in 2012. The second was with the Greater Ridgewood Youth Council, a community center where a group of fourteen- and fifteen-year-olds participating in a teen employment program were conducting a community documentation project involving oral history and photo digitization.

The trainings focused on the digitization process and workflow, and included technical explanations of resolution, bit-depth, color space, compression, and file format. Although Queens Memory provides a list of technical standards that are both professional and responsive to the reality of the situation and the resources available, it is also very important for participants to learn how and why to choose particular standards and settings. When community members learn about the technology behind the process of digitization, they are empowered to make their own decisions about best practices, as well as applying this knowledge to other scenarios. At the beginning of the training in Breezy Point, none of the participants could explain the concept of resolution. Only two hours later, participants not only understood resolution, but could also come up with multiple analogies to explain the difference between lossy and lossless compression!

The trainings included sections on metadata, and provided suggestions as to how to collect and record metadata for material being digitized. In this section, it was particularly successful to use age-appropriate examples: card catalogs for the older adults at the Breezy Point Historical Society, and Instagram for the teenagers at the Greater Ridgewood Youth Council. Additionally, this portion of the training proved to be a great opportunity to talk about the historical value of the collections, and how others might interact with these materials in the future. Ultimately, these trainings aimed to empower individuals and communities through technical knowledge, allowing them to be better custodians of their historical materials by digitizing and sharing their collections.

CONCLUSION

The PDA teaching tools employed by Queens Memory at community scanning events and digitization trainings extend the reach of the program's community archiving focus. PDA knowledge provides additional meaning and context for participants, as well as expanding the volunteer base for the program: "By engaging individuals in the identification and preservation of their own personal, digital objects, it may be possible to increase awareness in, and commitment to, community repositories that reflect a community's diversity and that will serve all."[16] After participating in the Queens Memory digitization training, youth at the Greater Ridgewood Youth Council hosted a community scanning day for neighborhood residents and they digitized materials from the community center's archive—and all these materials are featured on the program's website. As the historical record becomes increasingly born-digital, it is imperative that Queens Memory donors gain the skills and knowledge to become stewards of the digital content that documents life in the borough of Queens, New York. Finally, teaching PDA as an integral part of Queens Memory aims to fulfill the service mission of the Queens Library by creating knowledgeable technology users. Teaching the underlying principles and best practices of PDA allows participants to move away from a consumer-driven relationship to technology and towards critical citizenship in the digital age.

NOTES

1. Toby Butler and Graeme Miller, "Linked: A Landmark in Sound, a Public Walk of Art," *Cultural Geographies* 12, no. 1 (2005): 77–88, doi: 10.1191/1474474005eu317xx.

2. Patricia K. Galloway, "Oral Tradition in Living Cultures: The Role of Archives in the Preservation of Memory," in *Community Archives: The Shaping of Memory*, ed. Jeannette A. Bastian and Ben Alexander (London: Facet, 2009), 78.

3. Galloway, "Oral Tradition in Living Cultures."
4. "About Knowledge River," University of Arizona, https://knowledge-river.mukurtu.net/about.
5. American University in Cairo, "University on the Square," Facebook, https://www.facebook.com/UniversityOnTheSquare/.
6. Michelle Caswell, "Seeing Yourself in History: Community Archives and the Fight against Symbolic Annihilation," *The Public Historian* 36, no. 4 (2014): 26–37, doi: 10.1525/tph.2014.36.4.26.
7. "Culture in Transit Toolkit," Metropolitan New York Library Council, https://mnylc.github.io/cit-toolkit/.
8. Andrea J. Copeland, "Analysis of Public Library Users' Digital Preservation Practices," *Journal of the American Society for Information Science and Technology* 62, no. 7 (2011): 1288.
9. Copeland, "Analysis of Public Library Users' Digital Preservation Practices," 1288.
10. Queens Library, "Technology Values Statement," 2016, www.queenslibrary.org/about-us/mission-statement.
11. Mike Ashenfelder, "The Library of Congress and Personal Digital Archiving," in *Personal Archiving: Preserving Our Digital Heritage,* ed. Donald T. Hawkins (Medford, NJ: Information Today, 2013), 44.
12. Horge-Ji Lai, "Information Literacy Training in Public Libraries: A Case from Canada," *Educational Technology & Society* 14, no. 2 (2011): 82.
13. Ashenfelder, "The Library of Congress and Personal Digital Archiving," 41.
14. Ashenfelder, "The Library of Congress and Personal Digital Archiving," 34.
15. "Activists' Guide to Archiving Video," WITNESS, https://archiving.witness.org/archive-guide.
16. Andrea J. Copeland and Deborah Barreau, "Helping People to Manage and Share Their Digital Information: A Role for Public Libraries," *Library Trends,* 59, no. 4 (2011): 637.

BIBLIOGRAPHY

"About Knowledge River." University of Arizona. https://knowledge-river.mukurtu.net/about.

"Activists' Guide to Archiving Video." WITNESS. https://archiving.witness.org/archive-guide/.

American University in Cairo. "University on the Square." Facebook. https://www.facebook.com/UniversityOnTheSquare/.

Ashenfelder, Mike. "The Library of Congress and Personal Digital Archiving." In *Personal Archiving: Preserving Our Digital Heritage,* edited by Donald T. Hawkins. Medford, NJ: Information Today, 2013.

Butler, Toby, and Graeme Miller. "Linked: A Landmark in Sound, a Public Walk of Art." *Cultural Geographies* 12, no. 1 (2005): 77–88. doi: 10.1191/1474474005eu317xx.

Caswell, Michelle. "Seeing Yourself in History: Community Archives and the Fight against Symbolic Annihilation." *The Public Historian* 36, no. 4 (2014): 26–37. doi: 10.1525/tph.2014.36.4.26.

Copeland, Andrea J. "Analysis of Public Library Users' Digital Preservation Practices." *Journal of the American Society for Information Science and Technology* 62, no. 7 (2011): 1288–1300.

Copeland, Andrea J., and Deborah Barreau. "Helping People to Manage and Share Their Digital Information: A Role for Public Libraries." *Library Trends,* 59, no. 4 (2011): 637–49.

"Culture in Transit Toolkit." Metropolitan New York Library Council. https://mnylc.github .io/cit-toolkit/.

Galloway, Patricia K. "Oral Tradition in Living Cultures: The Role of Archives in the Preservation of Memory." In *Community Archives: The Shaping of Memory,* edited by Jeannette A. Bastian and Ben Alexander. London: Facet, 2009.

Lai, Horge-Ji. "Information Literacy Training in Public Libraries: A Case from Canada." *Educational Technology & Society* 14, no. 2 (2011): 81–88.

"Technology Values Statement." Queens Library. www.queenslibrary.org/about-us/ mission-statement.

LOTUS NORTON-WISLA
AND MICHAEL WYNNE

8

Community-Based Digital Archiving

The Plateau Peoples' Web Portal
at Washington State University

DIGITAL ARCHIVES CAN INTRODUCE a new layer of challenges related to the sustainability, preservation, and access of collections for everyone from a seasoned professional managing hundreds of collections to an individual or family managing their own files. This is true whether the files are born digital or digitized from a physical item—and many personal collections are a mixture of both. The ecosystem of digital archival work includes the preservation, management, curation, and circulation of digital files—all of which are important issues in tribal and non-tribal environments. Our work at Washington State University's Center for Digital Scholarship and Curation (CDSC) is focused on the ethical use of technology to further mutually beneficial collaborations, especially with tribal partners throughout the region. In this chapter, we will share our experience with the next step of personal digital archiving: using digital tools to allow people to share personal and family collections within a larger context of shared community history.

This chapter demonstrates how digital platforms can be used to support communities, individuals, and families as they organize, describe, and add value to their digital content. Personal digital archiving often connects to broader themes of sharing digital content between family and community, which is influenced by a broad range of histories. This chapter will provide library, archives, and museum professionals with guidelines for how to evaluate and use digital platforms to engage specific groups of interested and invested individuals in managing and sharing their own digital content.

First, we provide a short discussion of the meaning and history of community archives and provide a base for further research. Next, we demonstrate the connections between the ideas of personal digital archiving and community-based archiving using an online sharing platform. Specifically, we discuss how engaging in these efforts in tandem can increase engagement and investment. Then we explain several factors to consider when choosing an online platform for a community-based archiving project. Finally, to show the specifics of how this type of work can be carried out, we will describe an ongoing collaborative project between several Plateau region tribes in the Inland Northwest and the Center for Digital Scholarship and Curation.

WHO WE ARE

At Washington State University's Center for Digital Scholarship and Curation, our mission is *to promote meaningful collaborations using technology in ethically minded and socially empowering ways.*[1] Technology is just one piece of a successful digital archiving project. Relationship building, project planning, and ethically conscious decision making are all steps that must happen before digital tools are implemented. A core part of the CDSC's mission is to partner with Native American and Indigenous communities to support the ethical curation of cultural resources. Through partnerships and collaborations with tribal institutions in the Northwest and beyond, we have learned from the unique opportunities and challenges that these communities face when managing digital content within their communities. Here are brief descriptions of our main projects at the CDSC.

Plateau Peoples' Web Portal (PPWP)

> The PPWP is, at the time of publication, a collaboration between the Spokane Tribe of Indians, the Confederated Tribes of the Colville Reservation, the Confederated Tribes of the Umatilla Indian Reservation, the Coeur d'Alene Tribe of Indians, the Confederated Tribes of Warm Springs, the Confederated Tribes and Bands of the Yakama Nation, the Salish-Pend d'Oreille Culture Committee, the Center for Digital Scholarship and Curation, and Native American Programs at Washington State University (WSU). The portal is a gateway to Columbia Plateau peoples' cultural materials held in multiple repositories, including WSU's Manuscripts, Archives and Special Collections, the Northwest

Museum of Art and Culture, and the National Anthropological Archives and the National Museum of the American Indian at the Smithsonian Institution. The materials in the portal have been chosen and curated by tribal representatives. Each item has one or more records associated with it as well as added traditional knowledge and cultural narratives to enhance and enrich the understanding of many audiences. CDSC staff provide training to PPWP tribal representatives on how to use the platform, teach others, and develop workflows to gather knowledge from their communities.

Mukurtu CMS[2]

Mukurtu CMS is a content-sharing and community archiving platform that enables communities to manage, share, preserve, and exchange their digital heritage in culturally relevant and ethically minded ways. As a team, we are committed to maintaining an open, community-driven approach to Mukurtu's continued development. Our first priority is to help build a platform that fosters relationships of respect and trust.

Tribal Stewardship Cohort Program (TSCP)

The TSCP is a yearlong training program for professionals working in tribal archives, libraries, museums, and cultural centers. Over the course of a year, participants come to WSU four times, with online education through the rest of the months in their home communities. The TSCP covers the life cycle of digital stewardship using a cohort-based educational model, discussion, and hands-on learning. Providing access to digital collections in each cohort member's community is a key topic throughout the year of training. The curriculum is tailored to each cohort's needs, and CDSC staff provide training that is flexible and adaptable to the group's priorities.

Sustainable Heritage Network (SHN)[3]

The SHN is a collaborative network and online platform that brings together communities, institutions, and professionals to support each other by sharing the knowledge, educational resources, and technology necessary for the responsible digitization and preservation of cultural heritage. The SHN provides hands-on and virtual topic-specific workshops and short courses; online educational resources relevant to tribal institutions; and access to experts, workspaces, and equipment through its network of workbenches to further digitization and preservation. CDSC staff host workshops at WSU and travel to present workshops to professionals working in tribal institutions.

The PPWP, Mukurtu CMS, TSCP, and SHN projects overlap in both practical and philosophical ways. With an emphasis on local curation, driven by community needs and an emphasis on technology use, these projects provide insight into the needs of tribal communities for their digital content. The common goals of these projects tie back into the CDSC's mission of ethical curation and collaboration, with an emphasis on "train-the-trainer" methods, flexible education and support, and accountable partnerships.

DEFINING "COMMUNITY-BASED ARCHIVING" AND "COMMUNITY ARCHIVES"

Community is a broad term that can denote a group of people with a shared culture, heritage, goals, or interests. In our experience, communities may be separated by distance, and many diverse voices can be part of a community. *Community archives* are usually organizations that are independent from institutions like universities, historical societies, or state or federal repositories. Michelle Caswell writes that *community-based archives* "serve as an alternative, grassroots venue for communities to make collective decisions about what is of enduring value to them and to control the means through which stories about their past are constructed."[4] In community archives, community members and community leaders make the decisions about selection, metadata, curation, and access—whether for physical or digital materials in their care. Representation in the existing historical record (found in state, federal, and other repositories) can be nonexistent, inaccurate, and even harmful to many communities due to the historical legacies of institutional collecting agendas. The work of creating equal and inclusive representation in our collections, staff, and messages is the responsibility of all informational professionals. Terry Cook envisions "a shift in core principles, from exclusive custodianship and ownership of archives to shared stewardship and collaboration."[5] Partnerships and joint projects with larger institutions are possible, but the self-direction and autonomy of community-based archives and archiving projects is an important priority for many groups engaging in this work. Examples of types of partnerships include joint projects, the sharing of digital surrogates or metadata, hosting, storage space, training, and consultation.

Communities that are not represented in the history of national and regional memory institutions can organize around the purpose of preserving, recontextualizing, and telling their histories from their own perspectives. In their detailed examination of community archives, Gilliland and Flinn write that community-based archives are "diverse, real world interventions into the field of local, regional and national, and even international archival and heritage narratives, often critical interventions, politically charged with notions of social justice and civil rights."[6] These "critical interventions" can correct, challenge, or provide a fuller picture of an incomplete historical record.

Consumer-priced digitization equipment, the Internet, and social media have made it easier and less costly to participate in the archival process, even across the geographical distances[7] that many communities face. Online plat-forms designed with community archiving in mind open up new possibilities for groups to manage, narrate, and share content on their own terms. With these thoughts in mind, we will discuss community-based archiving as an effort that academic institutions can work to support while respecting the independence, values, and vision of the community in question.

HOW A COMMUNITY ARCHIVING PLATFORM RELATES TO PERSONAL DIGITAL ARCHIVING

Personal digital archiving projects that start at an individual level can take on new meaning if individuals and families are given the opportunity to col-laborate with others in their community. Often, the goals of PDA are limited to what a single person or family can envision for their records. Community archiving allows a given community to combine their ideas and resources in support of a shared goal for the cultural heritage materials they can add. In many tribal communities, tribally managed digital archives are an expression of sovereignty, while also supporting local needs for access, protection, and description that are specific to the community. It is important to remember that these digital cultural heritage materials that families and groups keep for generations are not only digital files; they are also meaningful and living languages, family stories and history, ceremonial or traditional practices, and traditional knowledge. The revitalization of language and culture in so many Indigenous communities means that digital materials can be used for lan-guage classes, by artists, and for youth programs to keep traditions alive.

Many tribal communities we have worked with are developing image digitization programs, not just for library and archives collections, but for collections in the community—in shoeboxes in closets, in attics, and under beds. When working to collect and preserve these collections, people are not necessarily ready or willing to make a physical donation to the tribal archives. This is not an end to the discussion, however, since many tribal institutions are willing to work with community members' needs. A common solution is to offer help with the digitizing, management, and preservation of materials, and to simply request a copy of the digital files and metadata. This concept of digitization assistance extends to many formats, and to managing born-digi-tal files as well, but most people will have a combination of materials, and will need help with multiple stages. These needs, and some considerations we have heard from people working in tribal institutions, are listed below.

Help with digitizing collections or transferring from digital media:

Tribal institutions can accomplish digitization work in several ways: (1) by providing on-demand assistance to community members on a case-by-case basis when contacted; (2) by hosting community scanning/

data days when people bring their materials during certain times or events; or (3) by traveling to community homes or senior centers to do digitization. Many individuals have identified visits as a strategy that is especially helpful for elders who might not be able to travel to another location, or who just feel more at ease in their homes.

Help with the preservation of physical materials:

Through storage agreements, or recommendations for home storage, tribal communities may have cultural practices that govern how materials should be stored, handled, protected and used, such as men or women only handling certain objects, prayers for certain items, and so on.

Help organizing and preserving digital files:

When files are created through digitization processes or are born digital, community members need the help of professionals to understand file management and digital preservation concepts. Tribal professionals can help people understand best practices for long-term storage at home and for future donations. This could be as simple as explaining the lower quality of a photograph pulled off of Facebook, or more complicated steps like choosing a way to back up a hard drive.

In addition to these technical needs, often a greater need is a place to view materials, histories, stories, and information produced by other community members, and the opportunity to contribute to them. If a community-based archiving project and platform is in place for community members to add to, the community archive will also benefit from their involvement. Beyond the digital items that are added, there are many valuable areas whereby individuals can expand the metadata and reach of the archive. Community members can identify people, places, and events that can provide critical context. This information is invaluable, especially when many people can bring their own perspective and family history to fill in gaps in knowledge of community history. A digital platform that has be thoughtfully designed can bring together appropriate sharing with the specific technical and cultural needs of a community.

FACTORS TO CONSIDER WHEN CHOOSING A COMMUNITY ARCHIVING PLATFORM

When planning a community archiving project, the collection, preservation, and access platform (or platforms) need to be selected early in the process. There are many factors that go into making this decision, and in some cases, they may differ from those that affect the decisions made for a larger institutional archive or repository. The deciding factors will always fall along a spectrum, but it can be useful to consider technical, logistical, and implementation concerns on one end, and user and community needs and concerns on the other. As an organization or institution, it can be easy to focus on factors such as cost, resources (both technological and personnel), and other implementation needs, but it is equally important to consider who the community is and what their needs, goals, and concerns are.

Cost

The costs for an archival platform or other content management system are rarely as straightforward as purchasing a piece of software off the shelf. While there are open source platforms, many systems are to a greater or lesser extent proprietary and require an ongoing license or subscription. In some cases, an annual license fee may also include some amount of training and/or ongoing user support, although these may also carry additional fees. That being said, full-service platforms where the provider covers installation, maintenance, and hosting can be convenient, especially if your organization does not have sufficient resources to maintain the infrastructure internally.

On the other end of the spectrum are open source systems which, depending on the specific license, users may be able to use and modify to best meet their needs. While there may not be fees associated with using an open source platform, these platforms should not be assumed to be without costs. The required infrastructure and physical equipment can be significant, as can the personnel costs, since qualified technical staff will be required (e.g., a system administrator and suitable server equipment). Initial setup costs will need to be factored in, as well as ongoing maintenance.

Depending on the nature of the organization, consider seeking out a larger institution for support or partnership. Regional or national organizations, or local universities may be willing to provide hosting or other access to their existing infrastructure and resources, and this may reduce (though it will probably not eliminate) some of the costs.

Features

The features and functions offered by any given platform will vary significantly depending on the intended use: a library or cataloging system will have a very different focus from a museum management system, a records management platform, or an archival or preservation system. If a project needs to support a wide range of features from multiple disciplines, multiple platforms may be required.

Assessing the needs of your organization is essential in choosing a suitable platform. Do you need to manage archival accessioning and processing workflows, or catalog and check out materials? Do you need to manage user and administrative permissions and access? Do you need to be able to work either remotely or off-line? What metadata standard do you use, and are you concerned about your content being in a proprietary format?

Ask if there are trial periods or introductory training available, and seek out existing or past users of any platforms being considered for their feedback and experience. Being able to explore an established project or speak to the staff responsible for maintaining one can be very helpful in answering any questions you might have.

Community Needs and User Experience

As stated earlier, *community* is a broad term that is often used to represent a diverse group. Every project will have different sets of stakeholders, each of which will have their own opinions, needs, and concerns. Addressing user needs means not just thinking about who the end users may be and attempting to anticipate their requirements, but rather going out and conducting community surveys, workshops, and focus groups. For a new archive or program, be sure to consider potential donors or content contributors in addition to the end user.

Will users want to access material remotely, or will it only be accessible on-site? Do staff and users need a different experience; that is, are the administration and data entry a different system than what the public sees? Are there any access restrictions that need to be in place, either through donor embargoes, legal concern, or cultural values? Who are your target, or most important, users, and what is their level of computer skills; can the most important users access and navigate the system? What kind of engagement do your users want; are they happy to browse content, or do they want to contribute to the records, or even add their own content?

Since there are many factors to consider, and every community archiving project is so unique, it is not practical to simply give a set of recommendations for making a final decision. Rather, reviewing the points above, take stock of your organization's resources, your internal needs, and your community's needs and interests. It is entirely possible that after taking a community survey, the wish list will be impractically long or detailed, and no single platform will meet all the identified needs; in such cases, a balance between community requests, organizational resources, and administrative needs will need to be struck.

SUMMARY OF THE PLATEAU PEOPLES' WEB PORTAL PROJECT, AND WASHINGTON STATE UNIVERSITY'S INVOLVEMENT

As introduced earlier in the "Who We Are" section, the Plateau Peoples' Web Portal is a collaboratively curated and reciprocally managed archive of Plateau cultural materials held in multiple repositories, including WSU's Manuscripts,

Archives and Special Collections; the Northwest Museum of Art and Culture; and the National Anthropological Archives and the National Museum of the American Indian at the Smithsonian Institution. The portal enables each tribal community to appropriately manage access to their cultural materials and narratives, and it supports rich descriptions, narratives, and storytelling provided by multiple community voices in addition to institutional records.

Washington State University has a signed Memorandum of Understanding (MOU) with fifteen tribes in the quad-state region (Washington, Oregon, Idaho, and Montana) that promotes sharing resources and expanding education opportunities.[8] The MOU included the establishment of a Native American Advisory Board to the President of WSU, and in 2009 the advisory board requested the development of an online portal to provide access to Plateau materials held at WSU and other institutions. At that time Kim Christen, working with the Native Programs Office and the Plateau Center for American Indian Studies, was asked to extend Mukurtu CMS, an indigenous content management system she developed while working with the Warumungu Aboriginal community in Tennant Creek, Australia, to meet these needs.[9] The initial version of Mukurtu CMS developed with the Warumungu community was an off-line archive focused on providing community access to photographs, and as such, needed to be modified to meet three additional criteria in order to meet the needs presented by the Native American Advisory Board:

1. Online access for tribal members across several states
2. Include WSU library collections
3. Incorporate multiple voices and stories when representing content

These needs provided direction for the development of Mukurtu CMS 1.5 (and later 2.0.x), which serves as the platform for the portal.[10]

The identification and selection of items for inclusion in the portal are driven by community needs. While the workflow varies with each tribe, the process starts by bringing tribal representatives into the holding institutions, so they can search for and review archival photos and documents, and museum objects. This process is also supplemented by the research staff at each institution, whose work is guided by feedback from tribal representatives. Once items are selected by the tribal representatives, they are then digitized (if not already), and the institutional metadata is formatted to fit the Mukurtu Core metadata scheme. No materials from WSU or other partner institutions are included in the portal that were not requested by a tribal representative. Once the initial portal records are uploaded by WSU staff, tribal members are able to add their voices and enrich the records. Crucially, the workflow involves community engagement at every stage, from development of the software, to identification and selection of materials, to curating and giving voice to the individual records.

For its metadata scheme, Mukurtu CMS (and by extension the portal) is built on "Mukurtu Core," which is an extended version of Dublin Core. While many fields map directly to Dublin Core, there are some unique features that were included to allow Indigenous communities to best represent their cultural heritage. Options include Traditional Knowledge and Cultural Narrative fields, and Traditional Knowledge Labels.

The Traditional Knowledge (TK) and Cultural Narrative (CN) fields complement the more general Description field. Where Description is well-suited to general, often institutionally provided information (e.g., physical description, cataloging notes), the TK and CN fields extend that, providing spaces for more specialized knowledge. Cultural Narratives are often more detailed descriptions of the content itself; in the case of a woven basket, for example, an experienced basket maker can provide more detail about the construction or materials used, the history of that particular basket, or traditional basket making in general. Traditional Knowledge usually encompasses information known only within a community, and not likely to be recorded elsewhere, such as the particular story or legend told by the item in question. All three of these fields support rich formatting, and the ability to embed additional media within them, so that an audio or video recording can be included, rather than relying solely on text.

Traditional Knowledge Labels are part of the Local Contexts project[11] and are a tool for Indigenous communities to add informational labels to digital cultural heritage materials. The TK Labels were developed for use where cultural heritage materials are either in the public domain, or held by a body other than the originating tribe, where these materials are divorced from their appropriate cultural context and protocols, allowing communities to correct the public historical record. There are thirteen labels which can be displayed in item records, all of which can be customized at the community level within Mukurtu, so that each tribe can customize the text of the labels that they choose to use.

One of the most important functions built into Mukurtu as a result of portal needs is the ability to include multiple voices or stories on each record or item through Community Records. Within the portal, each item is uploaded by the holding institution or individual, and is populated with available metadata. Once an item has been uploaded, any of the tribes affiliated with that record can then add Community Records. Community Records share the same media file as the initial record (e.g., a photo of a basket), but all of the metadata fields can be completely distinct from the initial record, allowing community members to correct, challenge, or enrich the record. Community Records are displayed non-hierarchically with respect to the initial records. That is, they are not supplementary records, nor is the information within them represented to be of any less significant value than that provided by WSU or other institutions. Multiple Community Records can be added to each item, and they can each have distinct Cultural Protocols to define access parameters.

The final unique feature provided by Mukurtu CMS is the ability to provide individual users with appropriate access to specific items, managed by

Cultural Protocols. While content provided by WSU and other partner institutions is generally public, information entered by community members may not all be appropriate for public dissemination. Each tribe can specify how their records are shared: some may be shared publicly to inform and educate both community members and the general public, some may be available only to tribal members, and some may be available only to smaller community groups such as a single family.

The portal is an active, ongoing project that the CDSC is committed to supporting, as part of a larger picture of engagement with local tribal governments and communities. Materials from WSU and other partners are continually being identified, selected, and added to the portal, records are being enriched by community members, and communities are also uploading content of their own—providing contemporary and current context. It is a collaborative project that, by providing online community access to materials that are otherwise difficult to engage with, is enriching public, institutional, and community records through community engagement and knowledge sharing.

CONCLUSION

This chapter provides a foundation of information to consider, and examples of how the CDSC has been involved in community-based efforts. Whether your institution or organization is an archives, public library, academic library, community archive, or any other resource center serving your community, there are many steps that can enhance personal digital archiving beyond preservation and management. In addition to these first steps of organizing and saving digital content, people, families, and groups have the need to access, share, tell, and retell personal memories and stories—especially when their histories have traditionally been told without their input. To conclude this chapter, we offer some lessons learned from projects at our institution.

Learn more about your institution's relationships with Indigenous communities in the region, currently and in the past. Understanding the positive *and* negative legacies of your institution (and the archives, libraries, and museum fields in general) is important to start any new endeavor. Think about what you, your project, or your department can do to strengthen those relationships, through formal and informal means. At Washington State University's CDSC, these ties and mutual support are a clearly stated part of our mission. We use Memorandums of Understanding to formalize projects and relationships, plan for sustainability, and make sure that we are showing our commitment in a tangible way.

From the projects we have been involved with, we have learned that each community will have specific goals for digital content. The goals and priorities could be general, like language revitalization, providing community voices in the public record, or making sure access is limited for culturally sensitive information. The goals and priorities could also be project-specific, like creating a fourth-grade class online curriculum, starting a photograph identification project, or digitizing a dictionary. Our experience with the PPWP has taught us that it is not our role at the university to decide on the goals and priorities for communities, but to respect decisions that tribal representatives make, and work with them to provide technical solutions.

With the PPWP and other projects, we continue to learn from working with individuals and communities about their needs for digital archiving. These projects push us to think about new ways of envisioning how the historical record is shaped and shared with future generations, and how to enhance and focus on community voices through digital tools.

NOTES

1. Center for Digital Scholarship and Curation, Washington State University Libraries & College of Arts and Sciences, 2017, http://cdsc.libraries.wsu.edu.

2. Mukurtu CMS, Washington State University Center for Digital Scholarship and Curation, 2017, http://mukurtu.org.

3. "Sustainable Heritage Network," Washington State University Center for Digital Scholarship and Curation, 2017, http://sustainableheritagenetwork.org.

4. Michelle Caswell, "Toward a Survivor-Centered Approach to Records Documenting Human Rights Abuse: Lessons from Community Archives." *Archival Science* 14, no. 3-4 (2014): 310.

5. Terry Cook, "Evidence, Memory, Identity, and Community: Four Shifting Archival Paradigms," *Archival Science* 13, no. 2-3 (2013): 115.

6. For a deep dive into what community archives are in the United States and United Kingdom, see Anne Gilliland and Andrew Flinn, "Community Archives: What Are We Really Talking About," presentation at CIRN Prato Community Informatics Conference 2013: Keynote, 3.

7. Gilliland and Flinn, "Community Archives," 13.

8. "Washington State University—Memorandum of Understanding," Washington State University Native American Programs, 2017, http://native.wsu.edu/tribal-liaison/mou.

9. Kimberly Christen, "Opening Archives: Respectful Repatriation," *The American Archivist* 74, no. 1 (2011): 185–210, 186.

10. For a more detailed discussion of the development of Mukurtu CMS, see Kimberly Christen, "A Safe Keeping Place: Mukurtu CMS Innovating Museum Collaborations," in *Technology and Digital Initiatives: Innovative Approaches for Museums*, ed. Juilee Decker (Lanham, MD: Rowman and Littlefield, 2015), 61–68.

11. Local Contexts, n.p., n.d., http://localcontexts.org.

BIBLIOGRAPHY

Caswell, Michelle. "Toward a Survivor-Centered Approach to Records Documenting Human Rights Abuse: Lessons from Community Archives." *Archival Science* 14, no. 3-4 (2014): 307–22.

Center for Digital Scholarship and Curation. Washington State University Libraries & College of Arts and Sciences. 2017. http://cdsc.libraries.wsu.edu.

Christen, Kimberly. "Opening Archives: Respectful Repatriation." *The American Archivist* 74, no. 1 (2011): 185–210.

———. "A Safe Keeping Place: Mukurtu CMS Innovating Museum Collaborations." In *Technology and Digital Initiatives: Innovative Approaches for Museums,* edited by Juilee Decker, 61–68. Lanham, MD: Rowman and Littlefield, 2015.

Cook, Terry. "Evidence, Memory, Identity, and Community: Four Shifting Archival Paradigms." *Archival Science* 13, no. 2-3 (2013): 95–120.

Gilliland, Anne, and Andrew Flinn. "Community Archives: What Are We Really Talking About." Presentation at CIRN Prato Community Informatics Conference 2013: Keynote. 2013.

Local Contexts. N.p., n.d. http://localcontexts.org.

Mukurtu CMS. Washington State University Center for Digital Scholarship and Curation. 2017. http://mukurtu.org.

Plateau Peoples' Web Portal. Washington State University Center for Digital Scholarship and Curation. 2017. http://plateauportal.libraries.wsu.edu.

Sustainable Heritage Network. Washington State University Center for Digital Scholarship and Curation. 2017. http://sustainableheritagenetwork.org.

"Washington State University—Memorandum of Understanding." Washington State University Native American Programs. 2017. http://native.wsu.edu/tribal-liaison/mou.

PART III

Personal Digital Archives and Academic Audiences

AMY BOCKO,
JOANNA DIPASQUALE,
RACHEL APPEL, AND
SARAH WALDEN McGOWAN

9
Personal Digital Archives Programming at Liberal Arts Colleges

WHEN IS THE "PERSONAL" THE PROFESSIONAL? For faculty and students who spend countless hours researching, writing, and developing new ideas, the answer (only sometimes tongue-in-cheek) is "always": the digital archiving of their personal materials quickly turns into the creation of collections that can span multiple years, formats, subjects, and versions. In the library, we know well that "save everything" and "curate everything" are very different. What role, then, could the liberal arts college's library play in helping our faculty and students curate their digital research materials and the scholarly communication objects that they create with an eye towards sustainability?

At Vassar, Wheaton, Bryn Mawr, and Amherst colleges, we designed Personal Digital Archiving Days (PDAD) events to push the boundaries of outreach and archiving, learn more about our communities' needs, and connect users to the right services needed to achieve their archiving goals. In fall 2014 we held sessions across each of our campuses (some for the first time, some as part of an ongoing PDAD series), using the Library of Congress's personal digital archiving resources as a model for our programming. Though our audiences and outcomes varied, we shared common goals: to provide outreach for the work we do, make the campus community aware of the services available to them, and impart best practices to attendees that will have lasting effects on their digital information management.[1]

Our successful on-campus Personal Digital Archiving Days grew out of the need we individually experienced to help members of our communities navigate the management, preservation, and stewardship of their digital content. The PDAD format that we implemented across our four college campuses was first developed in 2012 by Joanna DiPasquale, the head of digital scholarship and technology services (at the time, the digital initiatives librarian) at Vassar College. Vassar College Libraries were increasingly receiving inquiries from faculty members expressing their need to manage their personal digital research. With a newly established Digital Initiatives Department, DiPasquale saw the opportunity to use the Library of Congress's guidelines for personal digital archiving in a professional, scholarly setting. While these guidelines had been developed for preserving such materials as born-digital photographs/audio/video, personal digital records, and e-mails, we found that they contained overarching lessons that could be brought into the college environment. We also found that the line between the personal and professional lives of our patrons was becoming increasingly blurred, and at times interchangeable, so to use the Library of Congress's PDA guidelines for digital scholarship was a natural progression.

The collaborative Personal Digital Archiving Days that took place at Amherst, Bryn Mawr, Vassar, and Wheaton (MA) colleges in fall 2014 grew out of our association in the Oberlin 17 Digital Group. The Oberlin 17 is a subgroup of the Oberlin Group, a consortium of liberal arts college libraries that are all located in the Northeast. With a new focus on building digital collections, scholarship, and support among the libraries of the Oberlin 17, a collegial network of digital library practitioners formed. We hold an annual unconference, maintain an electronic discussion list, and regularly collaborate together. DiPasquale approached the group about a collective initiative to present PDAD programming in our libraries, and found three additional partners, Rachel Appel (Bryn Mawr College), Amy Bocko (Wheaton College, formerly of Vassar College), and Sarah Walden McGowan (Amherst College). They shared resources and ideas, and each tailored their PDAD to best serve the needs of their college communities. DiPasquale and Bocko focused on faculty scholarship, while Appel and Walden McGowan turned their attention to the student population, working with student groups and thesis writers, respectively. In each case, we focused on bringing best practices to our communities, identifying and connecting campus resources to the process, and discussing recommended software options and strategies for common problems.

In the following case studies, we each expand upon our experiences with Personal Digital Archiving Days at our colleges, including our PDAD formats, successes, and findings.

Vassar College Case Study

JOANNA DIPASQUALE

Head of Digital Scholarship and Technology Services

In fall 2012 the Vassar College Libraries explored ways to begin discussions among the faculty about preserving their research materials. While many faculty knew the various repositories that their disciplines provided for them (e.g., arXiv for physics research), they were unsure what the campus could provide to support their short- or long-term needs—and they often did not know which department to ask or how to best articulate their needs. I began my job as digital initiatives librarian for the college in May 2011 as part of a newly formed department, and by September 2012, when our faculty conversations began, it was clear that we needed a wider discussion that connected our faculty to the resources they needed to begin the task of preserving their documents, field notes, recordings, and more. The need to provide this advice came at a great time: the Library of Congress had launched its new digital preservation site, www.digitalpreservation.gov, complete with "starter kits" to host what it was calling Personal Digital Archiving Day events.[2] As every researcher knows, though, the terms *personal* and *professional* are frequently interchangeable—faculty dedicate their lives to their subjects, and their passion for their subject material is not just for the latest findings but also for the information they have accumulated to date. Could I adapt the best practices of personal digital archiving to common academic library workflows for institutional repositories, combine them with campus resources, and create an event that would disseminate high-quality information to our faculty?

The obvious answer was "yes," but getting to "yes" was only half the challenge. As I began my work, with significant input from the digital team (most notably Amy Bocko), it became clear that we had traditionally taken important administrative details for granted. Differences between our campus information technology services, media resources, academic computing, archiving, and digital library groups were clear to all the members of those teams, but were not at all clear to the faculty. Highly specific terms such as *institutional repository, digital library, data management plan,* and *archiving* had been used (and misused) interchangeably, exacerbating the confusion. Perhaps worst of all, faculty from different departments did not realize that their concerns about their materials' short- and long-term longevity had much in common with one another, as these faculty had had little opportunity to discuss them. Thus our digital initiatives group at the Vassar College Libraries joined forces with the college archivist and the Academic Computing and Media Resources departments (both of which are in our Computing and Information Services area) to design our first Personal Digital Archiving Day.

The planning process identified three important features that we knew we had to emphasize:

1. *Multiple session times.* We identified multiple times when members of a variety of departments were available, in order to foster as much interdisciplinary conversation as possible.

2. *Collaboration between departments on campus.* We ensured that multiple members of our departments were on hand to answer questions. Academic computing consultants could provide information about exporting materials from our learning management system, Moodle, while our Media Resources team skillfully answered questions about VHS reformatting (a service they perform in-house!). Meanwhile, I could answer questions about redundant backups and file-naming schemes, while our archivist could discuss records management issues.

3. *Presentation materials that connected advice to resources.* I designed a series of handouts and a presentation that mapped Library of Congress best practice guidelines to a service available on campus. For example, when we discussed the "3–2–1 Rule" (have 3 copies of your data, in 2 different media, 1 in a separate location), we provided information about CrashPlan and Google Drive, two freely available resources that our campus supported—and which were frequently confused (see figure 9.1). When we discussed reformatting, our handouts clearly showed labs on campus where equipment was available and personnel who could consult with faculty.

The 3-2-1 Rule

- Make 3 copies
- Have at least 2 of the copies on two different types of media
- Keep 1 copy in a different location from where you live/work

Ask: "What types of media do I have? What is the longevity of that media?"

Vassar resources:

- Media Resources Department
- Digital Media Zone computer lab
- CrashPlan software
- Google Drive

FIGURE 9.1

An example presentation slide showing how to connect the best practice of the 3-2-1 Rule to resources readily available on campus

To advertise, we brainstormed a list of faculty who might be good candidates for our sessions and then sent them a personal invitation through their library research liaison or academic computing consultant. We believed that targeted e-mails and personal invitations would go a long way in helping our professors understand what type of information we wanted to disseminate and why. If the topic was not relevant to them, then most likely they would not devote their free time to come to our event. For example, if a faculty member had recently approached an academic computing consultant about storing field notes, that faculty member was on our list of invitees; without that personal invitation, the faculty member might not have noticed our event in the many e-mails received that day. We then asked that faculty member to forward the e-mail to anyone else who might be interested. This model was sustainable for us because, as a small liberal arts college, personal connections between the faculty, librarians, and academic computing consultants are common, and worked well to lay the foundation for our audience.

Our sessions were initially designed as an "open house" model, where we imagined that each of our departments would have its own table, and faculty could walk from table to table to ask questions. When we started the event, however, we wanted to set the stage with a brief introduction, and so I began a basic presentation that provided an overview of personal digital archiving principles. Almost immediately, faculty began asking questions—and interesting conversations emerged right away. Thus, the open house model was quickly abandoned at our first event in favor of an open forum, where everyone could discuss questions and challenges at the same time. This approach proved incredibly useful, for each of us could provide our own perspectives on the challenges at hand. For example, a question about saving e-mail was much richer because our campus archivist could talk about records management principles, while one of our academic computing consultants could discuss Google's tagging feature in Gmail. Faculty began to discover connections with one another about similar problems they were having and how to tackle those problems, either on their own or with the right combination of people and resources.

As our Personal Digital Archiving Days took shape and we began hosting more lunchtime discussions for our faculty, the other half of our PDAD takeaway emerged: lurking under the surface of "digital archiving" (a weighty and fraught term!) were digital scholarship projects that the faculty did not explicitly realize they were doing. Thus PDAD became an excellent way to begin collaboration questions among librarians, academic computing consultants, and the faculty. A department on campus with many years of lab data, in a variety of formats, sought a way to preserve their materials—but they also wanted to provide an open-access way for researchers around the world to find those materials. Another faculty member had a series of high-quality TIFFs on ancient Roman funerary tablets; did the library work with standards like Epi-doc, a papyrology- and epigraphy-specific version of TEI? (Why, of course we can help!) Other faculty members asked questions that showed the challenge of creating data dictionaries or researching metadata standards, and PDAD provided an opportunity to connect librarians to these needs.

Subsequent PDAD events introduced a new and generally effective tool: the case study. We invited two faculty members who had attended a past event to come to another one and discuss how the principles and practices they had learned had helped to meet (or at least get the ball rolling on) their digital archiving needs. Our choice of faculty members was key: one of the most important pieces of feedback that we heard from our faculty was that digi-tal archiving was not just for the technophiles among them, and that faculty liked to hear about cases or circumstances where their colleagues might be more conservative about their technology use. To that end, our faculty mem-bers discussed how PDAD and our consultations had helped them, or how their materials were challenging enough that we needed more time to think through all of the aspects. Our case studies came from the History Depart-ment and the Art Department, and both involved faculty research. Neither case study talked about cutting-edge technology or solved problems, but instead they highlighted the workflows and resources used to get each faculty member to the next step in her digital archiving challenges.

After our first PDAD experience in October 2012, the libraries began a few outreach opportunities. First, we polled the faculty to see if the materials were useful and if we should host similar events, and the answers were affirmative. We continued our PDAD events for two additional years, eventually creating a more formal digital scholarship group on campus to continue extracting projects and meeting demand. Second, I presented our results to the Oberlin 17 group of libraries, which, as previously stated, is a regional group from the wider Oberlin Group,[3] a consortium of liberal arts colleges across the United States. The presentation resonated with other colleges, many of which found opportunities to connect students as well as faculty to digital archiving materials and services. Finally, the success of the first and subsequent events allowed us to take stock of the resources we had and where we could continue to meet our faculty's needs. For example, we had an institutional repository on campus, but few faculty knew about it or how it could help them. PDAD showed that the demand existed on campus to roll out broader institutional repository services and find new ways to make them resonate on campus. We also found that confusing terminology exacerbated a confusing set of services, and so we helped to make those services a bit clearer. Though we have much more to do, it was wonderful knowing that "personal" and "professional" dig-ital archiving brought so many of us together to take up these challenges and uncover exciting projects in the process.

As our PDAD events continue, we have continued to collect best practices on our digital library project blog,[4] always providing links to the Library of Congress and "real-world" examples whenever we can. We frequently distill the information down to the basics right away, because we want to use the events as ways to connect faculty to the appropriate on-campus resources and people. My wonderful coauthors helped me realize that we want faculty to think, "What is one thing you can do today to improve your 'digital life?'" And we want them to remember concepts such as the "3-2-1 Rule" in the context of our cloud services, metadata practices, or best practices about disk storage and reformatting, when they answer that question.

Bryn Mawr Case Study

RACHEL APPEL

Former Digital Collections Librarian (currently Digital Projects and Services Librarian at Temple University Libraries)

I began my position at Bryn Mawr College in spring 2014. In this position I oversaw digitization, digital asset management, and preservation. I was also part of a grant-funded project, College Women,[5] which is a coordinated effort between the colleges formerly known as the Seven Sisters. This project is a web-based portal built on Drupal for digitized college archives, specifically for items relating to student life at women's colleges before World War II. Interested users can search among trends in the experiences of students at that time. This project encouraged me to do two things. I wanted to partner with students to work on collecting their archives for their enduring value and for future access to them. If we were centering entire digital projects on student life from the first half of the twentieth century, we needed to become more active stewards in order to ensure the viability of born-digital student life materials. I also wanted to spread awareness about digital preservation to help fulfill the prior goal, which became tied in with PDAD events.

The College Archives in Bryn Mawr College Special Collections are meant to collect, preserve, and provide access to institutional records. The College Archives has traditionally been equipped to acquire administrative and faculty records on a semi-regular schedule, but documenting student life has been ad hoc. We have small collections of rich scrapbooks, letters, and diaries from alumni, but most of our student life while students are on campus and working on exciting initiatives has gone largely uncollected over the years. Paradoxically, these gaps may be due to the growth of digital records: both archivists and librarians' inability to keep up with such records as they are generated, as well as the extensive investment and labor needed to preserve digital collections. I started providing outreach to students to create informed donors and enable them to have an active voice in the archiving process for the history of the college.

In order to do outreach and start building relationships across departments and student groups, I started giving PDAD workshops, which I had learned about through Joanna DiPasquale. My initial goal was to get people to be knowledgeable about their digital information generation and to provide best practices for the extra maintenance that born-digital materials might need. In pulling together my workshop materials, I combined the Library of Congress materials with the lecture and hands-on activity components from the Society of Georgia Archivists' Train the Trainer PDA Workshop.[6]

Digital preservation is an abstract concept for many communities, so I looked for interesting ways to advertise the workshop. I found an image of a woman holding a floppy disk and wearing a T-shirt that read, "No Bad Memories." I call her "Floppy Disk Girl."[7] She became my mascot for the event; I used the ad for my flyers and in my introduction to the workshop. I thought this ad showed the irony in how technology has been touted as an answer to preservation instead of in support of it. The ad also showcases the humor of the idea that we can save our memories forever using OPUS floppy disks, since these are almost obsolete now. Last, in the picture Floppy Disk Girl is touching the magnetic media on the disk—clearly another preservation issue. Students were quick to identify these ironies.

In conceiving this project, I had a number of considerations that determined many aspects of the program's eventual design. First, I realized that what I was sharing must be relatable to students. I felt that it was important to have interactivity at all stages of the presentation, so as to make the too-often latent concepts of digital preservation and file taxonomy part of a discussion rather than a lecture. And third, I wanted an activity that would allow me to know whether or not the participants had critically grasped the concepts. My general workshop overview is described below.

To start, I often begin the lecture component of the workshop with some higher-level concepts. I define digital preservation and explain technological obsolescence (giving the example of a floppy disk). Most students have told me that they do know what a floppy disk is, and some have even used them. I discuss media degradation and point to a scratched DVD as an example. While we are in the early stage of the workshop, I ask the attendees if they have any data-loss horror stories. Data-loss stories are an excellent bonding exercise to get a group comfortable with the fact that maintaining digital objects is hard for everyone. I often use the examples of family photos, important coursework they want to save for the long term, saving documents for financial reasons, important e-mails, and so on. I explain how digital files are created and how they work in conjunction with software and hardware and dependencies between the three layers. Describing retention schedules is where I really start to use the language in the field and introduce the students to it. I suggest to the students that they develop guidelines or lists that include what should be saved and what should be deleted on a regular basis.

I then go through PDA best practices more explicitly. I ask them, "Where is your information?" Taking an inventory can help keep students organized and allow them to more easily clean up their files. I discuss file-naming best practices such as avoiding spaces and special characters in file names. I explain what metadata is and suggest several programs to add metadata to their files. I go through file formats and tell students to be aware of file formats that are attached to specific software programs and go through the process of migration. Storage is one of the biggest topics, and one that I get the most questions about. I explain to participants that whatever storage platform they use, they need to have an exit strategy and they also need to make sure that all of their records are in at least two or three places, such as the cloud and an external hard drive, depending on their resources. I also make sure to explain what the cloud is and what it means when your materials are in the cloud, since it has become a rather ubiquitous term.

Storage naturally leads into a discussion about copyright. Most students understand copyright, but not necessarily the nuances of copyright and its variables. We go through some terms of service agreements like those of Google and Facebook to understand it. Because these agreements are always changing, it's important for me as the instructor to read them as well, so I can dispense the most up-to-date advice.

Copyright leads into privacy. As with the copyright section of the workshop, we go over terms of service agreements for platforms such as Google Drive and DropBox. A terrific teaching tool to use is called I Know Where Your Cat Lives.[8] This website has taken the metadata from one million public pictures tagged with the word *cat* and used the geolocation information to place them on a map. Not all of these pictures show a cat—for example, some images show people with cat ears on, but the picture is still tagged "cat." This humorous website reveals how often we publicly post information that can be used to identify our location, illuminating online privacy loss to the workshop attendees.

Then, after this huge information dump, which does include some discussion, I do a walk-through of how students can export and normalize their e-mail. I explain what the Internet Archive is, then demonstrate how to crawl a website using HTTrack or upload it to the Wayback Machine. I show the very first Bryn Mawr website too, which students find either charming or alarming. I hope that viewing these processes gives students a glimpse of what is often needed to preserve born-digital materials.

Last, in addition to the lecture, I sometimes use the Find the Person in the Personal Digital Archive: Murder Mystery Edition! game, which is the second component of the Train the Trainer PDA Workshop (http://soga.org/involvement/advocacy/professional). This is a wonderful resource! There is a zip drive available for download on the website that contains a fictional murder victim's personal digital archive on a thumb drive, plus group discussion questions. Participants break up into groups and go through the files on this person's thumb drive with the knowledge that it was left at a crime scene. Some files are in obsolete formats, others have passwords, and some have poor file names with little to no metadata. This is a way for the workshop attendees to try out what they have just learned and see how it can work firsthand under the auspices of a murder mystery game. Participants were very engaged, demanding the passwords from me and arguing among themselves. This also gave me a nice way to finish up the workshop: if the students could articulate their issues in solving the mystery through the discussion questions, it meant they had learned something.

The first workshop was open to everyone, but my end goal was to use it as a way to connect with student organizations. I also facilitated this workshop for staff and faculty groups and tweaked it to focus on those groups' needs. Attendance generally ranged from 10 to 25 participants. As a deliverable that attendees could refer to after the workshop, I made a LibGuide.[9] The LibGuide shows different types of materials such as images, e-mails, social media, and websites and offers advice on how to retrieve your data and preserve it— again, a lot of it is taken from the Library of Congress and Society of Georgia Archivists' resources. Bryn Mawr is part of a Tri-College Consortium with Haverford College and Swarthmore College. It was exciting to watch these colleges opt to hold their own successful PDAD event for Archives Month 2015.

There are many current and forthcoming issues that I will have to grapple with as I continue to adapt my workshop. One main consideration is the ebb and flow of interest in student club or organization archiving. Will all of these resources and workshops about personal digital archiving stick? A generation at Bryn Mawr is considered every four years, so I have no idea how the new generation of students will feel about records collection.

I also have serious concerns about privacy, a topic that requires further exploration when working with student organization records. I have set the stage to accession student records into Special Collections, but at this point, it has become less important to me to do that than I originally envisioned. I think now it is more important to give students the tools to create their own record collections and have their own archives; however, that brings me back to the question of long-term preservation that is done well and consistently. One of my next steps is to look into additional post-custodial models.

So far, PDAD events have achieved the relationship-building goals that I initially hoped for. While these events' long-term impact is hard to measure, I regularly receive e-mails from students, staff, and faculty who have questions about personal digital archiving. We are having more conversations about electronic records management, and I think campus community members are more knowledgeable about their digital information generation. I now give the workshop by request, rather than annually, because of the similar content and the value in focusing the workshop to meet the group's needs.

Wheaton College (MA) Case Study

AMY BOCKO

Former Digital Initiatives Librarian (currently Digital
Initiatives Librarian at Emerson College)

After participating in two very successful PDAD events at Vassar College, I was eager to duplicate that success in my new position at Wheaton College. I was tasked with creating a digital initiatives program at Wheaton, and with a new department comes the challenge of establishing yourself in the larger library structure, as well as finding your niche in the college community as a whole. The position of digital asset curator (later changed to digital initiatives librarian) was repurposed from the post of a visual resources curator that had previously worked exclusively with the art faculty; the scope of my new position was much broader, with potential service areas to faculty members throughout the college. The challenge lay in how to publicize this new area of service and create faculty buy-in and partnerships. I thought a natural path would be to offer a workshop on personal digital archiving, which I also publicized as an event about managing one's own digital content.

I invited all faculty to the workshop, and since I realized that scheduling a large group of faculty members could be difficult, I crowdsourced the interested faculty members with a variety of potential times to get the greatest buy-in. Since I knew that getting a large body of faculty members in diverse disciplines together to converse with one another about their "digital lives" would be most beneficial, I was open to conducting multiple sections to best serve our community. We designated one afternoon that was the best fit for interested participants, and I designed my materials in a way that they could either work as takeaways for attendees, or I could provide those who could not attend with materials to help them begin organizing their digital materials and open the door for further conversations.

In addition to the faculty members who were invited to the workshop, I extended an invitation to my colleagues in the library's Research & Instruction, Archives, and Technical Services departments. Each successful digital project/initiative had a group of talented library personnel working together to ensure its success, so it was a good opportunity to introduce these staffers who might not have a very public (but very important) role and offer a platform for my library colleagues to add their expertise to the faculty-driven conversation.

As a former contributor/participant at Vassar College's PDAD events, I was familiar with the materials and format that Joanna DiPasquale followed, and I had seen how these were a pathway to successfully reach faculty members. She kindly shared her current materials with me,[10] which proved to be a jumping-off point and a refresher that resonated with the liberal arts faculty we work with. The refined, in-depth LibGuide[11] that Rachel Appel generously shared was an invaluable resource when expanding upon the content most valuable to our users. With Rachel's focus on working with student groups, I appreciated how she addressed a diverse body of materials, such as social media, archiving your Google content, and text messages, that would play a larger role in the more junior audiences we work with. Both of these librarians' web resources proved an important inspiration while I created a Google website for the Wheaton community (since I've left Wheaton and the proxy that I transferred ownership to, the site is no longer available). While the website I created was a valuable resource, I also made available a PDF version of the presentation I gave that contextualized some of the basic principles we were imparting to our participants, provided examples of these principles in practice, and offered the expanded "menu" of digital services the Wheaton College Library was offering now that we had launched a Digital Initiatives working group. This PDF version was a valuable resource to send to follow up with faculty who were unable to attend because of previous commitments but were interested in the PDAD programming.

The structure of the workshop was a brief presentation about best practices, an illustrated example of how I manage digital assets (I used a photo shoot of an on-campus seashell collection that subsequently was made into a library digital collection as an example), and a brief rundown of the digital services the library was now pleased to offer. After the formal presentation, I facilitated a discussion among faculty members about their particular concerns and questions. This offered a platform for their peers to commiserate about similar problems, and offer some solutions about how they overcame their issues. I wanted to promote the new area of library services that I had been hired to offer, and to reassure the faculty that they would have library assistance in navigating the overwhelming task of stewarding their professional and personal digital content. I was also hoping that through this discussion, some potential hidden collections could be discovered that the library could partner with faculty to digitize.

The highest number of attendees at the workshop were from the Art History Department, so the conversation was somewhat skewed towards managing a large number of digital images. While this may have been an issue that was particular to the discipline of art history, the other attendees were interested in the solutions their colleagues were employing successfully and the potential crosswalk into managing their own content. The faculty members who attended were very engaged with managing their content effectively in order to maximize their scholarship.

While I knew that taking in the entirety of managing personal digital content is overwhelming, I asked my participants to think of one thing today that they could do to better manage their digital life. Replies ranged from backing up their computer, to being more mindful of how they name files, to investing in an external hard drive (to be kept in a separate location from their computer!). My goal was to break down the overwhelming array of best practices into a set of smaller, achievable goals and to offer my support where needed. PDAD was an excellent opportunity to interface with the faculty at Wheaton College, offer support in digital library services, and create relationships that strengthen the bond between the library and faculty members.

Amherst College Case Study

SARAH WALDEN MCGOWAN

Former Digital Projects Librarian (she now serves as Digital
Collections and Preservation Librarian at Amherst College)

During the fall 2014 semester, the Amherst College Library's Digital Programs Department had an opportunity to focus on department promotion and outreach while we had a part-time post-baccalaureate position. That post-bac, Criss Guy, and I were inspired by the discussion about personal digital archiving that Joanna DiPasquale started on the Oberlin 17 e-mail list. Because Criss had graduated from Amherst in 2014 after finishing a thesis, we felt that a workshop aimed at students, particularly seniors writing theses, would be a good match for his experience and insight, my digital preservation expertise, and also the resources that were being shared by our colleagues at other institutions.

The resources that most contributed to our workshop were the Library of Congress's personal digital archiving resources[12] and a Train the Trainer PDA Workshop from the Society of Georgia Archivists.[13] We decided to frame the workshop around the four steps used in the Library of Congress's brochures: identify, prioritize, organize, and back up.[14] In order to illustrate the difficulties caused by disorganized files, we used some screenshots of the files provided by the Society of Georgia Archivists' hands-on murder mystery game,[15] as well as some actual research files from Criss's own thesis work. In a second iteration of the workshop, we had attendees install and use a free demo of Hazel,[16] a file cleanup tool for Mac computers, on lab computers.

Our goal was to expose students to immediate preservation concerns surrounding a large research project like a thesis, as well as to give them just a little exposure to the idea of longer-term preservation. We offered two versions of our workshop: one in the fall, which was purely lecture-style, and a second during Amherst's January interterm that added a hands-on activity in which the students organized a set of sample files using Hazel.

We had some trouble drumming up student interest in the topic of digital preservation. Attendance at both iterations of the workshop was sparse (despite the fantastic posters designed by our post-bac).[17] Criss and I theorized that we were advertising our workshop too narrowly, and that we might have more luck casting a broad net aimed at all students, rather than focusing on thesis writers. Reaching out to and partnering with specific student organizations, as Rachel did at Bryn Mawr, could have also helped us.

The attendees who came to our workshops were very interested in being better-organized and having better control over their files, both personal and academic. Though we had low turnout, our attendees were all very enthusiastic about the topic and seemed to find what we had to say very helpful. One conceptual stumbling block that we ran into was that students seemed to want a piece of software or an app that would be a one-stop fix to digital preservation. When they learned just how complex the task before them was, they seemed overwhelmed by the idea of doing all this work just to gain control of their files. Amy's method of asking workshop attendees to identify one thing that they could do today could be a good solution to this problem: it reminds attendees that although personal digital archiving is a very large task, they can tackle it one piece at a time.

When our department has sufficient staffing levels to offer personal digital archiving workshops again, I would like to expand our target audience: either to all students, or revamping the workshop to cater to faculty or staff. Our Alumni & Parent Programs Department has also expressed interest in offering a workshop for alumni during reunion week. I see many possibilities for partnering with other departments on campus in order to do targeted outreach about personal digital archiving.

PDAD RESOURCES

One of the helpful features of working together on PDAD events was the ability to pool resources, as well as incorporating additional materials that resonated with our communities and interests. As a planning exercise, consulting our colleagues' materials was useful as a way not to duplicate our efforts when compiling resources, as well as providing inspiration on how to distinguish our individual PDADs in our communities. While our PDAD events were focused on our communities and their specific needs, a cornerstone of all four Personal Digital Archiving Days was the Library of Congress's website on personal digital archiving.[18] This website both provided the inspiration for DiPasquale to create PDAD programming on a liberal arts college campus, and provided us with a wealth of specific resources to reference for our audiences. In particular, the LOC website's breakdown of format-specific best practices was helpful and offered expert guidance to our patrons on the materials most valued by them. While we were able to put the LOC's personal digital archiving materials into practice during our sessions, the LOC website is also an online resource that we could refer our audience to when further questions arose.

With Vassar College's first Personal Digital Archiving Day taking place in 2012, there have been many years for the PDAD resources we have collected to evolve. While it is easy to expand upon the online resources and handouts we've compiled and to update format-specific information as it changes, there are basic principles/rules for digital organization and preservation that we've held at the forefront and continuously impress upon the audiences we serve. By understanding and giving weight to both the "3–2-1 Rule" and "Six Important Steps," we're imparting principles of digital best practices that our users can carry over into any digital content they are consuming or managing.

The "3–2-1 Rule" came to us courtesy of the American Society of Media Photographers.[19] Peter Krough lays out cursory information about the importance of "backing up" your work, how-to's, and best practice principles to adhere to. While created in response to the challenges faced by digital photographers and the nature of their work, we believe the "3–2-1 Rule" is an important concept to implement for digital content of any genre. The rule is as follows:

The 3–2-1 Rule

- Make *three* copies
- Have at least *two* of the copies on two different types of media
- Keep *one* copy in a different location from where you live/work

Six Important Steps (Michel)	Six Important Questions for the PDAD Attendee
1. Identify where you have your information. Keep this list handy. 2. Decide what is important to you. 3. Get organized. 4. Make copies of your data. 5. Understand the trade-offs of placing objects in various websites, and so on, and what is helping you to accomplish digital preservation. 6. Embed extractable metadata whenever possible.	1. Where is your information? 2. What is most important to you? 3. Are you organized? (And can someone else tell?) 4. Do you have backups? 5. Are your copies viable short- and long-term? 6. Can you get information in/out of your system?

SOURCE: "Personal Archiving: Keeping Personal Digital Photographs," Digital Preservation (Library of Congress), www.digitalpreservation.gov/personalarchiving/photos.html.

FIGURE 9.2
PDAD takeaway: steps and questions

In addition to the "3–2–1 Rule" being a core takeaway from our PDAD events, Joanna DiPasquale compiled a list of "six important questions" based on the "six important steps" to consider when managing/preserving digital objects from the advice of Phil Michel, digital conversion coordinator from the Prints & Photographs Division of the Library of Congress. The steps and questions, shown in figure 9.2, helped frame the conversation with the goal of making digital preservation more manageable.

By having our participants reflect on the above-mentioned steps, we found a good jumping-off point to tackle the monumental tasks of digital preservation and adopting best practices as routine.

MAJOR TAKEAWAYS

Although our workshops had varying audiences and goals, they empowered attendees to become more aware of their digital data management and the records continuum, as well as become critical thinkers regarding technology, rather than simply consumers. The workshops also provided an outreach opportunity for the digital library to address issues of sustainability in digital scholarship. PDAD events helped convey that the library and campus IT groups had a set of practices that could help scholars keep their materials well-organized and manageable, and could illustrate such services as institutional repositories, instructional classes, and available software licenses at the point of need.

One of the greatest concerns that each of us faced when we began our PDAD events was the potential to over-promise to our constituents. Asking questions such as, "Are your digital materials safe?" could easily lead to questions about how much the library could aid in storing digital materials or inquiries about the library's interest in accessioning digital data. It was important to frame each event from the perspective of consulting and good advice, with a "do it yourself" ethos pervasive in each iteration. We wanted our information to be empowering, not cumbersome; we wanted attendees to leave feeling armed with the tools they needed to keep their digital files in the best shape possible for at least the short term. At the same time, it was important to provide each community—whether faculty or student—with information about available library and campus resources to help them with this process. We wanted to be able to point attendees in the right direction in an incremental way, and sharing materials and experiences with each other and tailoring the Library of Congress's PDA kits to our college communities went a long way in framing language and identifying resources.

Additionally, the PDAD events helped each library move forward in identifying the library as a major source of high-quality, relevant information for a timely and critical need. We found that our students and faculty had the same concerns that the library did about how to manage an ever-growing amount of digital materials, but the underlying assumptions that the library negotiated so fluidly were welcome news to our attendees. Librarians can perhaps underestimate their expertise in such facets of digital archiving and preservation as file-naming schemes or well-documented organizational structures because these skills are "second nature" to them—but to a scholar with a personal file system that has not scaled up along with the digital age, or a student who is concerned about the course materials that might get lost upon graduation, our expertise is critical to their success.

We found that connecting faculty and students to relevant information only worked if they also connected their experiences to a broader information landscape. Bryn Mawr students saw their own lack of a paper trail in contrast to the archival materials that prior students had left behind. Amherst students framed digital preservation problems in their own and others' thesis materials. Wheaton's art history faculty were challenged: "What is one thing you can do *today* to improve your 'digital life'?" while reviewing the incremental steps that the library had taken to answer that very question for its own digitization efforts. Vassar faculty were presented with best practices to help organize their scholarly communication materials, but also with resources such as the institutional repository to challenge their notions of sustainability. In each case, that connection to the big picture contributed greatly to the PDAD events' success.

Finally, we found that, if at all possible, we should secure a small budget for these events, enough simply to provide snacks or lunch! Though it is often a light-hearted notion on campus that students and faculty will always show up at events that have food available, we found that our attendees appreciated this small gesture; it was our way of telling them that, with the many events that compete for their time on campus, we were happy they came to ours.

DIRECT BENEFITS TO DIGITAL SCHOLARSHIP EFFORTS

We found that our PDAD events had significant benefits for both the scholars (whether just beginning as undergraduates or longtime tenured faculty) and the library in the realm of potential digital scholarship projects. This was an unanticipated but welcome consequence that was first observed at Vassar, and it is interesting to note that the principles of digital curation dovetail well with digital scholarship when approached from a library context, at least at our liberal arts colleges. The potential for sustainable digital scholarship increases when we can bring our own best practices to our constituents, particularly when we introduce PDAD as a set of incremental steps in a larger plan for the sustainability of the project (e.g., identify your materials that you wish to save; choose a good file-naming scheme; find campus resources that can help). We believe that PDAD events like ours provide an opportunity for college libraries to meet their scholars in multiple project phases:

- While they are potentially worried about their past digital materials
- While they are actively creating (and curating) their current digital materials
- When they move beyond our campus services (particularly for students)

While we dispense good advice, we also raise awareness of our libraries' digital preservation skills, our services, and our best practices, and we only see that need growing as digital scholarship flourishes. On the college campus, the *personal* heavily overlaps with the *professional*.

DIRECT BENEFITS TO COLLEGE ARCHIVES

We believe that an important long-term effect of PDAD events is the understanding that the personal and professional materials which our students and faculty are collecting might one day find their way to a college archives—if, of course, that material is maintained in a sustainable way. Attendees learn how to take care of their materials so those materials last longer; in turn, the archives lay the foundation for more robust accessions in the future, and importantly, fewer gaps in collections.

PDAD FOR THE FUTURE

We anticipate that we will be holding more targeted workshops for specific groups of attendees, and we would like to hear experiences from other institutions on how their PDADs evolved.

Bryn Mawr has started giving PDAD workshops upon request, which has helped shape the scope and goals of each workshop to match the audience. The Self-Government Association[20] has requested various trainings (and helped lead some) and has begun managing their own archives as a result. Bryn Mawr's college archivist, Christiana Dobryznski, will continue to keep college record-keeping practices transparent and provide guidance for personal digital archiving. Rachel Appel anticipates looking for new opportunities to incorporate Personal Digital Archiving Days in her new role at Temple University, which she started in fall 2016.

Having left Wheaton College in fall 2015, Amy Bocko is enthusiastic about bringing PDAD to Emerson College, where she has been tasked with creating a library digital initiatives program. Emerson is a liberal arts college that is focused on communications and the arts, and with that media-based focus, new challenges are created in working with tech-savvy students, faculty, and multimedia collections. Amy is currently strategizing with the college's digital archivist, Micha Broadnax, on developing PDAD programming for the Emerson community and exploring sub-communities for outreach opportunities. Broadnax has been focused on student outreach and cultivating mutually beneficial partnerships between student organizations and the archives; the archives is currently exploring working with student groups on managing, preserving, and archiving their original content and developing new digital collections of student-generated materials.

Although Amherst College Digital Programs has not had the opportunity to offer a PDAD event or workshop since January 2015, they have been able to incorporate their knowledge of personal archiving and experience with educating students into several other projects. For example, in the summers of 2014, 2015, and 2016 they offered a digital scholarship summer internship, which was an immersive, hands-on introduction to digital humanities for undergraduate students.[21] After the first year, they realized (partly because of our PDAD events) that they needed to do more education during the internship about the long-term sustainability of the students' projects, and help the students manage and organize their working documents throughout the summer. Every summer, Amherst has been able to improve the amount and quality of the documentation that the interns leave behind, and also show them the value of following archival principles in the process.

Vassar's PDAD events have been absorbed into a more broadly defined digital scholarship strategy in the college's libraries. In collaboration with campus partners such as Academic Computing Services and the College Archives, they hope to continue their PDAD events and broaden their audience. Faculty, in particular, asked that the library deliver information on PDA to students, and given the successful student-focused initiatives at Amherst and Bryn Mawr, PDAD materials seemed like they would resonate well. Vassar began incorporating this consulting work into student interactions, particularly for summer programs such as Vassar's Mellon Foundation–funded Creative Arts across the Disciplines, in 2015. They hope to continue along this student-focused road, and also begin faculty events again in the near future.

CONCLUSION

Overall, we believe that our collaboration to present personal digital archiving programming to our liberal arts colleges was successful. It raised awareness about best practices in managing and stewarding digital content, created community buy-in for our digital programs, and established the library as an on-campus resource for our community members to address questions about preserving their digital content. While we have tailored our PDAD outreach efforts and presentations to best fit the communities we work with, the core takeaways for all of our participants, whether a new student or a long-tenured faculty member, were best practices to implement as they navigate personal digital content throughout their careers. We also found that the short-term and long-term benefits were mutual, as we aided current digital content providers to maintain their own scholarly records—and, in turn, our own future materials. Our belief is that, with a solid understanding of the overarching principles used to guide the management of digital materials, the communities we serve are well-prepared to take on the monumental task of managing their materials. And with this effective management and the understanding of preserving their materials for our colleges' digital scholarship programs and archives, we are able to aid in creating the most thorough record of our colleges' scholarly landscapes.

NOTES

1. Rachel Appel, Amy Bocko, Joanna DiPasquale, and Sarah Walden McGowan, "Digital Archiving Programming at Four Liberal Arts Colleges," *The Signal* (Library of Congress), https://blogs.loc.gov/thesignal/2015/05/digital-archiving -programming-at-four-liberal-arts-colleges/. This chapter extends our initial writing about these events, and the first two paragraphs of this chapter also appear in that article.

2. "Personal Digital Archiving Kit: Suggested Handouts and Videos," Digital Preservation, Library of Congress, www.digitalpreservation.gov/ personalarchiving/padKit/handouts.html.

3. "About the Oberlin Group," The Oberlin Group: A Consortium of Liberal Arts College Libraries, http://oberlingroup.org/about-oberlin-group.

4. "Digital Archiving and Preservation Information," Vassar College Digital Library, http://pages.vassar.edu/digitallibrary/resources-and-links/digital -archiving-and-preservation-information/.

5. "College Women," College Women: Documenting the History of Women in Higher Education, http://collegewomen.org/.

6. "Professional Outreach and Advocacy," Society of Georgia Archivists, http://soga .org/involvement/advocacy/professional.

7. Benj Edwards, July 18, 2008, "[Retro Scan of the Week] Floppy Girl Doesn't Remember," *Vintage Computers and Gaming: Adventures in Classic Technology* Blog, www.vintagecomputing.com/index.php/archives/481/ retro-scan-of-the-week-unflappable-floppy-girl.

8. "I Know Where Your Cat Lives Map," I Know Where Your Cat Lives, http:// iknowwhereyourcatlives.com/.

9. "Personal Digital Archiving: Home," Tri-College Libraries Research Guides, http:// libguides.brynmawr.edu/pdad.

10. "Digital Archiving and Preservation Information," Vassar College Digital Library, http://pages.vassar.edu/digitallibrary/resources-and-links/digital -archiving-and-preservation-information/.

11. "Personal Digital Archiving: Home," Tri-College Libraries Research Guides, http://libguides.brynmawr.edu/pdad.

12. "Personal Digital Archiving Kit: Suggested Handouts and Videos," Digital Preservation, Library of Congress, www.digitalpreservation.gov/personalarchiving/padKit/handouts.html.

13. "Personal Digital Archiving: A Train the Trainer Webinar," Georgia Library Association Vimeo, https://vimeo.com/georgialibraryassociatio/review/109735555/e07279a1c2.

14. "Preserving Your Digital Memories Brochure," National Digital Information Infrastructure and Preservation Program: A Collaborative Initiative of the Library of Congress, www.digitalpreservation.gov/personalarchiving/documents/PA_All_brochure.pdf.

15. "Professional Outreach and Advocacy," Society of Georgia Archivists, http://soga.org/involvement/advocacy/professional.

16. "Hazel: Automated Organization for Your Mac," Noodlesoft, www.noodlesoft.com/hazel.php.

17. "Personal Digital Archiving," Amherst College, https://www.amherst.edu/library/services/digital/personal-digital-archiving.

18. "Personal Digital Archiving Kit: Suggested Handouts and Videos," Digital Preservation, Library of Congress, www.digitalpreservation.gov/personalarchiving/padKit/handouts.html.

19. "Backup Overview," American Society of Media Photographers: Digital Photography Best Practices and Workflow, www.dpbestflow.org/backup/backup-overview#321.

20. "Welcome to the Bryn Mawr Self-Government Association Website," Bryn Mawr Self-Government Association, http://sga.blogs.brynmawr.edu/.

21. "Digital Scholarship Summer Internship," Amherst College, https://www.amherst.edu/library/services/digital/DSSI.

BIBLIOGRAPHY

"About the Oberlin Group." Oberlin Group: A Consortium of Liberal Arts College Libraries. http://oberlingroup.org/about-oberlin-group.

Appel, Rachel, Amy Bocko, Joanna DiPasquale, and Sarah Walden McGowan. "Digital Archiving Programming at Four Liberal Arts Colleges." *The Signal.* Library of Congress. https://blogs.loc.gov/thesignal/2015/05/digital-archiving-programming-at-four-liberal-arts-colleges/. This chapter extends our initial writing about these events, and the first two paragraphs of this chapter also appear in that article.

"Backup Overview." American Society of Media Photographers: Digital Photography Best Practices and Workflow. www.dpbestflow.org/backup/backup-overview#321.

"College Women." College Women: Documenting the History of Women in Higher Education. http://collegewomen.org/.

"Digital Archiving and Preservation Information." Vassar College Digital Library. http://pages.vassar.edu/digitallibrary/resources-and-links/digital-archiving-and-preservation-information/.

"Digital Archiving Programming at Four Liberal Arts Colleges." Available at https://blogs.loc.gov/thesignal/2015/05/digital-archiving-programming-at-four-liberal-arts-colleges/.

"Digital Scholarship Summer Internship." Amherst College. https://www.amherst.edu/
library/services/digital/DSSI.

Edwards, Benj. July 18, 2008. "[Retro Scan of the Week] Floppy Girl Doesn't
Remember." *Vintage Computers and Gaming: Adventures in Classic Technology*
Blog. www.vintagecomputing.com/index.php/archives/481/retro-scan-of-the
-week-unflappable-floppy-girl.

"Hazel: Automated Organization for Your Mac." Noodlesoft. www.noodlesoft.com/
hazel.php.

"I Know Where Your Cat Lives Map." I Know Where Your Cat Lives. http://iknowwhere
yourcatlives.com/.

"Personal Archiving: Keeping Personal Digital Photographs." Digital Preservation. Library
of Congress. www.digitalpreservation.gov/personalarchiving/photos.html.

"Personal Digital Archiving." Amherst College. https://www.amherst.edu/library/services/
digital/personal-digital-archiving.

"Personal Digital Archiving: Home." Tri-College Libraries Research Guides. http://
libguides.brynmawr.edu/pdad.

"Personal Digital Archiving: A Train the Trainer Webinar." Georgia Library Association
Vimeo. https://vimeo.com/georgialibraryassociatio/review/109735555/e07279a1c2.

"Personal Digital Archiving Kit: Suggested Handouts and Videos." Digital Preservation.
Library of Congress. www.digitalpreservation.gov/personalarchiving/padKit/
handouts.html.

"Preserving Archiving: Preserving Your Digital Memories." Digital Preservation. Library of
Congress. www.digitalpreservation.gov/personalarchiving/.

"Preserving Your Digital Memories Brochure." National Digital Information Infrastructure
and Preservation Program: A Collaborative Initiative of the Library of Congress.
www.digitalpreservation.gov/personalarchiving/documents/PA_All_brochure.pdf.

"Professional Outreach and Advocacy." Society of Georgia Archivists. http://soga.org/
involvement/advocacy/professional.

"Welcome to the Bryn Mawr Self-Government Association Website." Bryn Mawr
Self-Government Association. http://sga.blogs.brynmawr.edu/.

10
Supporting Artists' Personal Archives

THE PRIMARY FOCUS FOR STUDENTS and faculty in academic art departments is the creation of artworks. Studio arts courses for both undergraduates and graduates help students to gain technical mastery in working with a variety of materials, and to develop critical and creative thinking skills to push their artworks to new levels. In addition to teaching, faculty in studio arts programs maintain their own practice as professional artists, actively creating and exhibiting new works while helping students to establish similar professional practices. While students and faculty are unsurprisingly focused intently on the creation of artworks, personal archives play a crucial role in all aspects of an artist's creative and professional practice—and increasingly, these archives are *digital*. Artists may use software programs to create work, connect with galleries and potential buyers via e-mail, and generate interest in their work through personal websites and social media platforms. Whether chaotic and unwieldy or carefully managed, personal digital archives are the by-product of all this digital activity, and artists depend on these digital collections to successfully create, exhibit, and sell their artworks.

Despite digital content's growing importance to them, artists have limited resources regarding techniques and best practices for organizing, preserving, and optimizing their use of personal digital archives. To address this need, academic libraries can strive to become a critical service point for both student and faculty artists, helping this population to develop skills to take control of their personal digital archives. Arguing that artists have long been "neglected patrons" in academic and research libraries, Laurel Littrell suggests ways that libraries can improve their access to information sources.[1] As a key to information access, academic libraries can provide services directed towards the unique needs of art students and faculty, supplementing the creative education gained in the classroom and studio with programs and resources designed to develop professional research skills. Recent literature has articulated the capacity for libraries to support research that is central to artists' creative practices,[2] but the development of professional and business skills constitutes a major information need for artists as well.[3] Primary among these, personal digital archiving techniques and knowledge are a crucial skill set.

In this chapter, I will highlight a daylong, intensive personal archiving workshop as a service model that academic libraries can consider in order to better address this information need. As a case study, I will draw on my experience with Learning from Artists' Archives (LFAA), an IMLS–funded collaboration between the Art Department and the School of Information and Library Science at the University of North Carolina at Chapel Hill with the express goal of devising strategies, tools, and means to support personal archiving efforts for North Carolina artists.[4] As a major component of the grant, the project team, consisting of four faculty members and six graduate student fellows, developed content for a daylong workshop for up to twenty-five local artists. The team delivered the workshop twice: first in October 2015 at the North Carolina Museum of Art in Raleigh, and second in October 2016 at the Mint Museum of Art in Charlotte. Although these workshops were conducted in museums, and for a diverse population of artists, I suggest that the model is flexible, easily applicable to a wide variety of institutions and organizations, and is especially suited for an academic library serving students and faculty in a fine arts program. Although the workshops addressed a wide range of both analog and digital personal archiving skills, I will largely focus on the workshops' digital archiving content for the purposes of this volume.

WORKSHOP OUTLOOK
Articulating and Achieving Goals

The overall goal of the workshop model is to empower artists to pursue and sustain personal digital archiving efforts. It is important to recognize that artists will likely not be able to develop digital archiving expertise over the course of a single day, but the workshop can help artists to establish a foundation of skills and knowledge necessary to develop and integrate practical archiving strategies as a core part of their studio practice. The overall goal of the workshop can be broken down into three action items:

1. Build a vocabulary of personal digital archiving terms and concepts, including storage solutions and preservation strategies
2. Develop a familiarity with resources and methods to gain more information and further build skills following the workshop
3. Realize the archival value and potential uses of their digital materials

Delivering this service in an academic library is, in many ways, using an ideal setting for achieving these action items. Because student and faculty artists have regular and ready access to the academic library, the workshop can serve to establish contact between the artists and librarians. By participating in the workshop, artists can receive the fundamental information and skills needed to tackle their digital materials and take concrete steps towards both the short- and long-term management of their digital archives, but also have the ability to return to the library to access information and further develop their digital archiving skills.

The content and structure of the workshop can vary, depending on the specific needs of the population of artists served. Even among a group of student and faculty artists, it is safe to assume a wide range of technological skills and varying levels of familiarity with digital technologies among workshop participants. It is also safe to assume that participants will come to the workshop with a diverse set of needs and expectations. These issues certainly factored into the planning of the LFAA workshops, both of which served artists at all career stages and from many different backgrounds. Academic librarians delivering a workshop to students and faculty will have the benefit of knowing their population beforehand, but they should still anticipate serving a varied group. The LFAA project team addressed this issue in several ways while planning the content and structure of the two workshops.

WORKSHOP CONTENT AND STRUCTURE
Meeting Artists' Information Needs

In the initial stages of planning and content development, the project team drew on a substantial base of knowledge about artists' personal archiving practices, grounded in professional experience and a body of research into artists' archives.[5] Because the LFAA workshops were open to all North Carolina artists, the project team did not know the specific population of participants from the outset, and thus had only a general idea of the needs and expectations of participants. As part of the application process, artists provided information regarding their creative practices, existing archiving habits, and topics they were particularly interested in learning about at the workshop.

The project team incorporated this information as much as possible, although the group of participants was finalized less than a month before the event in both cases. At the end of both workshops, participants were asked to fill out a survey, which offered invaluable feedback regarding the sessions and helped the project team to continue to develop the workshop's content and structure in order to better meet the needs of the artists served. I will go over these surveys in more detail later, but I want to highlight here the importance of using both pre- and post-workshop surveys as mechanisms to learn more about the specific needs of workshop participants.

Using these various sources of feedback and professional experience, the project team developed content for the workshop sessions with the aim of bridging the information gaps that were impeding artists' current personal archiving efforts. What are artists struggling with, and how could the workshop address these struggles? While the project team began with some idea of the personal archiving challenges that artists face, the team's sense of artists' specific information needs significantly developed by working directly with the artists at both workshops. The following are some of the major issues that emerged with digital materials:

- Building artwork inventories, especially with specialized database software
- Strategizing digitization efforts, deciding what to digitize, and how best to digitize it
- Managing copyright over digital materials, for both materials generated by the artist as well as materials generated by other entities, such as museums or galleries
- Gaining basic digital preservation skills, like updating obsolete file formats and regularly backing up materials
- Integrating a variety of artwork documentation into personal digital archives
- Developing manageable file organization schemes
- Weighing different storage media and cloud storage options
- Legacy planning, especially regarding the donation of materials to institutional archives

The artists' personal digital archiving concerns ranged from everyday practices to the scope of an entire career, and from specific technical skills to more complex workflows and processes. This is a lot of ground to cover, especially since each individual artist may have his or her own unique problems with any given issue. Depending on the career stage and nature of an artist's practice, there can be some clear differences in the digital archiving goals among the participants. Any personal archiving workshop for artists will need to respond to the specific challenges of the participants, while also accounting for a potentially wide range of needs and abilities.

The project team addressed this difficulty by building flexibility into the structure of the overall workshop, as well as each session. Over the course of each workshop, artists could choose among different breakout sessions, selecting the sessions that best met their needs. Workshop sessions were structured to include both core content delivery and participant-driven discussion. For each session, project team members delivered content through mini-lectures, informative slides, and handouts summarizing key concepts and techniques; sessions also included time for artists to raise questions and join in discussion. This structure ensured that the workshop served all participants and accommodated varying levels of expertise.

While the delivery of core content provides all participants with a foundation of personal digital archiving concepts and skills, the emphasis on participant-driven discussion allows artists to voice concerns specific to their practice. During discussions, artists were able to not only engage with session leaders, but also to hear from other artists. In many sessions, artists helped each other to troubleshoot particular issues, sharing and developing personal archiving strategies on the spot. For the second workshop, the project team built in further spaces for artists to raise unique and individual challenges. In one of the concluding sessions for the day, all of the project leaders set up personal stations with name cards listing specific areas of expertise, and artists were able to roam from station to station to engage in one-on-one or small group discussions. From my own experience as a project leader, this session sparked some of the most interesting and productive discussions of the entire workshop.

To help address long-term and legacy issues, the project team sought out the involvement of professional archivists from area institutions. Both workshops included a session in which local archivists offered advice on working with institutional archives, and (eventually) donating personal materials to an archives. For both workshops, the archivists spent time with the artists during lunch to engage in one-on-one conversations and address specific questions and concerns. The involvement of local archivists provided artists with insight into the long-term archival value of their materials. Many of the participants had not previously considered how their materials might fit in an institutional archives, and realizing that professional archivists deemed their materials of great value was a revelation.

Increasingly, artists recognized that their materials not only have use in their day-to-day careers as artists, but might also hold value as part of the cultural memory of their communities. Although personal archiving was the focus of the workshops, the discussions with professional archivists illustrated the role that institutional archives might play in legacy planning and longer-term considerations for personal archival collections. Participants of all ages and career stages valued the involvement of professional archivists. The interaction with professional archivists may be especially beneficial for early-career and student artists. Even though these artists are far removed from thinking about their legacy as artists, such interaction can instill a sense of the value of personal archival materials early on. Early-career materials that might otherwise have been tossed out or disregarded might now be saved with an eye towards a more comprehensive personal archives.

WORKSHOP TAKEAWAYS
Benefits for Artists and Information Professionals

Whether in a museum, academic library, or other setting, the workshop model promises many benefits for both artists and the information institution. Although personal archives can play a significant role in both creative and professional activities, artists rarely receive any formal education intended to develop their personal archiving skills and knowledge. Especially for students in studio arts programs, personal archiving workshops can deliver this content alongside—and even as an integrated part of—formal artistic training. Students can then develop good archiving habits early on, incorporating these skills into their studio practices that persist beyond school and into their professional careers.

In order to be motivated to develop and implement personal archiving practices, artists need to recognize the value of their personal materials. For both student and faculty artists, a workshop can raise awareness of this archival value in concrete ways. By initiating discussions among artists and with information professionals, participants can learn about the myriad ways that well-maintained personal archives can support their artistic practice. LFAA workshop participants shared how they used their archives as key resources to apply for grants and shows, keep track of sales and commissions, and inspire the creation of new works. Many of the participants discovered unanticipated uses for their personal archives; for instance, the conversations with professional archivists brought to light the potential that personal archives have to contribute to broader processes of communal memory-making. Beyond merely imparting information about personal archiving skills and techniques, a workshop can excite artists about the potential for their personal archives. In turn, this energy can move participants to articulate and implement a workable game plan to tackle the challenges of their own personal archiving.

A major benefit of the workshop model for information professionals is the opportunity to forge meaningful connections with artists, the value of which has long been recognized in the literature if not in practice.[6] The professional archivists at the LFAA workshops enjoyed conversing with artists from their local communities. For these professionals, the workshop was a chance to learn about the personal archiving challenges that artists are currently facing, and to reach out to those artists as a viable resource. In an academic library setting, librarians can take advantage of ongoing contact with students and faculty to build upon the energy generated by the workshop, and sustain connections beyond the life of one particular information service. As touched on above, participants are not expected to gain digital archiving expertise over the course of a single day, but can develop skills and knowledge through continued access to digital archiving resources and information professionals who do possess this expertise.

For librarians serving student and faculty artists, a personal digital archiving workshop may be part of an effort to attract artists into the library in the first place. As Hannah Bennett suggests, art students are among the hardest populations for art libraries to attract and, in turn, serve.[7] In a recent survey of academic libraries regarding services for graduate students, Andrea Baruzzi and Theresa Calcagno found that graduate students responded well to workshops focusing on professional skill development, and also to workshops directed towards a specific discipline or domain area.[8] While workshops on conducting literature searches and writing research articles serve students in many academic disciplines, the information needs of art students may not be adequately met by these kinds of services. Based on the enormous outpouring of interest the LFAA project team has received from artists, arts educators, and information professionals, personal archiving *is* an area in which artists genuinely and adamantly have an information need.

Academic librarians can meet this need not only by offering personal archiving workshops to student and faculty artists, but also by building on these relationships to offer sustained support in response to the specific issues and challenges raised by workshop participants. If an artist is unsure about which cloud storage service to use, a librarian may offer to conduct a follow-up consultation to review different options and find an optimal storage solution for that artist. Academic librarians have a well-developed set of tools for helping students and faculty at all levels to meet a variety of information needs. Librarians can put these tools to work in assisting artists with their personal archiving efforts; a workshop is an ideal method to establish contact with this population and gain a deeper understanding of these information needs.

WORKSHOP ASSESSMENT
Evaluating and Improving the Service

In the information and library science literature, artists' personal archiving efforts (and services supporting these efforts) have not been thoroughly examined. Even over the course of two workshops, the LFAA project team learned a great deal to contribute to this growing body of knowledge. To facilitate a better understanding of how information professionals can support artists' personal archiving, and to improve services for artists, it is important to assess the personal archiving workshop for artists from a number of angles. I will review the methods that the LFAA team used to assess the two workshops, and go over some of what we learned from these assessments.

Immediately following the first workshop, the project team held a debriefing session. As soon as the participants left, the group circled up to discuss how the day went, highlighting what went well and considering what could be improved for future workshops. Although we were thoroughly worn out and still very much caught up in the hectic happenings of the day, we found this debriefing enormously helpful, as we were able to express our most raw impressions, much of which might have faded from memory if we had not articulated them in the moment. We followed up on this post-event debriefing a month later with a more in-depth debriefing at our next team meeting, at which point we had more perspective on our experiences of the event. We reviewed our initial impressions and added further thoughts now that we had had a chance to reflect on the workshop.

In addition, artists were asked to fill out surveys in the closing session of the workshop. The survey gathered both qualitative and quantitative information from the participants. For the quantitative data, the survey asked participants to indicate which sessions they attended and to mark the applicability of the session to their needs on a scale from one to five; the survey also asked participants to mark how well the overall workshop met their expectations on a scale from one to five. For the qualitative data, the survey asked participants how they see themselves implementing the tools and strategies from the workshop, and also solicited any suggestions about how we might improve the workshop to better meet artists' needs. Although I will not go into a detailed analysis of the survey here, the results were—on the whole—incredibly positive, as 94 percent ($n = 17$) of the respondents said that the workshop overall exceeded their expectations. All of the individual sessions were also overwhelmingly well received, as respondents reported that the individual sessions were somewhat applicable (3 out of 5 on the scale) to extremely applicable (5 out of 5 on the scale) in 98 percent ($n = 109$) of responses.

While these results indicated that the workshop was well received by the artists, we also used the survey to revise and improve our approach for the second workshop. We evaluated the quantitative data to determine which sessions were heavily attended and which were more lightly attended. We used this information to restructure the schedule for the second workshop and provide more time for the popular sessions. For instance, we found that nearly all of the participants attended a breakout session on building artwork inventories and databases, and so we made this a longer, full-group session for the second workshop. As noted above, the needs and interests of participants will vary depending on the population of participating artists at any given workshop. While this information was useful to better serve the attendees at the LFAA workshops, the needs of artists attending a workshop at another institution may significantly differ.

Our group discussed our own reflections as well as the survey responses in team planning meetings, but several of the student fellows also wrote blog posts recapping and reviewing both of the workshops.[9] These blog posts act almost as informal reports, not only making public many of the lessons learned from the first to the second workshop, but also serving as a tool for self-reflection. These posts provided a space for project fellows to clearly articulate what worked well and what we needed to improve for future iterations of the workshop. As artists and arts information professionals continue to come across the project site, the blog posts are also a visible means to communicate to a wider audience about both the successes and the areas for improvement of the workshops.

As a final mechanism for assessment, project fellow Elizabeth Grab conducted follow-up interviews with three of the artists six months after the first workshop.[10] In the follow-up interviews, we wanted to gauge the extent to which participants were still energized about pursuing personal archiving efforts, and how they had been using the skills and knowledge gained from the workshop. Although Grab was only able to conduct interviews with 3 (of the 21 total) participants, the interviews were informative, and affirmed that the overall goals for the workshop were met—at least for these three participants. The three interviewees reported that they routinely put into practice many of the skills learned from the workshop, developed a better understanding of archival terms and concepts, and had a new appreciation for the archival value and potential uses of their personal archival materials. Participants recognized that their personal archives can meaningfully contribute to a broader, communal cultural history and can also add significant context to their own body of work. One participant remarked that "maintaining a studio archive brings my work process into broader focus. It adds perspective to the life of my paintings and . . . ultimately has an effect on productivity and creativity."[11]

All of these assessment mechanisms could be easily integrated into a similar workshop provided in an academic library setting. In fact, these modes of assessment can actually be carried out more easily in an academic library setting, and librarians can readily incorporate insight gained from assessment into the improvement of workshop services. As discussed above, student and faculty artists will hopefully return to the library for further information, offering librarians the opportunity to organically follow up with individual artists regarding particular concerns and issues. In addition to these informal follow-ups, academic librarians can also integrate the formal assessment mechanisms described above. Debriefings with other library staff, participant surveys, reports published on blogs or library discussion lists, and formal follow-up interviews can all provide valuable feedback. If a library offers personal archiving workshops as an ongoing service, then these assessment mechanisms become critical for ensuring that this service remains responsive to the needs of the specific population.

SUPPORTING ARTISTS' PERSONAL ARCHIVING
Today and Tomorrow

Many artists today struggle to manage an increasing amount of personal digital materials, all of which play a central role in all facets of their artistic careers. Artists rely upon their archives to support the day-to-day business of creating artworks, applying for grants and shows, and connecting with galleries and potential buyers. Beyond these daily uses, artists' personal archives carry great significance as historical documentation of those artists' careers. Artists' personal archives enrich the cultural heritage record, providing insight into the context and meaning of artists' works. However, all of the enormous potential benefits of these archives hinge upon artists having the skills, resources, and support necessary to support their personal archiving efforts.

Personal archiving workshops designed specifically for artists are an ideal method for addressing the unique challenges that artists face in managing and utilizing both their analog and digital materials. The LFAA workshops that I present as a case study were held in art museums and were open to artists at all career stages. However, I suggest that this model can be implemented in a variety of institutions, and would be especially effective in an academic library setting where information professionals are in direct and ongoing contact with a population of student and faculty artists. This information service is extremely valuable for student artists: receiving personal archiving training early on can establish core skills and habits that will pay dividends throughout an artistic career. For a population that may have less motivation to use the library, a personal archiving workshop can also get student artists through the door, and raise their awareness of the wealth of information resources the library has to offer.

Although artists face a number of challenges in their personal archiving efforts, the workshop model is sufficiently flexible to meet this diverse range of information needs. The specific content of the workshop sessions may be subject to change depending on the particular needs of the participants, but in any case the workshop model succeeds insofar as it operates through discussion, participation, and exchange. The great virtue of the workshop is that it affords participants and session leaders alike the opportunity to offer and receive information in a direct and immediate way: artists can work with each other, building upon common struggles to develop shared strategies; information professionals can learn about artists' information needs firsthand, and improve services and resources for this population; and artists and information professionals can forge relationships that can evolve even after the workshop ends. Nurturing these relationships will ensure that artists can continue to effectively sustain their personal digital archiving efforts, aiding artists in their creative and professional pursuits today, and promising a richer cultural record for future generations.

NOTES

1. Laurel Littrell, "Artists: The Neglected Patrons?" in *Crossing the Divide: Proceedings of the Tenth National Conference of the Association of College and Research Libraries* (Denver, CO: Association of College and Research Libraries, 2001).

2. Kasia Leousis, "Outreach to Artists: Supporting the Development of a Research Culture for Master of Fine Arts Students," *Art Documentation: Journal of the Art Libraries Society of North America* 32, no. 1 (2013): 127–37; Effie Patelos, "Research Intersections within Practice: Artists and Librarians," Art Documentation: *Journal of the Art Libraries Society of North America* 32, no. 1 (2013): 43–53.

3. William S. Hemmig, "The Information-Seeking Behavior of Visual Artists: A Literature Review," *Journal of Documentation* 64, no. 3 (2008): 343–62; Helen Mason and Lyn Robinson, "The Information-Related Behaviour of Emerging Artists and Designers: Inspiration and Guidance for New Practitioners," *Journal of Documentation* 67, no. 1 (2011): 159–80.

4. For more information, see www.artiststudioarchives.org.

5. See, for example, Sue Breakell and Victoria Worsley, "Collecting the Traces: An Archivist's Perspective," *Journal of Visual Arts Practice* 6, no. 3 (2007): 175–89, doi: 10.1386/jvap.6.3.175_1; Darlene I. Tong, "Artists' Archives: Preserving the Documentation and Collections of an Artist Organization," *Art Libraries Journal* 27, no. 2 (2002): 22–27; Judy Vaknin, Karyn Stuckey, and Victoria Lane, eds., *All This Stuff: Archiving the Artist* (Oxfordshire, UK: Libri, 2013).

6. D. C. Stam, "Libraries as a Bridge between Artist and Society," *Inspel* 29, no. 4 (1995): 275–82; Ruth Wilcox, "The Library's Responsibility in Collecting Source Material Concerning Local Art and Artists," *Bulletin of the American Library Association* 18 (1924): 296–98.

7. Hannah Bennett, "Bringing the Studio into the Library: Addressing the Research Needs of Studio Art and Architecture Students," *Art Documentation: Journal of the Art Libraries Society of North America* 25, no. 1 (April 1, 2006): 38.

8. Andrea Baruzzi and Theresa Calcagno, "Academic Librarians and Graduate Students: An Exploratory Study," portal: *Libraries & the Academy* 15, no. 3 (July 2015): 403.

9. Erin Dickey, "Starting the Conversation," http://artiststudioarchives.org/2015/10/12/starting-the-conversation-impressions-from-the-first-asa-workshop/; Kim Henze, "What the Students Learned," http://artiststudioarchives.org/2015/10/29/what-the-student-learned/; Kelsey Moen, "A Few Final Thoughts," http://artiststudioarchives.org/2015/11/15/a-few-final-thoughts-on-the-1st-asa-workshop-before-we-move-on/.

10. Elizabeth Grab, "2015 Workshop Follow Up," http://artiststudioarchives.org/2016/04/19/2015-workshop-follow-up-where-are-we-now/.

11. Grab, "2015 Workshop Follow Up."

BIBLIOGRAPHY

Baruzzi, Andrea, and Theresa Calcagno. "Academic Librarians and Graduate Students: An Exploratory Study." portal: *Libraries & the Academy* 15, no. 3 (2015): 393–407.

Bennett, Hannah. "Bringing the Studio into the Library: Addressing the Research Needs of Studio Art and Architecture Students." *Art Documentation: Journal of the Art Libraries Society of North America* 25, no. 1 (2006): 38–42.

Breakell, Sue, and Victoria Worsley. "Collecting the Traces: An Archivist's Perspective." *Journal of Visual Arts Practice* 6, no. 3 (2007): 175–89. doi: 10.1386/jvap.6.3.175_1.

Dickey, Erin. "Starting the Conversation." http://artiststudioarchives.org/2015/10/12/starting-the-conversation-impressions-from-the-first-asa-workshop/.

Grab, Elizabeth. "2015 Workshop Follow Up." http://artiststudioarchives.org/2016/04/19/2015-workshop-follow-up-where-are-we-now/.

Hemmig, William S. "The Information-Seeking Behavior of Visual Artists: A Literature Review." *Journal of Documentation* 64, no. 3 (2008): 343–62.

Henze, Kim. "What the Students Learned." http://artiststudioarchives.org/2015/10/29/what-the-student-learned/.

Leousis, Kasia. "Outreach to Artists: Supporting the Development of a Research Culture for Master of Fine Arts Students." *Art Documentation: Journal of the Art Libraries Society of North America* 32, no. 1 (2013): 127–37.

Littrell, Laurel. "Artists: The Neglected Patrons?" In *Crossing the Divide: Proceedings of the Tenth National Conference of the Association of College and Research Libraries.* Denver, CO: Association of College and Research Libraries, 2001.

Mason, Helen, and Lyn Robinson. "The Information-Related Behaviour of Emerging Artists and Designers: Inspiration and Guidance for New Practitioners." *Journal of Documentation* 67, no. 1 (2011): 159–80.

Moen, Kelsey. "A Few Final Thoughts." http://artiststudioarchives.org/2015/11/15/a-few-final-thoughts-on-the-1st-asa-workshop-before-we-move-on/.

Patelos, Effie. "Research Intersections within Practice: Artists and Librarians." *Art Documentation: Journal of the Art Libraries Society of North America* 32, no. 1 (2013): 43–53.

Stam, D. C. "Libraries as a Bridge between Artist and Society." *Inspel* 29, no. 4 (1995): 275–82.

Tong, Darlene I. "Artists' Archives: Preserving the Documentation and Collections of an Artist Organization." *Art Libraries Journal* 27, no. 2 (2002): 22–27.

Vaknin, Judy, Karyn Stuckey, and Victoria Lane, eds. *All This Stuff: Archiving the Artist.* Oxfordshire, UK: Libri, 2013.

Wilcox, Ruth. "The Library's Responsibility in Collecting Source Material Concerning Local Art and Artists." *Bulletin of the American Library Association* 18 (1924): 296–98.

SARA MANNHEIMER
AND RYER BANTA

11

Personal Digital Archiving as a Bridge to Research Data Management

DATA LITERACY IS QUICKLY GAINING IMPORTANCE for undergradu-ate students who are preparing to enter the workforce. This chapter brings together three key concepts to address undergraduate data literacy: research data, research data management, and personal digital archiving (PDA).

1. Research data is the material that is collected, observed, or created, for purposes of analysis to produce original research results.
2. Research data management is the practice of organizing, preserving, and providing access to research data.
3. PDA is the practice of organizing, maintaining, using, and sharing per-sonal digital information in daily life.

Working directly with research data can be an ideal way for students to develop their data literacy. However, most undergraduates do not collect or manage research data regularly. In this chapter, we draw upon the princi-ples of constructivist learning theory to suggest that PDA can be used as an instructional bridge to teach research data management to undergraduates. PDA closely parallels research data management, with the added benefit of being directly relevant to undergraduate students, most of whom manage complex personal digital content on a daily basis. By teaching PDA, librarians encourage authentic learning experiences that immediately resonate with students' day-to-day activities. Teaching PDA builds a foundation of knowledge that not only helps students manage their personal digital materials, but can be translated into research data management skills that will enhance students' academic and professional careers.

THEORETICAL BACKGROUND

The Rise of Data

Data-driven research is growing both in academia and in the private sector. In 2009, Director John Marburger of the White House Office of Science and Technology Policy asserted that "our Nation's continuing leadership in science relies increasingly on effective and reliable access to digital scientific data."[1] Since then, the perceived power of digital data has only continued to grow— so much so that data scientists have been touted as having "the sexiest job of the 21st century."[2] Beyond this glamorous reputation, data science and data management skills are increasingly valued by employers who are looking to take advantage of the insights that big data can provide.[3] In fact, in 2016 the job of data scientist topped several "best jobs" lists—as measured by factors like the number of job openings, salary, and outlook.[4]

Research Data Management in Academic Libraries

Research data management has also grown in importance in academia as federal agencies,[5] private funders,[6] and academic journals[7] increasingly require data management plans and research data archiving. Across professions, there is a growing perception that data is a valuable commodity that can help us understand the world in new ways, and this places increasing relevance on research data management skills. Anyone planning to enter data-driven professions—including students at the undergraduate level—will benefit from opportunities to develop research data management skills. Shorish[8] calls research data management a "critical competency" for undergraduate students en route to the workforce, and she maps out a plan for promoting that competency within universities. She suggests that discipline-specific faculty can provide students with training in data comprehension and data analysis, while librarians—with their expertise in teaching information literacy—are well-positioned to provide expertise in research data management and preservation. Indeed, working with data has been viewed as an important element of information literacy for some time. A 1998 progress report from the

American Library Association's Presidential Committee on Information Literacy emphasized the importance of data literacy in a global marketplace,[9] and the Association of College and Research Libraries' Information Literacy guidelines (including the 2016 Framework for Information Literacy for Higher Education[10] and its predecessor, the 2000 Information Literacy Competency Standards for Higher Education[11]) include data literacy as a component of information literacy. Building from this foundation, academic libraries have identified a need for library services relating to research data management and preservation.[12]

Academic libraries are beginning to incorporate research data management into their instructional programs, teaching best practices like data management planning; metadata and documentation; organization; storage, backup, and preservation practices; and data publication and sharing.[13] Instruction programs on research data management often focus on faculty and graduate students, who commonly work with research data and can therefore find immediate utility in improving their data management strategies.[14] When working with undergraduates, many of whom do not encounter research data on a regular basis, librarians are challenged to find ways to communicate the relevance of research data management.

Applying Constructivist Learning Theory to Research Data Management Instruction

To make research data management relevant to undergraduates, librarians can look to constructivist learning theory for strategies that create meaningful learning experiences. Constructivist learning theory encompasses several principles, but in this chapter the authors focus on its principles of active, student-focused discovery. As articulated by Good and Brophy,[15] two core tenets of constructivist learning theory specify the following:

> *New learning builds on prior knowledge.* By tapping into students' past experiences, educators can create a learning sequence that extends from prior knowledge to the current lesson to a lifelong pattern of curiosity and learning.

> *Meaningful learning develops through "authentic" tasks.* According to Cooperstein and Kocevar-Weidinger, activities conducted in class should "simulate those that will be encountered in real life or in an assignment."[16] This strategy ensures that the skills students learn in the classroom have direct relevance to their lives outside of the classroom.

Applying these tenets to research data management instruction for undergraduates provides some guidance for librarians. Given that *new learning builds on prior knowledge,* librarians should aim to understand undergraduates' prior knowledge regarding data, tap into students' past learning experiences, and then build upon that knowledge in the classroom. Given that *meaningful learning develops through "authentic" tasks*, librarians should teach concrete, relatable skills that can be practiced during instruction and afterwards. Librarians need to position research data management skills in the context of students' current lives, rather than promising a theoretical applicability to an abstract future career. One promising way to relate research data management skills to students' lives is through the lens of personal digital archiving.

Personal Digital Archiving as a Bridge to Research Data Management

Personal digital archiving is a field of study that investigates how people organize, maintain, use, and share personal digital information in their daily lives, with a particular focus on preservation and access.[17] PDA has key similarities to research data management. Both PDA and research data management address the information literacy needs of users in their role as information producers;[18] both address how users manage and preserve their digital materials;[19] and both focus on digital stewardship, storage, long-term access, and the value of digital materials by providing practical strategies for the management, description, and preservation of those materials for future use.[20] Where PDA differs from research data management is in its broad applicability—PDA strategies focus on all personal digital materials, not just research data. The universal relevance of PDA suggests that librarians can teach PDA strategies as a bridge to research data management.

Following the principles of constructivist learning theory can inspire creative connection points between research data management and PDA. PDA taps into undergraduates' prior knowledge and is immediately relevant to students' daily lives. Students have likely worked with personal digital materials for most of their lives. By learning to manage their digital documents, photographs, music files, and other digital materials, students can build on their prior knowledge of handling these materials. PDA also has immediate relevance to undergraduate students, and facilitates learning through authentic tasks. By applying PDA techniques to their digital possessions, students see the clear, concrete benefit that research data management practices have on the organization of their digital lives.

Learning to manage digital assets like personal digital information and research data is an important skill for a thriving digital life and, as already discussed, is becoming a core competency in many emerging professions. Now that the theoretical background has been established, this chapter will transition to a discussion of practical instructional methods based on the authors' experience teaching undergraduates at Montana State University. This section aims to guide instructors in creating lesson plans and learning materials that connect the immediate benefits of PDA practices with the potential future benefits of research data management. By building a bridge from PDA to research data management, instructors can enhance learning and foster digital stewardship skills that can be broadly applied to students' futures—both personal and professional.

PRACTICAL INSTRUCTION STRATEGIES

In aiming to introduce undergraduate students to research data management at Montana State University, the authors put constructivist concepts into practice by developing lessons that activated students' prior knowledge and engaged them in authentic learning tasks. At the beginning of instruction we *set the stage* for learning by activating students' prior knowledge related to working with personal digital files, such as photos, word-processing documents, music files, and other media files. In particular, we asked students to provide examples of problems they had encountered when managing their personal digital files. Acknowledging these problems not only activated students' prior knowledge, but it also established the need and relevance of the lesson. Once students' prior knowledge was activated, we presented the *basics of PDA* as a set of useful strategies for avoiding common file management problems, particularly the problems students had identified. After the basics of PDA were presented, we engaged students in authentic tasks that gave them the opportunity to *apply learning with activities*. For these activities students apply PDA principles to their own digital files. Finally, through discussion, students *debrief to connect PDA to research data management*. In these discussions, students predicted the relevance and applicability of PDA principles to their potential future work with both their own personal data and with research data in their future studies and professions. During this discussion section, instructors and students highlighted parallels between the principles and strategies of PDA and those of research data management.

This section on practical instruction strategies details the highlights from these lessons. These lessons have been used with both face-to-face and online classes, and the components of these lessons can be adapted to either context with only slight adjustments. The lesson highlights in this section can be combined in different configurations depending on the context, the audience, and their needs. The instruction and outreach strategies in this section are designed primarily for undergraduate audiences, but they can be adapted to graduate and professional audiences with minimal adjustment.

The lessons presented here are organized into four key sections:

- Set the Stage
- Basics of PDA
- Apply Learning with Activities
- Debriefing to Connect PDA to Research Data Management

Each section is recommended to be completed in the order as presented because the sections build on each other and culminate in a complete lesson. That said, instructors can develop novel ways to deliver the sections in this suggested sequence. For example, for blended classes, the instructor may wish to do the first two sections online and use the face-to-face class time to complete the activity and debriefing. Regardless of how the instructor redesigns and customizes these sections, we hope that the highlights from these sections will provide instructors with a solid, road-tested starting point for developing useful, engaging lessons that develop the PDA and research data management skills of learners.

Set the Stage

In this lesson students describe the use, importance, and challenges of data within their discipline or other personally relevant contexts.

We have found it useful to set the stage for instruction by providing readings and videos for learners to review prior to the session. Based on our experience, we recommend selecting readings and viewings that have a relevant connection to the course discipline and are intended for a fairly general, popular audience. For example, when we worked with a Health and Human Development course, we selected an article from a popular magazine that discussed the complexities of health data from patient, family member, and caregiver perspectives.

At the beginning of the session, engage the class in a discussion about the readings and viewings. Having this discussion allows the instructor to demonstrate how the readings will relate to the day's lesson, build a rapport with the students, refresh the students' memory of the preparatory material, and clear up any confusion or misconceptions. Hearing students' reactions and thoughts can also reveal new insights into what they find interesting and their life experiences. Later in the session, the instructor can use these insights as the basis of examples to illustrate a point.

Connecting to the next section on the basics of PDA, the instructor can ask for student examples of how they name and organize their coursework-related files. For in-person courses, these examples could be shared orally; for online courses, they can be shared in writing on discussion boards or via other online tools. For more in-depth exploration of student examples, the instructor can devise a short activity where students diagram, share, and then discuss their current file organization and naming structure of a set of their own files. With either approach, students should be given enough time to engage in detailed reflection on their current practices. It is important that several different student examples are shared with the class so that variations and differences can be brought to light. This activity should lead students to consider the benefits and drawbacks of various approaches to organizing common files, like coursework files.

The Basics of PDA

In this lesson, students discover basic PDA strategies and principles that are also used to manage research data.

The PDA basics that we have found to be most relevant to undergraduates are naming conventions, folder structure, metadata/description, and backup, which are also fundamental for research data management. The students will explicitly explore the connections and similarities between PDA and research data management during the debriefing section at the end of the lesson, so this section can focus solely on the basic PDA practices. For each of these concepts, instructors can use an interactive presentation technique that first lays out the general concept and rationale, then asks for student-provided examples, and finally provides additional examples. Depending on time, instructor style, and the capabilities of the instructional space, the instructor may wish to use presentation slides for this section. Example slides can be found on Project Cora.[21] When students provide examples, instructors can ask them to share these verbally, write examples on whiteboards, or write on live collaborative slides. Online instruction will likely need to provide more details in slides or accompanying audio, but will still benefit from engaging students in providing their own examples of each PDA concept. Online discussion boards are one readily available option in major course management systems for collecting and distributing student examples. Beyond the course management system, there is a constantly evolving set of online tools that enable groups to collaborate and share ideas in a way that is complementary to the aim of this section. To facilitate student-generated examples online, beyond the content management system, we recommend searching for current tools for brainstorming, discussions, polling, or mind mapping.

Apply Learning with Activities

In this lesson, students apply PDA strategies and principles to organize and document their own files and data.

In this section of instruction, students will get hands-on experience applying the PDA strategies already discussed to their own data and files. Even if students do not have their own computers or access to their own files, the instructor will ask them to work with a set of files that they know they store on their computer or in the cloud. To focus the students, the instructor should suggest they work with a set of their files rather than all files on their computer. For students who have difficulty selecting a viable set of their own files, they should consider the files for their schoolwork. These students can be reminded of the variety of files they may have from their schoolwork, such as various versions of papers they wrote, instructor-supplied readings, their own presentations and associated media, and presentations provided by the instructor. Students may need some additional structure in order to focus on the various PDA strategies and principles. To provide this structure, we recommend initially asking students to devise a folder structure that is at least three levels deep, with folders that conform to naming conventions. Following this, students can then be asked to focus on developing naming conventions that account for similar types of files, various versions of files, and the preservation of dates.

The following are some questions to ask students at the completion of this activity:

- What naming conventions did you use and why?
- What were some challenges of the activity?
- What questions were raised by the activity?
- Which of the strategies you learned today do you think will be most useful to you and why?

Instructors should provide ample time to address these end-of-activity questions. Larger groups typically require more time to address questions than smaller groups. These questions about the activity typically segue naturally into the final section of instruction, in which the group debriefs in order to connect PDA to research data management.

Debriefing to Connect PDA to Research Data Management

In this lesson, students reflect upon the value of PDA principles and practices for their own personal data and discover the connection and similarities between PDA and research data management.

To get the most out of putting constructivist theory into practice, after providing students with activities based on authentic tasks, students need space in order to reflect on their learning. One widely used method for student reflection is post-activity debriefing.[22] Post-activity debriefing can take many forms, but the basic aspects to consider are immediate or delayed, and individual or group (see figure 11.1). Depending on the depth of reflection desired, instructors may wish to use more than one combination of these aspects of debriefing. For example, directly after the activity an instructor could use an immediate, group debriefing strategy, like a group discussion reacting to a simple prompt, and then later in the week students could write a multi-paragraph reflection that responds to more in-depth prompts. Any combination of these aspects (immediate/delayed, individual/group) can leverage online technologies, like online survey tools or discussion boards, or can use time-tested offline approaches, like writing by hand or having a group discussion.

To create this reflective space, instructors can designate some class time to debrief as a group, or provide an online discussion prompt to activate reflection. For this particular lesson, instructors need to develop a two-step

	IMMEDIATE	DELAYED
Individual	**Example:** Students complete online survey in class. **Good for:** Checking individual understanding. Quickly clearing up misconceptions. Students can learn from their peers if responses are reviewed. **Drawbacks:** Superficial reactions that may miss deeper con-nections. Although some peer learning can happen if responses are reviewed, students have less opportunity to build on the reflections of their peers than when working in groups.	**Example:** Short reflection paper **Good for:** Checking individual understanding and providing individual feedback and support. Deep, complex reflection that connects disparate concepts. **Drawbacks:** Students cannot take advantage of collective wisdom or build on the ideas of their peers. Due to the time delay, students may not carefully consider instructor feedback.
Group	**Example:** Small group discussion in class. **Good for:** Checking collective level of understanding. Quickly clear up misconceptions. Stu-dents learn from each other and build on the reflections of each other. **Drawbacks:** Superficial reactions that may miss deeper connec-tions. Difficult to check individu-al's understanding.	**Example:** Online discussion board **Good for:** Deep, complex reflec-tion that connects disparate ideas. Students can learn from their peers and build on each other's ideas. **Drawbacks:** Difficult to determine that students have engaged with the comments of their peers, unless the prompt specifically requires reaction to a peer comment.

FIGURE 11.1
Types of debriefings

prompt. The first prompt enables students to connect PDA strategies to their own personal data management, and the second prompt connects PDA strat-egies to workplace, professional, and research settings.

At the beginning of the debriefing section, instructors can ask students to reflect, and then describe which PDA strategies they predict will be most useful for their personal use. There are a few options for how to facilitate this kind of activity (see figure 11.2). The most simple and direct way to do this is to give students a minute to think about which strategies they will use in the future, then ask for volunteers to share their thoughts verbally. In this case, instructors should allow time for several students to voice their predictions and thoughts. Some students may wish to build on the comments of others,

---

Quick Reflect and Share Method

Benefits: Easy to implement; quick, immediate feedback; can be extended with additional questions.

Drawbacks: More gut reactions; do not reveal deeper motivations.

Example Prompt: Take a minute to think about which of the strategies we talked about today that you will most likely use in the future. After you've thought about it, I'll be looking for some volunteers to share.

Tips: Let students respond to each other. Avoid voicing judgments. Use additional prompts if you need more diverse responses. Aim for a representative sample of student thoughts.

Two-Minute Writing Activity

Benefits: This is a quick way to get students thinking more deeply about the topic so that they are better prepared to discuss it.

Drawbacks: Students can become too focused on quality writing and less focused on exploring the ideas if they don't fully understand the intent of the activity.

Example Prompt: We're going to do a quick two-minute writing activity. This is about gut reactions, and your writing doesn't have to be elegant. The writing is just for you, as a way to process your thoughts, and afterwards we can have a productive discussion. I would like you to write about which of the strategies we talked about today you will be most likely to use in the future.

Tips: Before giving the prompt, let students know that they will write for two minutes so that they can explore the idea, and then they will be expected to share their thoughts with the class. This does not have to mean that they will read aloud what they wrote.

FIGURE 11.2

Debriefing options

or they may offer contrasting opinions. Instructors should avoid voicing judgments on student comments about which strategies they think they will or won't use in the future. Instructors should be aware that student comments from a simple reflect-then-share activity will only reveal the PDA strategies that resonate most immediately, and may not reveal deeper motivations for why some resonate and others do not. Instructors who wish to dig deeper into the motivations behind these comments will need to use a more in-depth reflection strategy, such as a two-minute writing activity with prompts that aim to uncover motivations and rationale.

Students can then be asked to estimate which of these strategies would be applicable to the data used in professional workplace and research settings. If the session is conducted with disciplinary faculty, the library instructor should encourage the faculty to share their experience and perspective.

OUTREACH STRATEGIES

The practical instruction strategies previously described will go a long way in helping librarians develop lessons that use PDA as a bridge to research data management. However, because librarians most commonly rely on working with students outside their own classes, outreach strategies are necessary to identify collaborators who are willing to invite outside instructors to their classes. Outreach strategies take different forms on different campuses, and they depend greatly on existing relationships, but there are some strategies the authors have used that will be broadly applicable to a variety of higher education settings.

Initially, librarians should look to match PDA lessons to the curriculum. Librarians can start by identifying programs and specific courses that require students to work with data and may even have outcomes that explicitly address data literacy in some form. Once courses and programs are identified, librarians can set up meetings with instructors and program coordinators, paying special attention to the timing of this lesson within the rest of the course. When reaching out to instructors about data instruction needs, librarians should also leverage existing relationships between instructors and the library. Even if courses with explicit data competencies are not readily apparent, librarians can look for courses in which students work with many digital files, like media production courses, or courses that produce digital projects and portfolios.

Another outreach strategy that we found to be successful was sharing learning materials like slides and lesson plans before meeting with interested instructors. Sharing learning materials can go a long way toward demonstrating the librarian's goals for a session. Concrete examples are powerful tools in convincing instructors of the value of these lessons, and will give both parties a tangible starting point for conversations about learning outcomes and how to achieve them.

KEY TAKEAWAYS AND CONCLUSION

Whether undergraduate students work in the public or the private sector after graduation, they will likely be asked to manage and analyze data at some point in their careers. Teaching PDA as a general introduction to research data management allows students to understand research data management strategies through activities that are tangible and relatable. This chapter suggests that librarians can use the following four steps to build an instructional strategy that works as a bridge from PDA to research data management.

Set the Stage. Students describe the use, importance, and challenges of data within their discipline or other personally relevant contexts. This step helps prepare students to apply the lesson to their own lives.

Basics of PDA. Students discover basic PDA strategies and principles that are also used to manage research data. This step provides a foundation of knowledge that informs in-class activities.

Apply Learning with Activities. Students apply PDA strategies and principles to organize and document their own files and data. This step provides students with hands-on experience with PDA strategies.

Debrief to Connect PDA to Research Data Management. Students reflect upon the value of the PDA principles and practices for their own personal data and discover the connection and similarities between PDA and research data management. This step allows students to process the lesson and consider future applications of the skills they learned.

Students have a tangible need for research data management skills—in their personal lives, academic pursuits, and future careers. Using constructivist learning principles, educators can respond to that need by presenting PDA as a bridge to research data management. PDA lessons build on students' prior knowledge of their digital belongings, and PDA allows students to learn through authentic tasks that have immediate relevance to their daily lives. The basic instructional strategies in this chapter can be applied, remixed, and customized to fit many different learning contexts.

Ultimately, the strategies outlined in this chapter establish a bridge from PDA to research data management. By encouraging undergraduates to think more critically about managing their digital materials—whether they are personal files or research data—librarians can provide important foundational skills that benefit students during their undergraduate education and in their future careers.

ACKNOWLEDGMENTS

The authors would like to thank the Skylight writing group (Doralyn Rossmann and Scott W. H. Young) for their feedback and support.

NOTES

1. National Science and Technology Council, Interagency Working Group on Digital Data, "Harnessing the Power of Digital Data for Science and Society," January 2009, https://www.nitrd.gov/About/Harnessing_Power_Web.pdf.

2. Thomas H. Davenport and D. J. Patil, "Data Scientist: The Sexiest Job of the 21st Century," *Harvard Business Review,* October 2012, https://hbr.org/2012/10/data-scientist-the-sexiest-job-of-the-21st-century.

3. Daniel Harris, "So You Want to Be a Data Scientist (Again)?" *NatureJobs* Blog, ed. Jack Leeming, May 23, 2016, http://blogs.nature.com/naturejobs/2016/05/23/so-you-want-to-be-a-data-scientist-again.

4. Glassdoor, "50 Best Jobs in America," 2016, https://www.glassdoor.com/List/Best-Jobs-in-America-2016-LST_KQ0,25.htm; Careercast, "The Best Jobs of 2016," 2016, www.careercast.com/jobs-rated/best-jobs-2016.

5. National Institutes of Health, "NIH Data Sharing Policy and Implementation Guidance," 2003, http://grants.nih.gov/grants/policy/data_sharing/data_sharing_guidance.htm; National Science Foundation, "Dissemination and Sharing of Research Results," 2011, www.nsf.gov/bfa/dias/policy/dmp.jsp.

6. Gordon and Betty Moore Foundation, "Data Sharing Philosophy," 2008, https://www.moore.org/docs/default-source/Grantee-Resources/data-sharing-philosophy.pdf; Bill & Melinda Gates Foundation, "Bill & Melinda Gates Foundation Open Access Policy," 2015, www.gatesfoundation.org/How-We-Work/General-Information/Open-Access-Policy; Wellcome Trust, "Policy on Data Management and Sharing" (n.d.), https://wellcome.ac.uk/funding/managing-grant/policy-data-management-and-sharing.

7. Dryad Digital Repository, "Joint Data Archiving Policy," 2011, http://datadryad.org/pages/jdap; PLOS, "Data Availability," 2014, http://journals.plos.org/plosone/s/data-availability.

8. Yasmeen Shorish, "Data Information Literacy and Undergraduates: A Critical Competency," *College & Undergraduate Libraries* 22, no. 1 (2015): 97–106, http://doi.org/10.1080/10691316.2015.1001246.

9. Patricia Senn Breivik, Vicki Hancock, and J. A. Senn, "A Progress Report on Information Literacy: An Update on the American Library Association Presidential Committee on Information Literacy: Final Report," March 1998, www.ala.org/acrl/publications/whitepapers/progressreport.

10. Association of College and Research Libraries, "Framework for Information Literacy for Higher Education," 2016, www.ala.org/acrl/standards/ilframework.

11. Association of College and Research Libraries, "Information Literacy Competency Standards for Higher Education," 2000, www.ala.org/acrl/standards/informationliteracycompetency.

12. Joyce L. Ogburn, "The Imperative for Data Curation," portal: Libraries and the Academy 10, no. 2 (2010): 241–46, http://doi.org/10.1353/pla.0.0100; Liz Lyon, "The Informatics Transform: Re-Engineering Libraries for the Data Decade," *International Journal of Digital Curation* 7, no. 1 (2012): 126–38, http://doi.org/10.2218/ijdc.v7i1.220; Andrew M. Cox and Stephen Pinfield, "Research Data Management and Libraries: Current Activities and Future Priorities," *Journal of Librarianship and Information Science* 46, no. 4 (2014): 299–316, http://doi.org/10.1177/0961000613492542.

13. EDINA and Data Library, University of Edinburgh, "Research Data MANTRA," EDINA, 2011, http://datalib.edina.ac.uk/mantra; Heather Henkel et al.,

"DataONE Education Modules" (Albuquerque: DataONE, 2012), https://www
.dataone.org/education-modules; Donna Kafel, Andrew T. Creamer, and Elaine R.
Martin, "Building the New England Collaborative Data Management Curriculum,"
Journal of eScience Librarianship 3, no. 1 (2014): e1066, http://dx.doi.org/10.7191/
jeslib.2014.1066; Ricky Erway et al., *Building Blocks: Laying the Foundation for a
Research Data Management Program* (Dublin, Ohio: OCLC Research, 2015),
www.oclc.org/content/dam/research/publications/2016/oclcresearch-data
-management-building-blocks-2016.pdf.

14. Jake Carlson, Lisa Johnston, Brian Westra, and Mason Nichols, "Developing an
Approach for Data Management Education: A Report from the Data Information
Literacy Project," *International Journal of Digital Curation* 8, no. 1 (2013):
204–17. http://doi.org/10.2218/ijdc.v8i1.254; Jennifer Muilenburg, Mahria
Lebow, and Joanne Rich, "Lessons Learned from a Research Data Management
Pilot Course at an Academic Library," *Journal of eScience Librarianship* 3, no.
1 (2014): e1058, http://dx.doi.org/10.7191/jeslib.2014.1058; Amanda L.
Whitmire, "Implementing a Graduate-Level Research Data Management Course:
Approach, Outcomes, and Lessons Learned," *Journal of Librarianship and Scholarly
Communication* 3, no. 2 (2015): eP1246, http://doi.org/10.7710/2162–3309.1246.

15. Thomas L. Good, and Jere E. Brophy, *Looking in Classrooms* (Boston: Pearson, 2008).

16. Susan E. Cooperstein and Elizabeth Kocevar-Weidinger, "Beyond Active Learning:
A Constructivist Approach to Learning," *Reference Services Review* 32, no. 2
(2004): 141–48, http://doi.org/10.1108/00907320410537658.

17. Catherine Marshall, "How People Manage Information over a Lifetime," in
Personal Information Management, ed. William P. Jones and Jaime Teevan (Seattle:
University of Washington Press, 2007), 57–75.

18. Jacob Carlson, Michael Fosmire, C. C. Miller, and Megan Sapp Nelson,
"Determining Data Information Literacy Needs: A Study of Students and Research
Faculty," *portal: Libraries & the Academy* 11, no. 2 (2011): 629–57, http://doi
.org/10.1353/pla.2011.0022.

19. Kathleen Fear, "'You Made It, You Take Care of It': Data Management as Personal
Information Management," *International Journal of Digital Curation* 6, no. 2
(2011): 53–77, http://doi.org/10.2218/ijdc.v6i2.190.

20. Amber L. Cushing, "Highlighting the Archives Perspective in the Personal
Digital Archiving Discussion," *Library Hi Tech* 28, no. 2 (2010): 301–12, http://
doi.org/10.1108/07378831011047695; Kristin Briney, *Data Management for
Researchers: Organize, Maintain and Share Your Data for Research Success* (Exeter,
UK: Pelagic, 2015).

21. Sara Mannheimer and Ryer Banta, "Everyday Data Management," Project Cora,
2016, www.projectcora.org/assignment/everyday-data-management.

22. Ann C. Baker, Patricia J. Jensen, and David A. Kolb, *Conversational Learning: An
Experiential Approach to Knowledge Creation* (Westport, CT: Greenwood, 2002).

BIBLIOGRAPHY

Association of College and Research Libraries. "Framework for Information Literacy for
Higher Education." 2016. www.ala.org/acrl/standards/ilframework.

———. "Information Literacy Competency Standards for Higher Education." 2000.
www.ala.org/acrl/standards/informationliteracycompetency.

Baker, Ann C., Patricia J. Jensen, and David A. Kolb. *Conversational Learning: An Experiential Approach to Knowledge Creation.* Westport, CT: Greenwood, 2002.

Bill & Melinda Gates Foundation. "Bill & Melinda Gates Foundation Open Access Policy." 2015. www.gatesfoundation.org/How-We-Work/General-Information/Open-Access -Policy.

Breivik, Patricia Senn, Vicki Hancock, and J. A. Senn. "A Progress Report on Information Literacy: An Update on the American Library Association Presidential Committee on Information Literacy: Final Report." March 1998. www.ala.org/acrl/publications/ whitepapers/progressreport.

Briney, Kristin. *Data Management for Researchers: Organize, Maintain and Share Your Data for Research Success.* Exeter, UK: Pelagic, 2015.

Careercast. "The Best Jobs of 2016." 2016. www.careercast.com/jobs-rated/best-jobs-2016.

Carlson, Jacob, Michael Fosmire, C. C. Miller, and Megan Sapp Nelson. "Determining Data Information Literacy Needs: A Study of Students and Research Faculty." *portal: Libraries and the Academy* 11, no. 2 (2011): 629–57. http://doi.org/10.1353/ pla.2011.0022.

Carlson, Jake, Lisa Johnston, Brian Westra, and Mason Nichols. "Developing an Approach for Data Management Education: A Report from the Data Information Literacy Project." *International Journal of Digital Curation* 8, no. 1 (2013): 204–17. http:// doi.org/10.2218/ijdc.v8i1.254.

Cooperstein, Susan E., and Elizabeth Kocevar-Weidinger. "Beyond Active Learning: A Constructivist Approach to Learning." *Reference Services Review* 32, no. 2 (2004): 141–48. http://doi.org/10.1108/00907320410537658.

Cox, Andrew M., and Stephen Pinfield, "Research Data Management and Libraries: Current Activities and Future Priorities." *Journal of Librarianship and Information Science* 46, no. 4 (2014): 299–316. http://doi.org/10.1177/0961000613492542.

Cushing, Amber L. "Highlighting the Archives Perspective in the Personal Digital Archiving Discussion." *Library Hi Tech* 28, no. 2 (2010): 301–12. http://doi.org/10 .1108/07378831011047695.

Davenport, Thomas H., and D. J. Patil. "Data Scientist: The Sexiest Job of the 21st Century." *Harvard Business Review.* October 2012. https://hbr.org/2012/10/data -scientist-the-sexiest-job-of-the-21st-century.

Dryad Digital Repository. "Joint Data Archiving Policy." 2011. http://datadryad.org/ pages/jdap.

EDINA and Data Library, University of Edinburgh. "Research Data MANTRA." EDINA. 2011. http://datalib.edina.ac.uk/mantra.

Erway, Ricky, Laurence Horton, Amy Nurnberger, Reid Otsuji, and Amy Rushing. *Building Blocks: Laying the Foundation for a Research Data Management Program.* Dublin, Ohio: OCLC Research, 2015. www.oclc.org/content/dam/research/publications/2016/ oclcresearch-data-management-building-blocks-2016.pdf.

Fear, Kathleen. "'You Made It, You Take Care of It': Data Management as Personal Information Management." *International Journal of Digital Curation* 6, no. 2 (2011): 53–77. http://doi.org/10.2218/ijdc.v6i2.190.

Glassdoor. "50 Best Jobs in America." 2016. https://www.glassdoor.com/List/Best-Jobs -in-America-2016-LST_KQ0,25.htm.

Good, Thomas L., and Jere E. Brophy. Looking in Classrooms. Boston: Pearson, 2008.

Gordon and Betty Moore Foundation. "Data Sharing Philosophy." 2008. https://www
.moore.org/docs/default-source/Grantee-Resources/data-sharing-philosophy.pdf.

Harris, Daniel, "So You Want to Be a Data Scientist (Again)?" *NatureJobs* Blog, edited by
Jack Leeming. May 23, 2016. http://blogs.nature.com/naturejobs/2016/05/23/
so-you-want-to-be-a-data-scientist-again.

Henkel, Heather, Viv Hutchison, Carly Strasser, Stacy Rebich Hespanha, Kristin
Vanderbilt, Lynda Wayne, Stephanie Hampton, Amber Budden, Yiwei Wang, David
Bloom, Amy Hodge, Gail Steinhart, Stephanie Wright, and Matt Mayernik. "DataONE
Education Modules." Albuquerque, NM: DataONE, 2012. https://www.dataone.org/
education-modules.

Kafel, Donna, Andrew T. Creamer, and Elaine R. Martin. "Building the New England
Collaborative Data Management Curriculum." *Journal of eScience Librarianship* 3, no. 1
(2014): e1066. http://dx.doi.org/10.7191/jeslib.2014.1066.

Lyon, Liz, "The Informatics Transform: Re-Engineering Libraries for the Data Decade."
International Journal of Digital Curation 7, no. 1 (2012): 126–38. http://doi.org/
10.2218/ijdc.v7i1.220.

Mannheimer, Sara, and Ryer Banta, "Everyday Data Management." Project Cora. 2016.
www.projectcora.org/assignment/everyday-data-management.

Marshall, Catherine, "How People Manage Information over a Lifetime." In *Personal
Information Management,* edited by William P. Jones and Jaime Teevan, 57–75.
Seattle: University of Washington Press, 2007.

Muilenburg, Jennifer, Mahria Lebow, and Joanne Rich. "Lessons Learned from a
Research Data Management Pilot Course at an Academic Library." *Journal of eScience
Librarianship* 3, no. 1 (2014): e1058. http://dx.doi.org/10.7191/jeslib.2014.1058.

National Institutes of Health. "NIH Data Sharing Policy and Implementation Guidance."
2003. http://grants.nih.gov/grants/policy/data_sharing/data_sharing_guidance
.htm.

National Science and Technology Council, Interagency Working Group on Digital Data.
"Harnessing the Power of Digital Data for Science and Society." January 2009.
https://www.nitrd.gov/About/Harnessing_Power_Web.pdf.

National Science Foundation. "Dissemination and Sharing of Research Results." 2011.
www.nsf.gov/bfa/dias/policy/dmp.jsp.

Ogburn, Joyce L. "The Imperative for Data Curation." *portal: Libraries and the Academy* 10,
no. 2 (2010): 241–46. http://doi.org/10.1353/pla.0.0100.

PLOS. "Data Availability." 2014. http://journals.plos.org/plosone/s/data-availability.

Shorish, Yasmeen. "Data Information Literacy and Undergraduates: A Critical
Competency." *College & Undergraduate Libraries* 22, no. 1 (2015): 97–106. http://
doi.org/10.1080/10691316.2015.1001246.

Wellcome Trust. "Policy on Data Management and Sharing." N.d. https://wellcome.ac.uk/
funding/managing-grant/policy-data-management-and-sharing.

Whitmire, Amanda L. "Implementing a Graduate-Level Research Data Management
Course: Approach, Outcomes, and Lessons Learned." *Journal of Librarianship and
Scholarly Communication* 3, no. 2 (2015): eP1246. http://doi.org/10.7710/2162
–3309.1246.

PART IV

Social and Ethical Implications of Personal Digital Archives

12
Avoiding a Gambit
for Our Personal Digital Archives

IN THE GAME OF CHESS, a *gambit* move is a calculated opening salvo to wittingly sacrifice one's own assets on the board in order to draw out an opponent and gain a strategic advantage over him throughout the game. The unassuming and expendable *pawns* are often the first-choice lambs, with the ultimate objective being to open up and expose an opponent's *king* to an inescapable series of advances.

The gambit is an apt analogy for the effort that today's tech giants—Apple, Google, Amazon, Facebook, and others—are making to build online platforms and content ecosystems wedded to the various smartphone, tablet, netbook, and wearable devices that users rely upon to an ever-greater degree. In this analogy, our personal digital documents—photos, audio/video, app data, and much else—are the king content. Little by little our pawns of control— choice, privacy, and ownership—are being drawn out, exposed, and taken down as we pipe our content more heavily into and through the aforementioned devices. Indeed, with each new device purchase and "digital locker" subscription, we appear to be slowly but surely migrating the full life cycle and strata of our personal digital libraries and archives into the domain of the cloud platforms that support them.

With this paradigm shift comes a host of questions and challenges. How can we collectively uphold a culture of ownership, control, and at-will sharing of our personal archives in the face of the mounting trends of remote storage, gated access, restrictive content licensing, copyright policing, pervasive online streaming, and digital rights management? Most importantly, how will libraries and archives contend with these ascendant platforms? What meaningful role, if any, will our public-oriented, public-minded curators play in the face of this corporately consolidated content life cycle?

This chapter explores these questions and challenges through a series of brief and concise case studies on recent media transformations—including those involving our personal documents, our digital photos/audio/video, and our vital app data. The chapter will shed light on the various corporate- and consumer-driven market forces that are consolidating this paradigm shift. The specific threats and challenges that are posed to our personal digital archives and, by extension, to the born-digital acquisitions of libraries and archives will be addressed. The chapter will then conclude with a summary of practical examples of curatorial strategies and grassroots initiatives that can be employed to help mitigate an encroaching personal "Digital Dark Age."

CASE STUDY
Personal Documents

We'll begin with personal documents—our word processor files, our spreadsheets, our presentation files. These all have a unique set of vulnerabilities when it comes to shifting our content to hosted online platforms for greater ease of access and use. Admittedly, as a class of digital materials it can be challenging to do them full justice in this conversation because the platforms that service their life cycle are only mildly interoperable and differ from one another across a number of features. However, against the backdrop of this paradigm shift, what can be said commonly about this class of materials is that they are squarely at the center of a significant corporate push to more robustly and elegantly sync our local document edits to a remote cloud storage environment.

Syncing, as it turns out, is a strategy that is not so much designed to ensure a thorough series of archived snapshots of our documents, but rather to ensure that only our most recent edits are successfully collected, stored, and pushed to the other devices that we may be using to complete our final editing. Leading platform services like Google's Docs/Drive, Apple's iCloud/Drive, and Microsoft's Office365/OneDrive have software schemes in place to save iterative working-draft versions of an edited document within their cloud storage environments. However, it is important to understand that these services are often then pruning these numerous snapshots down to a more limited set of stored changes that are in turn available to the document author at a later date. These limited but retained versions are the sum of what the author can return to for reference purposes and use as a basis for restoring an older version to take the place of the author's most recent edits.

The dilemma, particularly for those who are editing and storing their documents solely in the cloud (e.g., Google Docs) as opposed to also syncing copies to their local "Drive" apps, is that downloading and saving any earlier versions as well as any annotations of their documents can often be somewhat fraught and time-consuming. Indeed, retrieving a full series of stored snapshots from document-hosting platforms often requires enterprise-level programming that utilizes advanced programming interfaces (APIs). Acknowledging that not all versions are necessary or equal, the current default export features of many hosted services do not typically support the download of document versions at all.

Archivists are only recently coming to terms with acquiring personal papers solely in electronic formats, and embracing the reality that acquiring working drafts of items like manuscripts and screenplays requires a combination of digital forensics, format migration, and emulation.[1] These sorts of strategies, along with outreach/education, will be imperative for archivists going forward when it comes to acquiring cloud-supported documents. With that in mind, it would help archivists to familiarize themselves with the various platform-specific Drive services and do the following:

- Be prepared to advise donors/creators on the trade-offs for choosing and using the above-mentioned services
- Learn about the enterprise-level APIs for the various services and how they might be leveraged to facilitate more robust document stewardship and transfer across platforms
- Understand how best to configure versioning settings to ensure that local copies are reliably synced and stored
- Educate donors/creators on good local document management practices in order to better guarantee that valuable changes to documents are saved and are distinguishable from other similar versions

When all is said and done, though documents created in proprietary cloud-oriented formats may not render the same way in their stand-alone app counterparts or in applications running on competing platforms, we can still be thankful at the present moment that when it comes to our personal documents, these commercial cloud platforms are supporting a locally synced storage option and several interoperable export formats. This gives users a measure of assurance, confidence, and control over their creations and ensures a point of free exchange between donors and archives. This chapter will have more to say on this below.

CASE STUDY
Personal Photos, Audio, and Video

When compared with personal documents, storage for personal digital photos and audio/video (AV) is getting steadily more complicated. For the average creator, the genesis of this sort of content has shifted rapidly to his smartphones and tablets. Users are getting all too familiar with the string of notifications from their devices alerting them to having reached their local storage limits and/or the need to purchase more remote cloud storage to continue with their device's automatic backup routines. Device manufacturers and service providers are scrambling to offer customers flexible options for managing this conundrum locally. For numerous smartphone and tablet owners, this means resorting to the previous scheme of saving born-digital photos and AV to removable microSD cards, which are unfortunately prone to being damaged and misplaced. This is also a scheme that introduces yet another step in the already challenging process of transferring content to another computer in order to accomplish a further chain of backup.

The other common strategy to which users are resorting is that of purchasing devices with larger storage allotments. This strategy forestalls the frequency with which users are receiving notifications about reaching their local limits, but it does very little to stave off notifications from any connected cloud storage services. The end result tends to be twofold: either users' reliance on increased tiers of device-connected cloud backup continues to grow, or they fall back on perpetually expanding their local storage in order to support transfers of content from their devices. The latter strategy, over time, hastens the rate at which we find ourselves in need of purchasing new computers with larger hard drives and creates a chaotic array of aging external storage media that tend to collect dust on our shelves.

From a consumer perspective, this state of affairs feels a bit stagnant and paralyzing. Where is the elegant, convenient, end-to-end solution to this quagmire of content management?

It is early days yet for a broad uptake of capacity and skills, but the archives community is making great strides when it comes to working on technical levels with collections of born-digital photos and AV materials that are donated to archives on external media. We are less prepared, however, for a future scenario wherein the paradigm flips more comprehensively toward users pushing waves of device-generated photos and AV solely to the cloud in order to avoid more frequent computer upgrades and managing stacks of dusty hard drives, SD cards, CDs, and DVDs. Storing off-line copies of photos and AV materials on such media could one day be the exception as opposed to the norm. What then?

At the risk of over-speculation, it may be in archives' interest to begin investigating and testing ways to make their acquisition processes more interoperable with cloud storage platforms, either through a particular service's sharing features or through the service's programmatic APIs. This was alluded to above in the section on personal documents. The intention is to meet users halfway while keeping a hand in the content pipeline—that is, asserting some influence and direction over how these services fit into the work of libraries and archives in the near future. Otherwise, institutional archives could very well find themselves without a stake in these commercial cloud services—all of which are seeking to extend their current enterprise-level support and features to everyday users in order to help them manage the full life cycle of this highly valued content—up to and perhaps including long-term preservation. Indeed, services such as Amazon Glacier, Google Near Line Storage, and Oracle's Archive Cloud Storage are all positioning these services as loosely defined archival end points within a longer chain of intermediary storage use on behalf of their customers. Partnerships between commercial giants like Google and state-level archives through the Google Cultural Institute, in just one such example, should also make clear to us that these entities see themselves as playing a meaningful role in collecting and servicing digital heritage materials.

In addition to becoming more conversant with the various services and APIs, further measures that archivists can undertake in this area would be to do the following:

- Become active learners when it comes to this rapidly changing space of digital imaging and time-based media, since we simply cannot continue to approach these objects as stand-alone files or static content—they are highly dynamic and complex
- Educate users on how they can proactively curate their digital photos and AV materials by leveraging the features and functionality of their mobile devices, social media accounts, and media libraries
- Raise more awareness about both the challenges and capabilities of removable and portable storage media, the need for active media refresh schedules, and encourage responsible local and geographically distant backup procedures

Ultimately, the end goal should be to better ensure that users can continue to work easily with archives to retain control of their content and have the means to transfer their personal photos and AV for the sake of independently preserving our broader collective history. At the same time, we can and should continue to ask critical questions along the way regarding the impacts to content quality and integrity as they pass through various cloud storage platforms and related sharing services. Concerns around compression and reformatting abound. Libraries and archives have to proactively engage the users, the services, and the issues.

CASE STUDY
Personal App Data

Finally, a neglected area of focus when it comes to addressing personal digital archiving is that of app data.

We can continue to conceive of documents in the context of traditional productivity software (e.g., Microsoft Office), and we can continue to conceive of photos and AV materials in the context of traditional media libraries (e.g., iTunes). But what happens as smartphone and tablet apps begin to play a more pivotal role in our intellectual and creative workflows—by way of note-taking apps, for example? Furthermore, what happens when the genesis of our personal photos is not only the default camera app on our smartphones, but the filter-rich camera features bundled within a social media app? Even thinking beyond text, images, and AV materials, we realize quickly that apps have penetrated the very surface of our biology by dint of wearable health monitors and other similar haptic-driven devices and related programs.

Where does all this data ultimately live, and how do we access it for the sake of longer-term archiving?

The first important thing to note is how fundamentally entangled apps are with very specific platforms, versions of operating systems, and remote databases and servers. Our smartphones, tablets, and wearable devices serve as content creation points, but they also store that content in formats highly unique to the apps that created them. These apps in turn also push our content over the Internet in the form of data to be remotely stored, analyzed (and in some cases enhanced), and served back to us within the confines of the creating app or another web interface.

This of course raises all sorts of questions for users around what rendition or elements of their data they might like to preserve, and in what ways they might like to interoperate with the data outside of the native confines of their devices and associated web services. In practice users will inevitably discover that they are often wholly at the mercy of app developers and service providers. Everything boils down to *if,* and *how easy or hard,* an app service makes it to export data and in which formats. Evernote, Instagram, and FitBit, to give just a few specific examples, provide several flexible options and formats for exporting user-generated data.

However, it is important to understand that the supported options and formats often dramatically restructure and re-contextualize the arrangement and organization scheme of the data itself. When attempting to access this same data outside of the app or in a separate app that might interoperate with the provided export formats, there are no sure guarantees that all of the information will survive or be easily accessible. One is at the very least promised an altogether different presentation and user experience with the newly exported/imported data.

Librarians and archivists can and should familiarize themselves with the range of different apps that users may be employing to create and manage data that falls under their desired collecting areas. A couple of ways of inventorying such apps and advising on best practices would be to do the following:

- Survey and interview existing donors/creators about what apps and platforms they may be using
- Seek out respectable online technology and app ranking sources to cross-reference
- Compile a list of recommended apps and services, preferably ones that are cross-platform—narrowing down apps that provide flexible options for exporting user data—data that is held in open or interoperable formats
- Build out statements in collection and digital preservation policies that communicate any and all adopted support strategies for donated app data sets
- Point out preferred export formats
- Be prepared to consult with donors/creators to help them avoid using apps that seek to lock up their data
- Drive home the message that apps and app features change rapidly and sometimes disappear altogether. It is imperative that users schedule routine manual exports and backups of their most crucial app data

Perhaps most importantly, libraries and archives need to prepare themselves to grapple with challenging provenance and arrangement questions, not to mention various format migration issues when it comes to donated app data. Endnote, for example, exports user notes and attachments into folder hierarchies that do not necessarily reflect a user's model for organizing the information. In addition, the exported note formats, though somewhat open in nature (HTML, Endnote-specific XML), are not necessarily immediately amenable to reproducing the information in other formats that would approximate the original look and feel—a common challenge that archivists and digital preservationists refer to as "significant properties," and which are merely the essential characteristics of a digital object that must be preserved over time for the digital object to remain accessible and meaningful.

THE PARADIGM SHIFT IN CONTEXT

These are by no means the full range of content genre and media-type transformations that archives and users are witnessing and experiencing through this paradigm shift. But they do provide a helpful starting point for understanding the forces and dynamics that are at the center of that shift.

The various tech giants are pushing more adoption of cloud platforms, cloud-dependent devices, and gated and licensed content ecosystems because this places more control in their hands for managing the complete life cycle of content with a view towards greater market dominance and monetization. The verdict is already firmly *in* that user adoption, attention, and consumerism are the keys to that monetization. Users' content and their interactions with it represent a rich source of metadata for tech giants, which enables these corporations to not only fine-tune the user experience and improve product uptake, but to also attract advertisers and publishers/distributors of content as a source of vital revenue. The more that these corporations can cordon off and control content distribution and user access/interaction, the more effective it will be for them to mine that use data and leverage it to market new services, and form partnerships with advertisers and content producers.

It is not just metadata related to our Netflix views or scans of our music library via iTunes that these corporations are interested in tracking. They are interested in the metadata (and in some cases even the content) related to our documents, and our photos, our AV, our notes. All of the case studies covered above represent vital sources of information about our interests, our productivity patterns, and our networks of friends and collaborators, among many other things. Bruce Schneier's 2015 book *Data and Goliath: The Hidden Battles to Collect Your Data and Control Your World* explains in good detail the widespread practice of corporate (and government) data mining of user content and the role of metadata.[2] All services approach data mining differently. For example, as of the writing of this chapter, Google does not mine the content of Google Docs for ad purposes, though it does in fact mine the content of Google Photos for the purposes of enhancing the app service itself.

Some of the targeted strategies employed for securing more control over the life cycle of this content include:

- Leveraging premiums on local mobile device storage and marketing cheaper (sometimes free) remote cloud storage as a means of funneling users to greater use of their cloud storage platforms
- Using digital rights management to manage and limit content access, sharing, and portability
- Impeding interoperability across platforms through the use of proprietary software and formats, controlled APIs, and siloed adoption and development of standards

All of these are measures that by design result in fewer choices and more lock-in for users, and fundamentally challenge the ongoing work of archivists and preservationists.

This chapter would be remiss if it did not acknowledge the role that users themselves are playing in driving these trends. For the vast majority of users, the convenience and short-term cost savings that this paradigm shift represents are of significant interest. Moving to simpler, lighter-weight, portable computing, and shifting the burden of managing digital storage to the cloud is a worthwhile prospect. For many users, this shift to hosted content and streaming services has opened up a whole new world of dynamic interaction and collaboration that is making the role of digital content in our lives exciting on a cultural, social, and even business level. Users cannot be faulted for taking advantage of these amazing developments in personal computing.

The fact remains, however, that in many cases users may not perceive their choices as a potential and deeply profound trade-off, or as I've framed it here, a gambit. It has already been alluded to, but what users sacrifice in increasing measure for this convenience and cost-savings are not just the pawns of control, choice, and privacy, but also the pawn of outright ownership. Users may be slowly but surely ceding their rights and ability to claim ownership over their king content and to determine how or whether it can be flexibly migrated, preserved, and accessed over time. They may also be ceding the ways in which that content can or should be shared, exchanged, or retrieved from within the walled-in confines of the platforms and ecosystems to which it is being entrusted. There are a number of vectors that threaten user ownership, among them:

Service agreements—these often contain obfuscating legal language that empowers the commercial provider to set and change the terms of use for uploaded and stored content at the expense of users' preferences

Lack of legal protections—this enables commercial providers to share our content and data with other commercial and governmental entities for their own profit or for their own indemnification without our prior knowledge or consent and with very little legal recourse for protection or compensation

Sudden service shutdowns—these result in hastened opportunities for data recovery and often the total loss and destruction of our hosted content

All of this amounts to a troubling gambit to be sure, but one that is thankfully not yet fully consolidated. Users, surprisingly enough, have a number of trends working for them, and unwitting allies in unexpected places. As just one example, we should recognize that even though Apple, Google, Amazon, Facebook, and others make money from consolidating their hold over the content uploaded by individual users, they also have had their sights set on increasing their market hold over larger enterprise-level customers and even government data. The latter bring with them stronger legal muscle for ensuring that data remains accessible, controllable, interoperable, and secure from within the commercial cloud. Attempts to overly gate intellectual content at these enterprise and government levels would likely prove counterproductive in the short term to many of the tech giants' efforts to capitalize on services to that market segment. Particularly in the area of personal documents and apps, the various commercial cloud service providers have bent over backwards to ensure that content created in the cloud can be stored locally and remain portable to other formats.

CHALLENGES AND OPPORTUNITIES AHEAD

Libraries, archives, and other cultural memory organizations are facing a new future when it comes to working with individual creators and donors. There is no telling what role, larger or smaller, that smartphone, tablet, netbook, and wearable devices will play in relationship to other more traditional computing solutions. That future situation will ultimately be settled out or become more consolidated along the lines of some of the trends described above. It is safe to say, however, that we are already at the doorstep of an established and growing paradigm. The greatest danger is that libraries and archives will confuse this new paradigm of computer media with previous generations of fixed technology. This new class of devices is not necessarily engineered to extenuate our already aging notions of "desktops," "file cabinets," "folders," and "documents," and they do not respect single points of locality or transfer. Nevertheless, our collections will only grow and acquire more richness insofar as we gain familiarity with these technologies and their users. Exploring and understanding points of interoperability and the best forms that outreach and advocacy should take are paramount.

In the best of scenarios, libraries and archives will have the time and presence to work closely with donors to maneuver their hybridized or more strictly cloud-based collections into a place (or places) of networked interoperable exchange—perhaps through the use of a variety of intermediary services (e.g., DropBox, WeTransfer, Google Drive, etc.). The real struggle will be securing the necessary financial and technology-related resources to advance testing and interoperability with the various cloud storage services that have been mentioned throughout this chapter.

Will the institution interoperate with users and their devices through only one cloud storage service, or a broad range of services? How will the institution sustain this paradigm of data acquisition and adapt to fluctuations in service subscription costs over time? What are the appropriate storage subscription tiers to handle programmatic transfers of data from donor devices? Will local computer workstations be configured with sufficient storage to download and receive any transferred data for further processing?

Along with the technical interoperability, there are also questions that will need to be explored on policy levels for working within such a framework. What data management requirements will need to be placed on users when it comes to transferring their personal digital archives via such services? Will data need to be packaged or placed in certain formats to meet archive specifications, or to avoid compression and other unstated transformations that might threaten the quality and integrity of the content during transmission?

In the worst-case scenario, libraries and archives will be handed this new class of devices in the absence of their owner/creator only to discover that their only access to the related data is through layers of passwords, encryption, digital rights management, and proprietary app data formats—all furthermore highly dependent upon an operating system that may be completely unsupported by the receiving computing environment.

Thankfully, the knowledge and skills that libraries and archives are beginning to amass through the acquisition of legacy computer media and the use of born-digital forensics tools and approaches can serve these new types of exchange. Through these methodologies curators are gaining experience with troubleshooting the intricacies of port connections and peripheral devices, engaging the research required to make sense of outdated operating and file systems, and learning to leverage metadata to sift for provenance and authenticity. Libraries and archives are also amassing more and more expertise in the areas of emulation and file format migration for born-digital materials. All of these skills are helpful starting points for navigating the approaching waves of donated smartphones, tablets, netbooks, and wearable devices that we are potentially liable to receive, not to mention the accompanying transfers of zipped-up export archives from various app services and/or extracted photo and media database files, among other similar esoteric content.

Libraries and archives are also well prepared to engage in the advocacy that will be needed to help everyday users understand their role in shifting these trends in directions that empower them on behalf of their king content. Volumes like this one are evidence of our community's passion to inform and provide guidance on issues of social and cultural importance as they pertain to technological change. This chapter itself in many ways owes its writing to inspiration from recent initiatives such as the Library Freedom Project, which is seeking to inform and equip libraries and their users with skills and technologies to protect patron privacy in our new age of surveillance.[3] The Electronic Frontier Foundation is another reliable partner organization for libraries and archives that is integrally involved in similar efforts, as well as others such as the Apollo 1201 Project, which is geared toward eradicating digital rights management.[4] Other previous advocacy work to be built upon would be that of the Library of Congress's coordinated outreach curriculum on personal digital archives,[5] and the Digital Preservation Outreach & Education "Train the

Trainer" series.[6] And this is not to mention the work of the Digital POWRR group based at Northern Illinois University.[7] Which is all to say that librarians and archivists clearly know how to rally on behalf of users and their content!

CONCLUSION

It is clear, then, that libraries and archives are well positioned to begin working with donors/creators to preserve personal digital archives that have their genesis and significant portions of their life cycle managed via smartphones, tablets, netbooks, and wearable devices. As we continue that work in earnest, there are a number of targeted strategies that we can undertake to solidify that position.

Libraries and archives must increase their familiarity with this unique class of devices, working hands-on and with donors to understand the ways in which the devices are becoming entangled with the online platforms and content ecosystems that support their use. More importantly, we must explore how to leverage the most open features of these devices and platforms to ensure that they have a meaningful place in our arsenal of acquisition pathways. To some degree the paradigm is set and the ship is sailing. The more that libraries and archives engage these technologies now, the better positioned we will be to shape them and continue curating collections into the future.

Libraries and archives should also be proactive in their outreach to creators and donors, educating them in how best to protect their vital pawns of control, choice, privacy, and ownership in support of their king content. Likewise, libraries and archives increasingly represent a powerful market segment to tech giants, and we should not undersell the role that we play in shaping the development of their online platforms and content ecosystems. When it comes to concerns around the consolidation of control over our content via their market-driven gambits, libraries and archives need to engage the issues, as individual institutions but also at consortial levels, through professional associations, and via grassroots initiatives, advocating for more control, choice, privacy, and ownership. The battlefront issues of digital rights management, interoperability, and industry support for more open nonproprietary formats should be paramount in those efforts.

With this new paradigm of devices and content wedded so intricately to online platforms and content ecosystems, in some ways the challenges for libraries and archives have never been more daunting. But as adept curators we've already accumulated a knowledge base and a set of expertise in the areas of format migration, digital forensics, and emulation. We are ready to engage the technical challenges. It is now time to get to work raising awareness within our institutions, piloting new acquisitions, appealing for needed resources, and adjusting our policies; in other words, continuing to do what we do best.

NOTES

1. Dan Rockmore, "The Digital Life of Salman Rushdie," *The New Yorker,* last modified July 29, 2014, www.newyorker.com/tech/elements/digital-life-salman-rushdie.
2. Bruce Schneier, *Data and Goliath: The Hidden Battles to Collect Your Data and Control Your World* (New York: W.W. Norton, 2015).
3. "Our Work," Library Freedom Project, https://libraryfreedomproject.org/ourwork/.
4. "About," Electronic Frontier Foundation, https://www.eff.org/about.
5. "Personal Archiving: Preserving Your Digital Memories," Library of Congress, www.digitalpreservation.gov/personalarchiving/.
6. "Digital Preservation Outreach & Education," Library of Congress, www.digitalpreservation.gov/education/index.html.
7. "About POWRR," Digital POWRR, last modified on January 6, 2016, http://digitalpowrr.niu.edu/.

BIBLIOGRAPHY

"About." Electronic Frontier Foundation. https://www.eff.org/about.

"About POWRR." Digital POWRR. Last modified on January 6, 2016. http://digitalpowrr.niu.edu/.

"Digital Preservation Outreach & Education." Library of Congress. www.digitalpreservation.gov/education/index.html.

"Our Work." Library Freedom Project. https://libraryfreedomproject.org/ourwork/.

"Personal Archiving: Preserving Your Digital Memories." Library of Congress. www.digitalpreservation.gov/personalarchiving/.

Rockmore, Dan. "The Digital Life of Salman Rushdie." *The New Yorker.* Last modified July 29, 2014. www.newyorker.com/tech/elements/digital-life-salman-rushdie.

Schneier, Bruce. *Data and Goliath: The Hidden Battles to Collect Your Data and Control Your World.* New York: W.W. Norton, 2015.

ISAIAH BEARD

13
Digital Photos, Embedded Metadata, and Personal Privacy

WHEN INDIVIDUALS ORGANIZE AND CURATE their own content, the ethical ramifications are generally the last thing considered. This is particularly true considering that most older adults doing such curation have spent most of their time creating content in a pre-digital age. In the past, analog artifacts were limited by their media in how far and wide they could be shared. Until very recently, photographs, sound, and moving image recordings used to be primarily physical, and creating them required dedicated, discrete equipment (a camera or recorder, and film or tape) as well as time, money, and labor (film developing and tape editing) to yield a finished product. The photographs and recordings themselves were limited in their tangible nature as well: for the most part, sharing these memories meant showing or passing the content around to a limited group of people in the same physical space, or having additional copies printed. As a result, the forethought and planning required often limited the spontaneity and volume of these artifacts, creating a limiting factor that kept the number of artifacts we created to an inherently low number, relative to what is achievable on more accessible, digital media. Meanwhile, the relatively limited sharing potential of analog formats made it possible for embarrassing, undesirable, or compromising photos or recordings to be more easily hidden or restricted in access, for the most part.

The landscape of documenting our personal histories—photography in particular—changed with the rise of digital creation tools. Their ease of use and additional features meant that not only could people create more photographs and recordings at massive volumes, but the information that these items contain is richer in detail, and provides ever more granular data about our daily lives. How we share these memories has changed as well, relying on third-party social networks to instantly distribute our memories—and the rich data they contain. Locations, dates, times, even the type of camera or smartphone you use and the software installed on it, are widely distributed with everything we share. This provides opportunities not only for our family, friends, and acquaintances to know more about our lives, but can provide useful and profitable information to the third parties with which we entrust our data.

These issues of data and privacy give rise to a whole new set of ethical concerns that must be considered as we archive and curate our own data, but are often overlooked or ignored by most of us. On the other hand, outright blocking of this data collection and boycotting the features and services of these social networks deprive the user of important and useful tools that can be legitimately used to organize and make sense of collections that are otherwise impossible to manage. Making personal preservationists aware of the issues, and educating them on both the benefits and pitfalls of data sharing, can help them make informed decisions on the ethical matters surrounding their content and what level of disclosure is prudent for them.

THE PRIMARY ETHICAL DILEMMA
Data Sharing and Privacy

The new capabilities afforded by high-quality digital cameras, smartphones capable of high-speed data, and social networks have no doubt enabled a transformational shift in how people interact with each other. Users of these tools now have the capability to engage in and maintain intimate social relationships with people anywhere—relationships that are purposeful and deliberate.[1] However, many of these same users who enjoy the beneficial aspects of the technology are concerned with its detrimental aspects. In fact, social network providers such as Facebook are keenly aware that there is at least a segment of their users who will actively modify their behaviors—including what they access and how—out of concerns for their privacy. Such behaviors include preferring not to install a social media app on their phone; this arises out of an awareness of that app's ability to collect data, threatening their sense of privacy.[2]

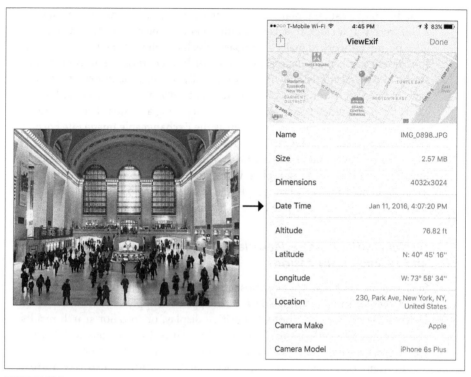

FIGURE 13.1

A digital photograph captured using a smartphone, and the technical metadata (time, date, location, smartphone make and model) embedded within the photo.

Most creators of digital content are primarily concerned with the substance and message of the work they're creating—the image they are trying to capture; the content of the document they're typing, drawing, or editing. What may or may not be known is that a wealth of additional, supporting metadata is being captured alongside the actual content of the work, and this metadata is being embedded into the digital file being created. It is this data that can store personal information, and in some cases this data may inadvertently be leaked by the tools we use to share and organize our personal digital archives. (See figure 13.1.)

Automatic Data Embedding: What Your Digital Camera Is Learning about You

The integration of high-quality cameras into smartphones has resulted in a fusion of these technologies into something that collects a great deal of data about the images captured, and by definition, about the user of each device.

In addition to a camera, many modern smartphones also come equipped with a GPS receiver; a clock that is constantly kept to the correct time using cellular phone network signals; a compass which can determine what direction the camera was facing; an accelerometer which can determine movement and speed; and an altimeter showing elevation.[3] By default, the information from each of these sensors gets collected automatically, and can be embedded in each photo and video taken by a smartphone, using a standardized metadata schema for digital photographs known as the Exchangeable Image File Format (EXIF). The result is a digital photograph or video which not only witnesses the scene before it, but also describes, with incredibly precise detail, the exact location where the photographer was standing and in what direction, the exact date and time the photograph was taken, and even the exact make and model of the smartphone itself.[4]

Social Media, Precise Metadata, and Privacy Implications

Smartphone apps, particularly those used by social media or by retailers, can also access location and usage data. Such apps then apply that information to provide the user with a context-sensitive display, or to tailor search results and content creation options. "Check-ins" also broadcast to your social group where you've been, and potentially who you were with at the time.[5]

Content organizing tools and social media platforms also rely a great deal on user interaction and crowdsourcing in order to gather more nuanced information. Most users of Facebook are familiar with "tagging," or digitally associating themselves and other users along with places, actions, and even moods, and applying these tags to created content such as a written status post, or a photograph or video.[6] Potentially even more definitive is facial and image pattern recognition based on such tagging. Social media platforms such as Facebook routinely analyze photographs uploaded by their users, and suggest automatically tagging individuals whose faces appear in each image, based on tags applied to previous photos.[7] Similar functionality exists for photo-organizing and sharing services like Google Photos, which even takes the capability a step farther, and can recognize common objects like "trees" or "cars" within photographs and index the photos under these contextual tags for later searching.[8]

Positive Aspects of Metadata

To be fair, many of the features discussed in this chapter were designed to be positive and helpful to the end user. Although the initial reaction upon first learning of these privacy and ethical concerns might be to disable all forms

FIGURE 13.2

Software such as Apple Photos constructively uses metadata tags
and embedded location information to help users organize their
content with ease.

of metadata collection, some careful consideration should be given to the
benefits that these same points of data can afford personal archivists in their
quest to organize and make sense of their digital collections. With the average
mobile phone user taking as many as 150 pictures per month,[9] such metadata,
invasive as it may seem, is often a vital and powerful tool to keep personal
media collections from becoming a disorganized mess. Such metadata encoding, for instance, can easily permit an archivist to recall all photos taken in a
specific location or date range; facial recognition algorithms can be used to
rapidly weed out photos taken of a specific person, or they can serve as a memory jogger when events call for it. (See figure 13.2.) Such actions can be done
far more rapidly than having an archivist painstakingly review hundreds—
or even thousands—of photos to manually organize them. Similarly, people
wanting to curate their social media postings will likely find it convenient to
search for content they've created while they were visiting specific places, or
while being with certain friends and acquaintances. Arguably, these are the
well-intentioned uses of these features that make them worth integrating.

Negative Aspects and Unintended Uses of Digital Content

Much of the consternation about creating and sharing digital content is that it may share too much, and provide a level of information about our whereabouts, habits, affiliations, and preferences that is beyond what a person could be comfortable with. This can be particularly true when someone tags his friends as appearing in certain photos, and being in certain places, without their prior knowledge or consent, thus making it more difficult for individuals to directly control what information is shared about them, and with whom that information is shared.

Much of the concern surrounding the use of these technologies, and the potential unwanted exposure of private information that can result, is fueled by very detailed demonstrations of the ability to retrace individuals' steps and carefully track their travels, activities, and routines, based solely on the data collected by their personal devices and social media content.[10] People have a tendency to make use of these convenience-adding features, in which location and other metadata are recorded, in order to better organize their collections, only to react with surprise and shock when they fully grasp the scope of the information collected, and how that data can be used to paint a picture of that person in an unsettlingly detailed fashion.

Rights, Ownership, and the Commoditization of Content

Adding to the ethical conundrum are the potential commercial aspects of this data, and how it can be monetarily exploited. Social media platforms like Facebook, Twitter, and Instagram, as well as online content-organizing services like Flickr and Google Drive/Photos, ostensibly provide much of their services at no cost to end users. However, these services are run by for-profit companies, whose investors expect them to eventually collect an income for providing such services. Naturally, the users of a particular service—and the unique content they provide—become a readily exploitable resource for monetization.

Most of these platforms provide a very clear explanation of the types of data they use and the methods with which they use it. However, the explanations aren't often in places where users are most likely to see them. Most users of Facebook, for example, are provided with a small link upon sign-up that gives them the opportunity to view Facebook's data policy before agreeing to it. However, based on self-reported user data, fewer than 16 percent of social media users claim to always read such privacy policies, and at least 12 percent never do.[11] Meanwhile, up to half of all Americans may not understand what a privacy policy is or does.[12]

Even so, if a user does decide to peruse Facebook's data use policy, how her data is utilized is very starkly laid out:

> Depending on which Services you use, we collect different kinds of information from or about you.
>
> **Things you do and information you provide.** We collect the content and other information you provide when you use our Services, including when you sign up for an account, create or share, and message or communicate with others. This can include information in or about the content you provide, such as the location of a photo or the date a file was created. We also collect information about how you use our Services, such as the types of content you view or engage with or the frequency and duration of your activities.
>
> **Things others do and information they provide.** We also collect content and information that other people provide when they use our Services, including information about you, such as when they share a photo of you, send a message to you, or upload, sync or import your contact information.
>
> **Your networks and connections.** We collect information about the people and groups you are connected to and how you interact with them, such as the people you communicate with the most or the groups you like to share with. We also collect contact information you provide if you upload, sync or import this information (such as an address book) from a device.[13]

Unfortunately, leaving the platform and deactivating your account does not make this data usage go away, since Facebook does reserve the right to retain user data even after they've stopped using it.[14]

To be sure, Facebook is not alone in this pervasive data mining. Twitter[15] and Google[16] have privacy policies in place which spell out similar practices in data aggregation and usage.

Knowing and Mitigating the Concerns

Admittedly, avoiding unwanted data sharing is an extremely difficult task, despite its presenting significant potential ethical quandaries. Most of the hardware and software we use for creating born-digital content is configured to "bake in" a significant amount of metadata that tells a great deal about the history of the object, including what some may deem sensitive, personal information. These features are by and large created with good intentions, and they provide powerful and useful tools for organizing, sorting, searching, and curating the content. However, disclosing this data may have unwanted consequences, such as disclosing the places people visited and at what time, or who may have authored sensitive data when they may have wanted to be anonymous. Some of these unwanted disclosures could be mildly embarrassing, or they could be seen as a nuisance when individuals are barraged with targeted advertising. Alternatively, such disclosures could expose individuals to more serious scrutiny, such as in cases where activists are making a political statement or performing activities not condoned by their government.

When performing digital curation activities, or organizing the born-digital content in our own personal collections or those of others, all of these concerns will need to be considered, along with the potential consequences of sharing this data. The potential risk and negative aspects of those consequences will need to be balanced against the positive benefits provided by location and other personal metadata, and the platforms which make use of them. Once users are made aware or educate themselves about the ethical and privacy concerns that abound, they must make decisions that strike a balance that is comfortable for them, a balance between security, privacy and convenience; they must balance which services and pieces of data they are comfortable with sharing against the potential results of undesired data sharing.[17]

Some editing methods and alternative platforms do exist to mask data, or avoid some of the privacy and ethical pitfalls befalling the more commonly used services. These include:

> Editing or wiping embedded metadata on digital files before they are shared. Software packages such as exiftool (multiplatform, www .sno.phy.queensu.ca/~phil/exiftool/) and AnalogExif (multiplatform, https://sourceforge.net/projects/analogexif/) permit users to view and edit the embedded information contained in various file types. Doing this will, of course, change or obliterate information that could be legitimately useful when organizing the content, or trying to search for it later.

> Eschewing common, commercial, and online-based tools for organizing digital resources in favor of open source platforms. Digital asset management tools such as Razuna (www.razuna.org) and Stuff Organizer (http://stufforganizer.sourceforge.net) can be used in place of the more common media platforms to curate content. However, setting up this software does require some knowledge of servers and infrastructure, and the convenience advantages associated with using the wider commercial platforms are lost.

CONCLUSION

Education and consent play a key role in enhancing technology users' awareness of these issues, and reducing or possibly even alleviating their concerns about what personal data they may accidentally be "leaking" to the Internet at large. When collecting and curating digital content, gaining knowledge of the type of metadata encoded in each resource, including what information these items may have about other people, will permit the curator to get a grasp of the potential impacts of disclosing that information, including who beyond the creator of the work may be affected due to identity tagging or the use of facial recognition tools. Making certain that affected individuals are aware of the tagging, and perhaps ensuring that these individuals find that to be acceptable, could help to avoid unwanted surprises when the collection is shared with others later.

As information professionals, we should encourage patrons to:

Familiarize themselves with technical metadata. Digital photographers and content creators understandably focus on their artistic expression, and less so on the technical nature of their output. There are tools built into the software and devices they use which can show them what is embedded in their digital photos, from the location data to anything personal they may want to filter out.

Not panic. When a patron has just realized that the location and other identifying metadata are being shared, his common response is to scrub the photos and digital collections of this information, and to take steps to disable recording it.

Understand situations where this technical metadata is useful. While knowledge and information control are certainly necessary, there are situations where this data is actually very useful for curating one's personal collection, and where desired features and functionality are lost in the rush to anonymize. Location, time, and other embedded metadata are incredibly helpful in organizing our content, jogging our memories, and rapidly retrieving photos from parts of our growing digital collections. As our smartphones grow bigger memories and our personal photograph collections grow into the thousands, finding "that one photo" can grow increasingly difficult without having metadata as a finding aid.

Make "sanitized" copies of photos and content. As information professionals, we should make ourselves familiar with software tools that are used to read as well as remove metadata from digital content. Patrons should be educated that these tools can be used to keep control of their personal data, and to make sure that only photos which don't contain sensitive information are shared on social media, when appropriate. And, rather than removing that data from their original files, they should adopt practices similar to those used in the digital preservation community: keep archival copies intact, and make separate, derivative "presentation" copies that contain all of the edits and modified information they wish to share.

We librarians and archivists have a unique opportunity to better educate digital content creators about how embedded metadata can affect them, in both constructive ways and in ways that may cause them privacy or ethical concerns. Holding seminars or classes on digital photography and creating content, as well as having one-on-one sessions with patrons, can go a long way toward making patrons aware of these issues, and having fruitful conversations with patrons about digital photos, content, and privacy matters can be extremely helpful.

NOTES

1. S. Choi, "The Flipside of Ubiquitous Connectivity Enabled by Smartphone-Based Social Networking Service: Social Presence and Privacy Concern," *Computers in Human Behavior* 65 (2016): 325–33.

2. P. Khusumanegara, R. Mafrur, and D. Choi, "Why Smartphone Users Accessing Facebook through Facebook Mobile Website?: Battery and Privacy Awareness," *International Journal of Multimedia and Ubiquitous Engineering* 10, no. 8 (2015): 339–46. doi: 10.14257/ijmue.2015.10.8.33.

3. Alasdair Alan, *Basic Sensors in IOS: Programming the Accelerometer, Gyroscope, and More* (Sebastopol, CA: O'Reilly Media, 2011).

4. Technical Standardization Committee on AV & IT Storage Systems and Equipment, "Exchangeable Image File Format for Digital Still Cameras: Exif Version 2.2, Technical Standard," 2002, Japan Electronics and Information Technology Industries Association, www.exiv2.0rg/Exif2–2.PDF.

5. Eunjoon Cho, S. A. Myers, J. Leskovec, "Friendship and Mobility: User Movement in Location-Based Social Networks," in *Proceedings of the 17th ACM SIGKDD International Conference on Knowledge Discovery and Data Mining* (New York: ACM, 2011), 1082–90. https://doi.org/10.1145/2020408.2020579.

6. Hyoryung Nam and P. K. Kannan, "The Informational Value of Social Tagging Networks," *Journal of Marketing* 78, no. 4 (July 2014): 21–40.

7. Facebook, "Facebook Help Center: How Does Facebook Suggest Tags?" 2016, https://www.facebook.com/help/122175507864081?helpref=uf_permalink.

8. Daniela Hernandez, "The New Google Photos App Is Disturbingly Good at Data-Mining Your Photos," Fusion.net, June 4, 2015, http://fusion.net/story/142326/the-new-google-photos-app-is-disturbingly-good-at-data-mining-your-photos/.

9. Janko Roettgers, "Special Report: How We Really Use Our Camera Phones," Gigaom, January 23, 2015, https://gigaom.com/2015/01/23/personal-photos-videos-user-generated-content-statistics/.

10. Kai Biermann, "Betrayed by Our Own Data," Zeit Online, March 10, 2011, www.zeit.de/digital/datenschutz/2011–03/data-protection-malte-spitz.

11. Stacey Higginbotham, "People Trust the Internet but Lie to It Anyway," Gigaom, November 27, 2012, https://gigaom.com/2012/11/27/people-trust-the-internet-but-lie-to-it-anyway/.

12. Aaron Smith, "Half of Online Americans Don't Know What a Privacy Policy Is," Factank: News in the Numbers, Pew Research, December 4, 2014, www.pewresearch.org/fact-tank/2014/12/04/half-of-americans-dont-know-what-a-privacy-policy-is/.

13. Facebook, "Data Policy," Facebook.com, September 29, 2016, https://www.facebook.com/full_data_use_policy.

14. Victor Luckerson, "7 Controversial Ways Facebook Has Used Your Data," *Time*, February 4, 2014, http://time.com/4695/7-controversial-ways-facebook-has-used-your-data/.

15. Twitter, Inc., "Privacy Policy," Twitter.com, September 30, 2016, https://twitter.com/privacy?lang=en.

16. Google, Inc., "Privacy & Terms," Google.com, August 29, 2016, https://www.google.com/policies/privacy/.

17. Il-Horn Hann, Kai-Lung Hui, Sang-Yong Tom, and Ivan Lee Png, "Overcoming Online Information Privacy Concerns: An Information-Processing Theory Approach," *Journal of Management Information Systems* 24, no. 2 (2007): 13–42, www.tandfonline.com/doi/citedby/10.2753/MIS0742–1222240202.

BIBLIOGRAPHY

Alan, Alasdair. *Basic Sensors in IOS: Programming the Accelerometer, Gyroscope, and More.* Sebastopol, CA: O'Reilly Media, 2011.

Biermann, Kai. "Betrayed by Our Own Data." Zeit Online. March 10, 2011. www.zeit.de/digital/datenschutz/2011–03/data-protection-malte-spitz.

Cho, Eunjoon, and S. A. Myers and J. Leskovec. "Friendship and Mobility: User Movement in Location-Based Social Networks." In *Proceedings of the 17th ACM SIGKDD International Conference on Knowledge Discovery and Data Mining,* 1082–1090. New York: ACM, 2011.

Choi, S. "The Flipside of Ubiquitous Connectivity Enabled by Smartphone-Based Social Networking Service: Social Presence and Privacy Concern." *Computers in Human Behavior* 65 (2016): 325–33.

Facebook. "Data Policy." Facebook.com. September 29, 2016. https://www.facebook.com/full_data_use_policy.

———. "Facebook Help Center: How Does Facebook Suggest Tags?" 2016. https://www.facebook.com/help/122175507864081?helpref=uf_permalink.

Google, Inc. "Privacy & Terms." Google.com. August 29, 2016. https://www.google.com/policies/privacy/.

Hann, Il-Horn, Kai-Lung Hui, Sang-Yong Tom, and Ivan Lee Png. "Overcoming Online Information Privacy Concerns: An Information-Processing Theory Approach." *Journal of Management Information Systems* 24, no. 2 (2007): 13–42. www.tandfonline.com/doi/citedby/10.2753/MIS0742-1222240202.

Hernandez, Daniela. "The New Google Photos App Is Disturbingly Good at Data-Mining Your Photos." Fusion.net. June 4, 2015. http://fusion.net/story/142326/the-new-google-photos-app-is-disturbingly-good-at-data-mining-your-photos/.

Higginbotham, Stacey. "People Trust the Internet but Lie to It Anyway." Gigaom. November 27, 2012. https://gigaom.com/2012/11/27/people-trust-the-internet-but-lie-to-it-anyway/.

Khusumanegara, P., R. Mafrur, and D. Choi. "Why Smartphone Users Accessing Facebook through Facebook Mobile Website?: Battery and Privacy Awareness." *International Journal of Multimedia and Ubiquitous Engineering* 10, no. 8 (2015): 339–46.

Luckerson, Victor. "7 Controversial Ways Facebook Has Used Your Data." *Time.* February 4, 2014. http://time.com/4695/7-controversial-ways-facebook-has-used-your-data/.

Nam, Hyoryung, and P. K. Kannan. "The Informational Value of Social Tagging Networks." *Journal of Marketing* 78, no. 4 (July 2014): 21–40.

Roettgers, Janko. "Special Report: How We Really Use Our Camera Phones." Gigaom. January 23, 2015. https://gigaom.com/2015/01/23/personal-photos-videos-user-generated-content-statistics/.

Smith, Aaron. "Half of Online Americans Don't Know What a Privacy Policy Is." Factank: News in the Numbers. Pew Research. December 4, 2014. www.pewresearch.org/fact-tank/2014/12/04/half-of-americans-dont-know-what-a-privacy-policy-is/.

Technical Standardization Committee on AV & IT Storage Systems and Equipment. "Exchangeable Image File Format for Digital Still Cameras: Exif Version 2.2, Technical Standard." 2002. Japan Electronics and Information Technology Industries Association.

Twitter, Inc. "Privacy Policy." Twitter.com. September 30, 2016. https://twitter.com/privacy?lang=en.

CAMILLE THOMAS

14

Black Folk Magic

An Autoethnography of Digitally
Archiving Black Millennialhood

THIS CHAPTER WILL SERVE AS AN OUTLINE for guidance on how information professionals can empower their communities to conduct personal digital
archiving. It is part autoethnography, part how-to, and part environmental
scan. I used the qualitative research approach of autoethnography to explore
the wider cultural understandings that can be drawn from individual reflection. I did not want to speak for others; rather, I wanted to speak for myself in
a way that may resonate with others.

I will start by discussing the mindful creation of personal records, explore
how personal records can be transformative for identity and community, and
end on practical applications through a cultural lens. My hope is that this
chapter will open the door for further research, perspectives, and projects on
the topic. I will discuss theories and experiences in order to highlight dispar-
ities in the records, collections, and services that information professionals
manage. If these topics are not discussed and acted upon, the consequences
could include incomplete collections, weak relationships with communities,
underserved users, and imbalanced historical evidence.

OUR RECORDS, OUR SELVES

In a global community, it is especially important for individuals from diverse ethnic backgrounds to make a habit of personal archiving. Now that it is easier than ever to make and preserve digital content, curating a personal collection can give much deeper insight into one's ancestry and history for the next generation. I will use some of my personal experiences to demonstrate the type and depth of insights to which I'm referring.

Once I had to tag along with my mom to the county courthouse. Bored out of my mind, I went around curiously looking in file cabinets. I realized we were in the department where birth and death certificates were kept. So naturally, a librarian in the making, I found birth and death certificates for my grandparents, aunts, and uncles—anyone I could think of who was from the county. My mom erupted with a mixture of surprise and joy. She asked the attendant at the desk to make copies of any records she did not have already. I made the connection at that time that in order to find records, they must be kept.

I learned to think about preservation from my mother and my home state of Florida. Flood and fire are very real threats there. I can only imagine the many personal records that were lost by families in New Orleans after Hurricane Katrina, and from other disasters in many places where damage to personal histories was irrevocable. My mother kept a fireproof box, backed up copies of our family records in other locations, and later would enlist a small conversion business in town to copy all of our important VHS and 8mm home movies onto DVDs.

My mother often took an interest in our family history. Both sides of my family have annual family reunions where I am often lost in a sea of almost-familiar faces. These days we are flung far and wide, but we have been concentrated for many generations in the American South. Through these reunions, I would hear oral accounts of our family history. One year they passed out packets with old photos of my mother's ancestors I had never seen before. Some of the people in these photos had the stern expressions of the rarely photographed, and others were outside of shack houses. Seeing their faces and what kind of lives they led made me feel connected to them. Like many African Americans, I treasure what information I can find, however real or legendary, because there just isn't much evidence to go on. There are usually no coats of arms, no castles in Europe you can trace back to, and often you are lucky to find the right records at all. Frankly, our record keepers lived in areas with low literacy, and they just didn't care if they got the records right for black people.[1] Many more tools for African American and genealogical research exist now.[2] Looking through my history, I sometimes find more through personal journeys than if the information had been presented to me by someone else (e.g., in the television series *Finding Your Roots* or *Genealogy Roadshow*, some found out that their great-grandparents had passed for white or had changed their names after the war to stay overseas). Black experiences, images, and legacies still impact how we see ourselves in the present and future. It shapes how the world sees us and how much we are still connected to America's history.

African Americans are deeply influential in the digital sphere.[3] Black people consume more media on average—for example, 52 percent read magazines compared to 22 percent of the general population, and they listen to 12 hours of radio compared to 6 hours of listening by the general population, according to a survey by Nielsen and *Essence*. The results showed that 81 percent of African Americans own smartphones, whereas the number decreases to 74 percent when looking at the general population. On a monthly basis, blacks spend close to 56 hours using apps or mobile Internet browsers on their smartphones and about 2.5 hours watching videos on their smartphones. Additionally, 81 percent of African Americans are more likely to show support for a favorite company or brand using social media, and 76 percent are more likely to share opinions by posting reviews and ratings online. Young African Americans set trends for what content or topics get buzz.[4]

While there are many people from generations preceding the Millennials who are interested in archiving digital artifacts, many from Gen X and Gen Y are not thinking about it. While it is common to archive items that illustrate slavery or the civil rights movement, there isn't much archiving that documents the rich, multifaceted, everyday lives of black people. Millennials, in particular, are busy multitasking, and consuming and creating multimedia interactive content.[5] They are idealistic and proactive, participating in how information about communities is disseminated. They have grown up in a world that is more diverse, digital, educated, and exploratory.[6] Less than 28 percent of adults aged 18 to 29 are loyal to their news sources, the lowest of any age group, and they are more likely than other age groups to sense media bias.[7] Many Millennials align with the framework of scholarship as conversation that reflects the gray, often narrative-based areas that Millennials encounter, rather than the black-and-white traditions of compliance, which we see in history, journalism, and social media.[8] People like me are creating, traveling, investing, achieving, and giving back in a way like never before, which explains why the Black Lives Matter movement arose—to protect the pursuit of happiness and healing, to create evidence, and to provide witnessing we may not find outside our communities.[9]

IDENTITY AND INDIVIDUALIZATION

Starting with my personal experience, I will explore how examining the digital self through a cultural lens plays a role in constructing identity. I will also discuss how fluid environments can foster intersectionality, active role discourse, and the development of values that were limited in static environments of the past.

My first memory of being on the computer was playing around on Microsoft Paint after school to pass time in my dad's office. There were dismantled computer parts everywhere. I also remember that my brothers and sisters in Atlanta would make banners of their names using the word processors of the mid-1990s and put them up on their walls. They knew how to make CDs and CD-ROMs work. This was Atlanta in the 1990s, often referred to as a "Black Mecca" in its prime of historically black colleges and universities, *Martin, Living Single,* TLC, and Outkast, among many other icons of the time. I was enthralled by my siblings and my community. I had only associated computers with Microsoft Paint, Jumpstart first grade, and later with Oregon Trail and Mavis Beacon Teaches Typing.

Though I began relying on the Internet for schoolwork, it was primarily my friends who influenced me to truly explore the online environment. AOL Instant Messenger was my entry to interpersonal communication between my friends and myself. I also began to take an active role in creating and sharing content. I used to keep a video diary and a diary in Notepad before I had a word processor or a blog. I had a Geocities free web page. I began to use Myspace, LiveJournal, Facebook, and Black Planet, an African American social networking site. I learned a bit of HTML and Java coding in order to manipulate profile designs and typography on my Myspace page. I went to fan site chat rooms (e.g., R&B boy bands like Lil' Bow Wow, Lil' Romeo, and B2K); I am a little embarrassed to admit this, but it was common at the time.[10] The freedom of designing a page and sharing information in the fluid "wild west" of the Web helped me to construct a sense of self.[11] These platforms were created with adults in mind, but we used them as teenagers. I was learning and trying on hats, as adolescents do.

I didn't realize how important these seemingly ephemeral mediums and "fads" were to my adolescence until looking back on them.[12] At times when I was feeling alone or marginalized, I could simply find things and people related to my interests on the Web. I could be judged on the content of my character in a world where no one could see the color of my skin. That being said, even online, I developed a deeper appreciation of the many facets of blackness because it was so much more than skin deep. I could form my own identity, instead of limiting it to how others perceived me. My involvement with the Internet also laid a foundation for connecting with others in my library science and information studies program, using Skype, and doing remote work. I'm not the only one. Our entanglement with digital and IRL (in real life) identities spans celebrity memoirs, TED talks, and scholarship alike. The writer, producer, and actor Issa Rae discusses similar experiences in her book *The Misadventures of Awkward Black Girl.*[13] Alexa Astrid Harris's "The Diary of a Black Female Millennial Blogger" examines digital components of personal identity as black women.[14]

Let's consider how access to technology influences the opportunity to construct one's identity. The digital turn is the growing power and influence of networked software, database logic and deep remixability, technological cultural analytics, and neurosciences. The digital turn can be a great tool for construction of the self. It can also be an obstacle for those who are not able to gain access to the online world. The digital turn begat the digital divide, as it's referred to by the library science and information profession. The digital divide is defined as where external power dynamics are reproduced, often in retrogressive ways that focus on re-inscription rather than regeneration.[15] In other words, those with access to the latest technology can continue to uphold existing structures and values. However, those who do not have access to that technology are not able to create structures for other values or experiences. Scholars such as Sowande and McPhail are reexamining these theoretical approaches to see how this affects black rhetoric, as well as the Afrofuturist movement, which examines the black experience in conjunction with the metaphysical and technological spheres. Rhetoric scholars believe that there still remains much to be seen about how these movements will capture or shift the digital historic moment. They show confidence in Banks's concept of the digital griot, which I'll discuss in more detail in the next section.[16]

Actively creating content, networks, and narrative not only shapes our own experiences but also how those experiences are portrayed in mainstream media. Last year, almost a quarter of teens used the now-defunct Vine. Of those surveyed, 31 percent identified as black (non-Hispanic) and 24 percent as Hispanic. These teens lamented the announcement given by Vine's parent company, Twitter, that there were plans to close the platform.[17] The closure wasn't nearly as unimportant as older people may perceive it to be; Vine had become how many young people map their place in the world. Now we see corporate entities profiting from the creative influence of black teenagers.[18] The most common praise I've seen for TV shows like Issa Rae's *Insecure,* Donald Glover's *Atlanta,* and *Dear White People* is how well they capture the current shared experiences of black Millennials. There haven't been many shows with multiple black characters that document different personalities, styles, and character development since the 1990s. It's what Boschma calls "the Shonda Rhimes Effect" where media aren't just diversified, but normalize complex narratives featuring people of color.[19] In other words, the everyday black folk magic we get to experience in our daily lives is reflected back to us.

Identity is a cornerstone for collective memory. This is evident, for example, in scholarly literature about leaving out historical information that can be considered objective or perspectives that add context in managing cultural heritage objects.[20] Rhetoric is also a point of access. The details, organization, syntax, and formality one uses in speaking or writing is a rhetorical act. Rhetorical acts within and outside academia limit the scope and development of studies concerning marginalized people.[21] As we've discussed, digital environments present the opportunity to highlight nuances of diverse experiences. Through these experiences, both myself and others like me learned new ways of belonging and having an active voice in the world around us. In cultural institutions, such as archives, there is a fallacy of objectivity. The failure to provide the degree of detail which reflects diverse experiences, in fact, supports the bias of the dominant culture.[22] Personal digital archiving can create partnerships that celebrate the values and identities of our cultural institutions' members on their own terms.

COMMUNITY

Now that I've discussed the self and its audience, we'll take a look at community. Community means different things to different people and can encompass multiple spheres. The family may be a private cornerstone of a community, while a church, an organization, or a museum can be a public cornerstone. In every sphere, there are those who take on leadership roles or act as a kind of historian. In black cultures, that person is the griot, a traveling class of storytellers, musicians, and poets who maintain a tradition of oral history. Cultural institutions can be influential in the development of potential leaders or potential griots in their communities. By equipping individuals with the tools to archive their personal digital records, using their own value judgments, information professionals can enrich the legacies of their communities.

This doesn't have to be a burden only for the individual. On March 24, 2016, the website was down for Dream Defenders, an organization that grew out of the transformational struggles of communities made up of black and brown people based in Florida.[23] Foul play was suspected when the site crashed suddenly and past blog posts were lost. I promptly contacted some of the members I knew and told them about the Internet Archive, which linked to past versions of the site.[24] I often have conversations with activist friends about the intersections of social justice and cultural institutions. I feel this connection is not as collaborative as it could be, though I know many are working to foster it.

Modern-day griots (e.g., preachers, DJs, and stand-up comics), when in the context of a digital, global community, help draw important connections.[25] Weaving performance, oral storytelling, writing, and multimedia together becomes especially useful as academic institutions pioneer into digital scholarship. In digital scholarship we begin to make decisions about how and with whom artifacts are created, collected, evaluated, and shared. St. Felix poses the questions, "What things come to those who innovate? And who can be called an innovator?"[26] Although several digital humanities groups have subdivisions dedicated to the inclusion of local and diverse culture, language, and geographical regions in digital scholarship, it certainly has not caught up with other media in terms of being normalized.[27] It is in the best interest of cultural institutions providing resources for personal digital archiving to consider seeking target audiences and incorporating cultural considerations in order to achieve the optimal "pre-custodial activities [which] are the principal sites of archival provenances."[28] However, digital humanities is still a radically open field and does not have the conflicting discourse or institutional expectations of established fields. The same can be said about personal digital archiving.

Institutions are archiving artifacts like Black Lives Matter tweets for their historical significance without engaging those communities. Cultural institutions have meeting spaces, expertise, and a love of community, even in crisis situations like those we have seen in Ferguson and Baltimore.[29] However, those communities are also managing information in their own right without engaging with cultural institutions. The goal is to create richer relationships with our communities by reconsidering Western notions of ownership and use in order to address the histories of our varied world. If institutions do not engage with communities, large groups or even generations of influential users may not become partners. Members of communities may see professionals as gatekeeping misers rather than as conduits, resulting in incomplete collections and imbalanced accounts of history. Furthermore, if community members are alienated by being underserved, notions that librarians and archivists are obsolete could become a self-fulfilling prophecy. Below are examples of community-centered projects from which information professionals can draw inspiration to localize in their community. In these examples, prominence is treated like it exists in the everyday lives of people, not that records of our lives should be collected if we are prominent:

> Archivists at the National Archives and Records Administration perform grassroots initiatives to collect experiences from the Washington, DC community.[30]

> "Diversifying the Digital Historical Record: Integrating Community Archives in National Strategies for Access to Digital Cultural Heritage" is a substantive series of forums organized by the Amistad Research Center at Tulane University, in collaboration with the Shorefront Legacy Center, the South Asian American Digital Archive, Mukurtu, and the Inland Empire Memories Project of the University of California, Riverside.[31] The forums are held on social media in order to be available to the public.

> Approaches like archivist Jarrett M. Drake's #ArchivesforBlackLives have taken the extra step to create A People's Archive of Police Violence in Cleveland, which considers how language and location (in physical and accessible terms) create barriers for the creators of content that is archived.[32] A People's Archive begins by addressing the biases in our practices concerning barriers with community members.

Documenting Ferguson is a freely available digital repository that seeks to preserve and make accessible community- and media-generated, original content that was captured and created following the killing of 18-year-old Michael Brown by police officer Darren Wilson in Ferguson, Missouri, on August 9, 2014.[33] The project is driven by participants, which is significant because it is set apart from what is provided by media outlets. All the content is born digital and publicly available.[34]

StoryCorps, created in 2003, is another interesting initiative that seeks to bring the archive to the people through oral history interviews in order to engage and preserve culture. [35] StoryCorps' permanent physical recording stations are in New York, Chicago, Atlanta, and San Francisco, and there is also a Mobile Booth and an app. Their records are housed in the Library of Congress. The StoryCorps Griot project is the largest collection of African American stories collected in history.

Compliance and sole authorship are large parts of Western culture, but the principles behind licenses like Creative Commons are much more in alignment with other cultural and contemporary notions of use.[36] Cultural sharing is ancient, and framing the Web as a Wild West where attribution and richness are inherently lost is a convenient amnesia.[37] Black people did not have input in copyright law in the past, which led to widespread imitation in order to transform a work into an unattributable idea. Entities like YouTube sometimes remove videos and accounts due to copyright infringement without consulting the artists, who are often glad for promotion among their peers.[38]

Personal digital archiving plays a role in helping us to avoid taking things out of context, or inversely, trying to place black rhetorical context into multimedia or records without giving attention to the traditions from which they emerge.[39] Black folklore and oral traditions (especially those concerning technology like Shine and the Titanic, Stagolee, John Henry, etc.) are often examined by scholars, but usually without the richness these sources possess because they have disrupted linear narratives by nature. We do not regard them in the same way as we do poets, faith leaders, or political activists, especially in selective acquisition.[40] Portable composition is the ability to compose media and contribute to participatory channels indicated by a permanent shift in practices and relationships. This is something that deserves significance because it demonstrates the networks to which a person belongs. Rhetoric scholars also believe it is important not to cut ties from cultural discourse in instruction in order to avoid alienation from one's culture and identity.[41]

It is crucial to not only recognize how race and technology are intertwined, but how this influences the production, consumption, and uses of technology in the present.[42] In libraries we often discuss openness, remixing, and reuse by experts who are usually often Anglo-American. However, we can do more to frame these initiatives toward community leaders who have been powerful vanguards in recontextualizing media. Users all have the potential to become digital griots in their own narratives and the rhetoric of their communities. Cultural institutions have the opportunity to facilitate this.

PRACTICE
The Personal Is Political, Professional, and Transformative

So how do we capture and draw meaning from our digital lives on our own terms? It's easy to get caught up in the workflow processes and skills that are needed to cultivate information. Much like my physical personal archives, my digital personal archives are basically semi-organized memory boxes backed up to the cloud (Dropbox, Google Drive, etc.). Initially, these were the things that came to mind when deciding how to best discuss PDA.

As I create this autoethnography, I have to admit there is a certain intimacy and validation in digging through the ephemeral and personal. There is an embodied experience for readers and authors as they perform "self" to an audience.[43] I am not excluded from this. I also have to admit, I feel a little relieved that personal digital archiving is not highly regarded in archival theory. For one thing, my practices and knowledge of theory are much closer to that of a user. Also, it makes me feel removed from the institutional notions of value and an inflated ego as an "expert." I realize I don't always share these values, which I now see as a benefit more than a concern.

Diversity is not abstract or academic.[44] It is personal and has local context. The literature encourages us to build tools in their local contexts; otherwise, practice becomes rooted in elitism and exclusivity.[45] Just as working papers are now more accessible and accounted for in the development of scholarship, new frameworks allow us to share traces of un-actualized projects, out-of-print masterpieces, and forgotten victories.[46] A great example of the historical implications of archiving the personal is Audre Lorde's personal diary. Access is not something to be acquired or achieved, but is instead a complex "practice."[47]

The second tenet of second-wave feminist theory asserts that the personal is political.[48] It is possible to consider personal digital archiving as an act of self-care and self-preservation on one's own terms and therefore as a radical act. One archivist interviewed caretakers (therapists, social workers, medical professionals, etc.) after seeing the impact that personal history had on patrons. Many people expressed their interest in personal history due to traumas such as illness, loss, nonbiological families, and lack of evidence of personal milestones. The archivist found that people's feelings of lost identity can have consequences that affect their psychological well-being and that the reparation of conflict can ease anxiety.[49] Healing oneself can mean healing the wounds that may pass down through the generations.

FROM PERSPECTIVE TO PRACTICE

Since working backwards is often the best way to be kind to our future selves, I want to borrow from scholars who offer the best practices for inclusivity and intersectionality in the digital humanities. Many digital scholarship projects draw from archived material, trying to save records as best they can to pave the way for future creative remixes and connections. Some goals were borrowed from successful projects listed in previous sections; others I created based on synthesizing the literature and personal experience. Although this chapter considers different perspectives, the ultimate purpose is to enable information professionals to provide their users with a sense of agency for their personal records. So, I'll discuss principles to keep in mind and provide a guided lesson plan in order to walk colleagues through what that process might look like in a workshop format (see figure 14.1).

We do not need to throw out archival principles; instead, we can take a holistic approach. A study compared and contrasted personal digital archival literature to archival theory in order to highlight how they might inform each other.[50] Archival literature emphasizes materials of institutional value and common practices of acquisition near the end of an individual's life. Instances of archival partnership with community members to perform personal digital archiving revealed that guidance from skilled archivists was much needed. Some examples of this are the Digital Life and PARADIGM projects. It should also be noted that the PDA literature examined was outside of the gallery, library, archive, and museum sector. Among the overlapping challenges such as long-term access and distributed storage, curation and appraisal were prominent.

As previously discussed, the values of marginalized groups vary from those of institutions, and individuals may have insightful demonstrations of value in how they construct the narrative of their lives. Graciously considering the values of community members is the best way to encourage agency. Successful projects like Documenting Ferguson and A People's Archive of Police Violence in Cleveland were designed with an acknowledgment of bias, creating accessible materials and locations for learning, as well as the facilitation of technical practices rather than curatorial judgments. We should focus on demonstrating how one curates, rather than spend our time making judgments on what to curate. Like StoryCorps, we still want to provide guidance on curation, but not on designating what should or should not be prominent. It may be helpful to think of it like facilitating a "folksonomy," rather than

Bias	1. Acknowledge any and all privilege, bias, and elitism that exists in individual perspectives and institutional perspectives
	2. Use intersectional content (work by diverse authors, collective biographies) to highlight intersectionality in the coding and invisible work of digital archiving
	3. Create structures for intersectional analysis by making technology and materials accessible
	4. Use multimedia and digital content in instruction
Value	1. Observe demonstrated worth through how often an artifact is replicated
	2. Observe creative effort invested in the artifact
	3. Observe any provenance (from where and how it originated)
	4. Utilize active learning to facilitate self-assessment of values
Curation/Editorial	1. Encourage members to privilege certain life events over others
	2. Have patrons list what they believe they have done to create a legacy
	3. Have patrons then list what they have done to preserve or curate their legacy
	4. Don't put off value judgments
	5. Avoid spontaneous cleanup
	6. Don't rely on periodic loss to limit the collection of digital items
Technical Criteria	1. Routine curation (e.g., virus checks and updates)
	2. Communal activities (e.g., add metadata)
	3. File naming
	4. Storage
	5. Privacy and encryption
	6. Copyright and sharing
	7. File types
Routine/Life Cycle	1. Curation of active content is ongoing
	2. Preservation of curated content is ongoing
	3. Create a plan or schedule for incorporating PDA into a personal routine
	4. Add to a project of cultural institution if it fits one's goals or prepare to do so in the future
	5. Cultural institutions as a resource for ongoing PDA

FIGURE 14.1

Holistic cultural principles for PDA

creating a controlled vocabulary. This is not only a matter of tools but also one of method. As Isabel Galina has noted, "Methods that have worked effectively in one cultural setting may fail spectacularly in another (and vice versa) and certain reasoning of how things should work does not apply similarly in other frameworks."[51]

Moreover, local cultural contexts influence practices; despite a general predisposition in the United States in favor of the idea that information wants to be free, not all communities want their cultural heritage digitized, whether because of cultural expectations of how knowledge should be transmitted, as in many Indigenous communities, or for matters of safety, as among trans communities.[52] So, when considering designing with a cultural lens, we should try to make the application as local and contextual as possible.

Let's draw from diverse digital scholarship practices in order to design our applications with reuse in mind. Most developed digital humanities projects are centered on the media of "dead white men" who are unlikely to be forgotten even without being included in new mediums. Although this can be attributed to the availability of works in the public domain and the use of institutionally approved prolific subjects in order to gain legitimacy from academia as a form of scholarship, it may end up omitting the works of marginalized people. This is one reason why it is important to take cultural considerations into account, since domination is often "routinized and multilayered."[53] For examples, Risam cites the book *Technicolor: Race, Technology and Everyday Life*, Afrofuturism, and Earhart's project The Diverse History of Digital Humanities in which she archives and recovers early work by diverse practitioners. We must prioritize these viewpoints to ensure that they are included in our curatorial approaches routinely and strategically, rather than being an afterthought.[54] These principles, just like digital content or pre-custodial accession, must be thoughtfully woven into the design of our outreach and workflows.

Technical considerations can be drawn from existing best practices in personal digital archiving. Tools such as ResCarta may create a threshold concept for an individual scanning documents or creating metadata; the Internet Archive may be helpful for someone archiving a website; and Dropbox might be a tool for someone looking to store family photos.[55] Also, when looking through a cultural lens, we want to consider the differences between those who may want to share (e.g., students, family members) and those who may not (e.g., activists, trans folk). Instructing on security basics and risk assessment can help expose someone to a new insight rather than static information.[56] We may also want to discuss the ongoing routine of curation and preservation as archival steps by taking the digital curation life cycle approach for technical best practices.[57]

HOLISTIC CULTURAL PRINCIPLES	ACRL FRAMES	UBD TYPES OF UNDERSTANDING
Bias	Authority is constructed and contextual; information creation is a process	Empathy; perspective
Value	Information has value	Interpretation; self-knowledge
Curation	Research as inquiry; searching as strategic exploration	Self-knowledge; application
Technical Criteria	Information creation is a process; scholarship as conversation	Application; interpretation
Routine/Life Cycle	Information creation is a process; scholarship as conversation	Application; interpretation

FIGURE 14.2
Mapping frameworks

In order to demonstrate learning outcomes for holistic cultural principles, I mapped two instructional design frameworks with the common threads from the literature we are discussing (see figure 14.2). I drew from Understanding by Design (Ubd)[58] and the Association of College and Research Libraries' Framework for Information Literacy for Higher Education.[59]

Let's put it all together in a workshop lesson plan.[60] Figure 14.3 is just an example for concrete application. In this table, learning assessment and evaluation are intentionally left blank in case individuals are encouraged to use the information on their own or if the workshops are ongoing. The assessment may depend on how you customize your approach; many different applications could be tested.

Place, Date, Time	• Face-to-face or online	
Librarian/Archivist		
Instructional Partner(s)		
Curricular Context		
Learners	• Community members/users (e.g., black Millennials)	
Preparation	• Accessible location • Prepare learner materials • Prepare examples and cases • Prepare handout of main points in lesson (optional)	
Digital Content	• Images • Social media • Born-digital text (e-mails, SMS text message, blog posts) • Digitized print content	
Instructor Materials	• Examples of community archive projects • Examples of digital content • Cases of value (e.g., family genealogy, activism, professional)	
Learner Materials	• Blank matrix template (Excel sheet or print worksheet)	
Learning Outcomes	• Learners will consider and evaluate culturally diverse examples and cases of value for archiving personal records • Learners will self-assess value (curation/appraisal) criteria • Learners will compare and contrast technical needs • Learners will create a plan for life cycle curation and routine technical management of personal records	
Introduction	• Welcome • Code of conduct • Acknowledgement of biases, diverse values, and intersectional identities • Provide overview of workshop	Time 5 min.
Teaching Strategy	• Show examples and cases to demonstrate the value of personal digital archiving • Provide sample questions for curation self-assessment • Note: Use intersectional content (work by diverse authors, collective biographies) to highlight intersectionality in the coding and invisible work of digital archiving. Create structures for inter-sectional analysis by making technology and materials accessible.	Time 10 min.
Comprehension Check	• Each person to create a matrix for their own cate-gories of personal value	Time 20 min.

Teaching Strategy	• Discuss multiple scenarios for technical considerations • Encryption and privacy • Copyright • Sharing • Active vs. inactive content • Storage and preservation • File naming, metadata, file types • Note: Multiple scenarios can take the form of personas (e.g., a student, an activist, a parent, a genealogy information seeker)	Time 15 min.
Comprehension Check	• Optional: Participants can record resource information or notes in a reminder mechanism of their choosing at this time (e.g., smartphone, e-mail, bookmark, notes)	Time 5 min.
Teaching Strategy	• Discuss tools and practices used in routine curation and preservation • Internet Archive • Photo album tools • Backing up copies • How to archive tweets • ResCarta toolkit • Library/archive resources • Dropbox • Note: The digital curation life cycle approach may be a good way to emphasize an ongoing routine.	Time 10 min.
Comprehension Check	• Each person creates an outline for a plan and schedule for curation and preservation of items	Time 10 min.
Closing	• Question and answer	Time 5 min.
Wrap-up	• Closing remarks • Contact information • Distribute handout of resources and workshop main points	
Student Learning Assessment		
Lesson Evaluation		

FIGURE 14.3

Lesson plan

CONCLUSION

There is still a lot to learn about cultural institutions' relationships to our community members. Through examining both the literature and my own experiences with personal artifacts, I hope to have demonstrated the great value of exploring ways to support our individual community members in order to form stronger communities. Hopefully, readers and the diverse communities they work with will take away the following messages for mindful practices:

- The process of personal information management or personal digital archiving can be a transformative act that means self and community care, especially for those who have not historically been able to participate in record creation.
- If you encourage your users to take care in creating, curating, managing, and preserving records, evidence of their lives has a better chance at existing in the future. Share with users the importance of this contribution for historical or cultural meaning in external spheres (family, community, public, etc.).
- Finally, it's more important to get started and keep going than to do it perfectly. Strive toward quality, but mostly strive.

The outline I've presented for how you might apply these ideas is not necessarily perfect: I am just one voice with only my own experience. It is important that these projects are not few and far between. Please continue to share your own experiences in this space.

ACKNOWLEDGMENTS

Thank you to my editor Brianna Marshall for her encouragement and patience as I wrote this chapter. Special thanks to Yvonne Ivey and Hannah Wiatt Davis for their particular perspectives as reviewers. Also, thank you to friends who helped me get to work in coffee shops or were otherwise supportive.

NOTES

1. Randall C. Jimerson, "Archives for All: Professional Responsibility and Social Justice," *The American Archivist* 70, no. 2 (2007): 252–81.
2. Geraldine Haile, "Resources for African American Research," presentation at the National Conference of African American Librarians, St. Louis, Missouri, August 6, 2015.
3. Janie Boschma, "Black Consumers Have 'Unprecedented Impact' in 2015," *The Atlantic,* February 2, 2016, https://www.theatlantic.com/politics/archive/2016/02/black-consumers-have-unprecedented-impact-in-2015/433725/.

4. Nielsen, "Multifaceted Connections: African-American Media Usage Outpaces across Platforms," February 3, 2015, www.nielsen.com/us/en/insights/news/2015/multifaceted-connections-african-american-media-usage-outpaces-across-platforms.html; Boschma, "Black Consumers Have Unprecedented Impact."

5. Sarah Harrison, "Y@ Our Library: What Do Millennials Want," *Access* 11, no. 2 (2005): 21–23; Joan K. Lippincott, "Information Commons: Meeting Millennials' Needs," *Journal of Library Administration* 52, no. 6-7 (2012): 538–48.

6. Alexa Astrid Harris, "The Diary of a Black Female Millennial Blogger: A Discourse Analysis of Theybf.Com," Order No. 3460672, Howard University, 2011, http://search.proquest.com/docview/878545845?accountid=7098.

7. Amy Mitchell, Jeffrey Gottfried, Michael Barthel, and Elisa Shearer, "The Modern News Consumer," Pew Research Centers, Journalism Project RSS, 2016.

8. Alexander J. Carroll and Robin Dasler, "'Scholarship Is a Conversation': Discourse, Attribution, and Twitter's Role in Information Literacy Instruction," *Journal of Creative Library Practice* (2015).

9. Patrisse Cullors, Opal Tometi, and Alicia Garza, "Black Lives Matter," Black Lives Matter, 2013, blacklivesmatter.com.

10. Shayla Marie Thiel, *Instant Identity: Adolescent Girls and the World of Instant Messaging* (New York: Peter Lang, 2007).

11. Christopher Poole, "Christopher 'moot' Poole: The Case for Anonymity Online," *Speech:* TED Talks, 2010.

12. Sharon R. Mazzarella, *Girl Wide Web 2.0: Revisiting Girls, the Internet, and the Negotiation of Identity* (New York: Peter Lang, 2010).

13. Issa Rae, *The Misadventures of Awkward Black Girl* (New York: 37 Ink/Atria, 2015).

14. Harris, "The Diary of a Black Female Millennial Blogger."

15. Reynaldo Anderson, Marnel Niles Goins, and Sheena Howard, "Liberalism and Its Discontents: Black Rhetoric and the Cultural Transformation of Rhetorical Studies in the Twentieth Century," in *A Century of Communication Studies: The Unfinished Conversation,* ed. Pat J. Gehrke and William M. Keith (New York: Routledge, 2015).

16. Anderson et. al., "Liberalism and Its Discontents."

17. Kat Chow, "A Moment of Silence for the Black and Brown Talent That Grew on Vine," National Public Radio, October 28, 2016, www.npr.org.

18. Doreen St. Felix, "Black Teens Are Breaking the Internet and Seeing None of the Profits," The FADER, December 3, 2015, www.thefader.com/2015/12/03/on-fleek-peaches-monroee-meechie-viral-vines.

19. Boschma, "Black Consumers Have Unprecedented Impact."

20. Wera Grahn, "Intersectionality and the Construction of Cultural Heritage Management," *Archaeologies* 7, no. 1 (2011): 222–50.

21. Anderson et. al., "Liberalism and Its Discontents"; Alexis Pauline Gumbs, "Seek the Roots: An Immersive and Interactive Archive of Black Feminist Practice," *Feminist Collections: A Quarterly of Women's Studies Resources* 32, no. 1 (2011): 17–20.

22. Ettarh, "Intersectional Librarianship."

23. "Dream Defenders," Dream Defenders, www.dreamdefenders.org/.

24. "Internet Archive," Internet Archive: About IA, https://archive.org/about/.

25. Adam J. Banks, *Digital Griots: African American Rhetoric in a Multimedia Age* (Carbondale, IL: Southern Illinois University Press, 2011). Laura Lisabeth, "Review: Digital Griots: African American Rhetoric in a Digital Age by Adam Banks," HASTAC, November 27, 2012, https://www.hastacorg/blogs/ lauralissju/ 2012/11/27/review-digital-griots-african-american-rhetoric-digital -age-adam-banks.

26. St. Felix, "Black Teens Are Breaking the Internet."

27. Roopika Risam, "Navigating the Global Digital Humanities: Insights from Black Feminism," 2016, *English Faculty Publications,* Paper 5, http://digitalcommons .salemstate.edu/english_facpub/5http://digitalcommons.salemstate.edu/english _facpub/5http://digitalcommons.salemstate.edu/english_facpub/5.

28. Lae'l Hughes-Watkins, "Filling in the Gaps: Using Outreach to Acquire Documentation of the Black Campus Movement, 1965–1972," Archival Issues: *Journal of the Midwest Archives Conference* 36, no. 1 (2014); Bass, "Getting Personal."

29. Megan Cottrell, "Libraries Respond to Community Needs in Times of Crisis," *American Libraries,* May 15, 2015, https://americanlibrariesmagazine.org/ 2015/05/15/libraries-respond-to-community-needs-in-times-of-crisis/.

30. "National Archives Explores Revolutionary Movements: Black Power and Black Lives Matter," National Archives and Records Administration, https://www .archives.gov/press/press-releases/2017/nr17–03.

31. "Diversifying the Digital," Diversifying the Digital, October 21, 2016, http:// diversifyingthedigital.org/index.html.

32. Jarrett M. Drake, "#ArchivesForBlackLives: Building a Community Archives of Police Violence in Cleveland—On Archivy," Medium, April 22, 2016, https:// medium.com/on-archivy/archivesforblacklives-building-a-community-archives -of-police-violence-in-cleveland-93615d777289#.wom2p5920.

33. "Documenting Ferguson," Documenting Ferguson, 2015, http://digital.wustl .edu/ferguson/.

34. "Documenting Ferguson," *Process: A Blog for American History,* October 22, 2015, www.processhistory.org/documenting-ferguson/.

35. "StoryCorps," StoryCorps, https://storycorps.org/about/.

36. Carroll and Dasler, "Scholarship Is a Conversation."

37. St. Felix, "Black Teenagers Are Breaking the Internet."

38. St. Felix, "Black Teenagers Are Breaking the Internet."

39. Banks, "Digital Griots," 20.

40. Bass, "Getting Personal."

41. Banks, "Digital Griots," 20.

42. Banks, "Digital Griots"; Risam, "Navigating the Global Digital Humanities."

43. Bass, "Getting Personal."

44. Ettarh, "Intersectional Librarianship."

45. Jimerson, "Archives for All."

46. Gumbs, "Seek the Roots."

47. Banks, "Digital Griots," 20.

48. Carole Mccann and Kim Seung-Kyung, "The Great Thrust of Radical Feminist Writing Has Been Directed to the Documentation of the Slogan 'The Personal Is Political,'" in *Feminist Theory Reader: Local and Global Perspectives* (London: Routledge, 2013), 191.

49. Judith Etherton, "The Role of Archives in the Perception of Self," *Journal of the Society of Archivists* 27, no. 2 (2006): 227–46.

50. Amber L. Cushing, "Highlighting the Archives Perspective in the Personal Digital Archiving Discussion," *Library Hi Tech* 28, no. 2 (2010): 301–12.

51. Roopika Risam, "Beyond the Margins: Intersectionality and the Digital Humanities," 2015, *English Faculty Publications*, Paper 4, http://digitalcommons .salemstate.edu/english_facpub/4.

52. Risam, "Beyond the Margins."

53. Risam, "Navigating the Global Digital Humanities."

54. Cushing, "Highlighting the Archives Perspective."

55. "The ResCarta Toolkit," ResCarta Foundation, www.rescarta.org/index.php; "Internet Archive"; "Dropbox," Dropbox, https://www.dropbox.com/.

56. Matt Mitchell, Cooper Quintin, Martin Shelton, and Rachel Weidinger, "Digital Security Training Resources for Security Trainers, Winter 2017 Edition," Medium, November 18, 2016, https://medium.com/@geminiimatt/security-training -resources-for-security-trainers-winter-2016-edition-4d10670ef8d3#.okhup1jy6.

57. Sarah Higgins, "The DCC Curation Lifecycle Model," *International Journal of Digital Curation* 3, no. 1 (2008): 134–40.

58. Ellie Dickson, Kate Dohe, Lisa Hinchliffe, Elizabeth Joan Kelly, and Chelcie Juliet Rowell, "Digital Library Pedagogy Incubator: A Workshop to Design Instruction with Digital Collections," Digital Library Federation Forum 2016, November 7, 2016, https://dlfforum2016.sched.com/event/8LGH/m3e-digital-library -pedagogy-incubator-a-workshop-to-design-instruction-with-digital-collections.

59. "Framework for Information Literacy for Higher Education," Association of College and Research Libraries, September 23, 2016, www.ala.org/acrl/standards/ ilframework.

60. Dickson et al., "Digital Pedagogy Incubator"; Megan Oakleaf, "Library Workshop Lesson Plan: Presentations," Megan Oakleaf, 2008, http://meganoakleaf.info/ presentations.

BIBLIOGRAPHY

Anderson, Reynaldo, Marnel Niles Goins, and Sheena Howard. "Liberalism and Its Discontents: Black Rhetoric and the Cultural Transformation of Rhetorical Studies in the Twentieth Century." In *A Century of Communication Studies: The Unfinished Conversation,* edited by Pat J. Gehrke and William M. Keith. New York: Routledge, 2015.

Banks, Adam J. *Digital Griots: African American Rhetoric in a Multimedia Age.* Carbondale, IL: Southern Illinois University Press, 2011.

Bass, Jordan Leslie. "Getting Personal: Confronting the Challenges of Archiving Personal Records in the Digital Age." PhD dissertation, University of Winnipeg, 2012.

Boschma, Janie. "Black Consumers Have 'Unprecedented Impact' in 2015." *The Atlantic*. February 2, 2016. https://www.theatlantic.com/politics/archive/2016/02/black -consumers-have-unprecedented-impact-in-2015/433725/.

Carroll, Alexander J., and Robin Dasler. "'Scholarship Is a Conversation': Discourse, Attribution, and Twitter's Role in Information Literacy Instruction." *Journal of Creative Library Practice* (2015).

Chow, Kat. "A Moment of Silence for the Black and Brown Talent That Grew on Vine." Code Switch: NPR. National Public Radio. October 28, 2016. www.npr.org.

Cottrell, Megan. "Libraries Respond to Community Needs in Times of Crisis." *American Libraries*, May 15, 2015. https://americanlibrariesmagazine.org/2015/05/15/ libraries-respond-to-community-needs-in-times-of-crisis/.

Cullors, Patrisse, Opal Tometi, and Alicia Garza. "Black Lives Matter." *Black Lives Matter*. 2013. Blacklivesmatter.com.

Cushing, Amber L. "Highlighting the Archives Perspective in the Personal Digital Archiving Discussion." *Library Hi Tech* 28, no. 2 (2010): 301–12.

Dickson, Ellie, Kate Dohe, Lisa Hinchliffe, Elizabeth Joan Kelly, and Chelcie Juliet Rowell. "Digital Library Pedagogy Incubator: A Workshop to Design Instruction with Digital Collections." Digital Library Federation Forum 2016. November 7, 2016. https:// dlfforum2016.sched.com/event/8LGH/m3e-digital-library-pedagogy-incubator-a -workshop-to-design-instruction-with-digital-collections.

"Diversifying the Digital." Diversifying the Digital. October 21, 2016. http:// diversifyingthedigital.org/index.html.

"Documenting Ferguson." Documenting Ferguson. 2015. http://digital.wustl.edu/ ferguson/.

———. *Process: A Blog for American History*. October 22, 2015. www.processhistory.org/ documenting-ferguson/.

Drake, Jarrett M. "#ArchivesForBlackLives: Building a Community Archives of Police Violence in Cleveland—On Archivy." Medium. April 22, 2016. https://medium.com/ on-archivy/archivesforblacklives-building-a-community-archives-of-police-violence -in-cleveland-93615d777289#.wom2p5920.

"Dream Defenders." Dream Defenders. www.dreamdefenders.org/.

"Dropbox." Dropbox. https://www.dropbox.com/.

Etherton, Judith. "The Role of Archives in the Perception of Self." *Journal of the Society of Archivists* 27, no. 2 (2006): 227–46.

Ettarh, Fobazi. "Making a New Table: Intersectional Librarianship." *In the Library with the Lead Pipe: An Open Access, Open Peer Reviewed Journal* 2 (July 2014). http:// www.inthelibrarywiththeleadpipe.org/2014/making-a-new-table-intersectional -librarianship-3.

"Framework for Information Literacy for Higher Education." Association of College and Research Libraries. September 23, 2016. www.ala.org/acrl/standards/ilframework.

Grahn, Wera. "Intersectionality and the Construction of Cultural Heritage Management." Archaeologies 7, no. 1 (2011): 222–50.

Gumbs, Alexis Pauline. "Seek the Roots: An Immersive and Interactive Archive of Black Feminist Practice." *Feminist Collections: A Quarterly of Women's Studies Resources* 32, no. 1 (2011): 17–20.

Haile, Geraldine. "Resources for African American Research." Presentation at the National Conference of African American Librarians. St. Louis, Missouri. August 6, 2015.

Harris, Alexa Astrid. "The Diary of a Black Female Millennial Blogger: A Discourse Analysis of Theybf.Com." Order No. 3460672, Howard University, 2011. http://search.proquest.com/docview/878545845?accountid=7098.

Harrison, Sarah. "Y@ Our Library: What Do Millennials Want." Access 11, no. 2 (2005): 21–23.

Higgins, Sarah. "The DCC Curation Lifecycle Model." *International Journal of Digital Curation* 3, no. 1 (2008): 134–40.

Hughes-Watkins, Lae'l. "Filling in the Gaps: Using Outreach to Acquire Documentation of the Black Campus Movement, 1965–1972." *Archival Issues: Journal of the Midwest Archives Conference* 36, no. 1 (2014).

"Internet Archive." Internet Archive: About IA. https://archive.org/about/.

Jimerson, Randall C. "Archives for All: Professional Responsibility and Social Justice." The American Archivist 70, no. 2 (2007): 252–81.

Lippincott, Joan K. "Information Commons: Meeting Millennials' Needs." *Journal of Library Administration* 52, no. 6-7 (2012): 538–48.

Lisabeth, Laura. "Review: Digital Griots: African American Rhetoric in a Digital Age by Adam Banks." HASTAC. November 27, 2012. https://www.hastac.org/blogs/lauralissju/2012/11/27/review-digital-griots-african-american-rhetoric-digital-age-adam-banks.

Mazzarella, Sharon R. *Girl Wide Web 2.0: Revisiting Girls, the Internet, and the Negotiation of Identity*. New York: Peter Lang, 2010.

Mccann, Carole, and Kim Seung-Kyung. "The Great Thrust of Radical Feminist Writing Has Been Directed to the Documentation of the Slogan 'The Personal Is Political.'" In *Feminist Theory Reader: Local and Global Perspectives*, 191. London: Routledge, 2013.

Mitchell, Amy, Jeffrey Gottfried, Michael Barthel, and Elisa Shearer. "The Modern News Consumer." Pew Research Centers, Journalism Project RSS. 2016.

Mitchell, Matt, Cooper Quintin, Martin Shelton, and Rachel Weidinger. "Digital Security Training Resources for Security Trainers, Winter 2017 Edition." Medium. November 18, 2016. https://medium.com/@geminiimatt/security-training-resources-for-security-trainers-winter-2016-edition-4d10670ef8d3#.okhup1jy6.

"National Archives Explores Revolutionary Movements: Black Power and Black Lives Matter." National Archives and Records Administration. https://www.archives.gov/press/press-releases/2017/nr17–03.

Nielsen. "Multifaceted Connections: African-American Media Usage Outpaces across Platforms." February 3, 2015. www.nielsen.com/us/en/insights/news/2015/multifaceted-connections-african-american-media-usage-outpaces-across-platforms.html.

Oakleaf, Megan. "Library Workshop Lesson Plan: Presentations." Megan Oakleaf. 2008. http://meganoakleaf.info/presentations.

Poole, Christopher. "Christopher 'moot' Poole: The Case for Anonymity Online." Speech: TED Talks. 2010.

Rae, Issa. *The Misadventures of Awkward Black Girl.* New York: 37 Ink/Atria, 2015.

"The ResCarta Toolkit." ResCarta Foundation. www.rescarta.org/index.php.

Risam, Roopika, "Beyond the Margins: Intersectionality and the Digital Humanities." 2015. *English Faculty Publications,* Paper 4. http://digitalcommons.salemstate.edu/english_facpub/4.

———. "Navigating the Global Digital Humanities: Insights from Black Feminism." 2016. *English Faculty Publications,* Paper 5. http://digitalcommons.salemstate.edu/english_facpub/5.

St. Felix, Doreen. "Black Teens Are Breaking the Internet and Seeing None of the Profits." The FADER. December 3, 2015. www.thefader.com/2015/12/03/on-fleek-peaches-monroee-meechie-viral-vines.

"StoryCorps." StoryCorps. https://storycorps.org/about/.

Thiel, Shayla Marie. *Instant Identity: Adolescent Girls and the World of Instant Messaging.* New York: Peter Lang, 2007.

ANGELA GALVAN

15
Absent Others

Contemporary Mourning and Digital Estates

USER EXPERIENCE AND DESIGN, law, and philosophy have discussed the fate of individuals' web and social media presence after death for some time.[1] This residual, postmortem presence is our digital estate. As the theoretical implications of digital estates continue to gain attention, librarians and information professionals of all kinds will receive practical questions about this topic from survivors.

This chapter has three functional purposes: first, to situate the digital estate within the current cultural experience of death and mourning in the United States; second, to offer introductory guidance for information professionals to proactively engage community members on this topic before one's own death; and third, to assist information professionals as their bereaved patrons try to make meaning out of the digital estate of the deceased.

CONTEMPORARY MOURNING

Physical death is for the most part *sequestered* or separated from our everyday experience in the United States. Our "engagement with death is increasingly mediated by a series of institutional and professional practices."[2] We encounter physical death in predictable ways: through end-of-life care, memorials, and cemeteries. While physical death remains sequestered, our engagement with the dead is now ever-present. Through their digital estates, the dead are as close to us as they were prior to their being sequestered.

Digital estates are dual natured as both *memory objects* and *mourning sites*. Memory objects are items passed down through generations: jewelry, tools, furniture, and other traditional heirlooms "hold" a record of previous use. For example, the peculiar shape of an earring, the acquired, aged form of leather goods, or the comfort of linen washed countless times; these record and make accessible for us both memories and the particular "knowledge" tied to the inheriting of such objects.[3] We hold a fine embroidered square and remember a family member's passing, but also recall her instruction on the stitching, and the complexities of our relationship with her. A site of mourning can be an altar, cemetery, monument, or other memorial area.[4] Digital estates have transformed both the object and the site, creating a haunted everyday reality.

After death the digital estate becomes an active space of grief and memory. Like spontaneous memorials, digital estates allow for "communication about, but directed towards the deceased."[5] Through this memorial communication, the metadata of the self is remixed and ultimately overwritten after death. These practices are now further mediated by technology and our experience of social networks. After the physical body decays, survivors experience a second loss as digital memory objects are overwritten through memorial communication, and are potentially lost through platform changes.

In a single generation, the geography of death and dying moved from the home to institutions. Contemporary death is ever more digital and public, as the same generation that encountered sequestered death embraces new systems of communication. Memories are now mediated through those systems, with relationships continuing and evolving after death as survivors uncover the paratexts[6] of a life.[7] Contemporary grief involves stratified acts of mourning as the bereaved may discover the departed's chat logs, forum posts, blogs, images, e-mails, music and video, websites crawled by the Internet Archive, projects with bits and bytes decomposing unattended, and various expressions of identity on now-deserted content platforms.

As our records move away from analog items and are ever more digital, the "shoebox" of letters and inherited memory objects becomes intangible, with heirlooms existing as bits and bytes. These are no less fragile and in fact may be more so because of cultural conceptions of what is "digital."[8] Digital estates are not necessarily bequeathed or given an executor, but rather persist online.

Social media allow the living and the dead to exist "through their presence in the experience of others."[9] In particular, platforms like Facebook, Twitter, and Instagram allow us to craft the metadata of the self in thoughtful ways, a curated exhibition of artifacts of the self to others. Though some scholars argue that our digital remains are more permanent and stable than a corpse, I suggest this is not the case because of how digital estates manifest in social media. By interacting with people who have passed away, the gestures of self we choose while alive are overwritten with time, moving beyond intended representations. Our relationships with the dead change through our interactions with the estate, and as a result our memories are "subject to ongoing revision."[10]

Social media are far from the first technology to complicate death. Early photography embraced memento mori because cameras' long exposure times made living subjects difficult to capture without blurring. Postmortem photography focused Victorian mourning ritual into the first widely available memory objects to offer an accurate representation of the dead.

Such images were "commonplace in the nineteenth century, where death occurred in the home and was an ordinary part of life."[11] Today, instead of losing entire branches of families to tuberculosis, influenza, or cholera, death is accessible whenever we check our social media feeds. After we die, someone somewhere "curates bits against our ruins."[12] When the living engage a digital estate, they encounter its lossy quality, its private grounds and open architectures, its inherent composite state as those interactions overwrite intention and become spaces for survivors to grieve. Physical death may be removed from our everyday experience, but we carry graveyards in our phones. There is a "common syntax of grief"[13] where librarians and information professionals can intervene.

Death as Spectacle

The contemporary experience of death is morphing into spectacle, particularly for the extrajudicial killing of black people at the hands of the state.[14] In these cases, intention and representations of self via the digital estate shift immediately; for example, the viral circulation of a photo of Trayvon Martin at an aviation program in response to media outlets portraying him as a criminal, or the many creative works depicting Martin that are distributed over social media networks.[15] Martin's public digital estate is further complicated by postmortem defacement from a white supremacist.[16] Michael Brown's digital estate was utilized in similar ways, as supporters distributed his high school graduation picture and images of his anguished father as narrative corrections.[17]

Death as spectacle acknowledges that all images are funerary. In engaging those estates, their deaths are transformed and public grief through social media becomes an act of solidarity.[18] For those estates-turned-spectacle, information professionals must be cautious and deliberate in their work to preserve the digital footprints of and about the deceased. In these cases, "spectacle swallows whole the story and spits back little to interrogate."[19] Working with these estates will involve great care and verification to determine the origins of individual objects, as well as identifying the assemblages and production of "mediated witnessing."[20] In these cases, art and other objects created *for* the deceased may be of equal importance to the estate itself for the bereaved. Although this topic is covered by other scholars, information professionals must consider how they will address patrons engaging these estates, and how the library itself might engage in possible acts of correction, collection, and mourning.

COLLECTING LOSS

Social Media and Websites

Memorial websites first appeared in the United States during the mid-1990s.[21] However, the use of social media for this purpose was not widely recognized until the 2007 Virginia Tech shooting, when university communities took to Facebook to process their grief.

Platform policy changes further complicate grief: Twitter now allows people to see their full private message history, previously limited to the last one hundred messages. After installing Facebook's mobile apps, some users report receiving unread messages from dead friends.

In her account of a friend's death mediated through Facebook, Julie Buntin expresses a desire to locate her grief in the known and accessible, lamenting: "The Internet has complicated the question of where to store my loss. How can I move on, if Lea's face is always lurking in my phone . . . With every Facebook upgrade it seems like the platform makes it easier for me to become an archeologist of Lea's past."[22]

Buntin's question about *storing loss* has multiple meanings here and is an expression of her desire to assign a place to Lea's memory, to locate her anguish in the known and accessible. Buntin's longing to store her loss is a wish for a memorial space or possession, a "guarantee of the presence of the absent other."[23] Unlike memory objects passed down through generations, digital lives are not consolidated in known spaces. They are scattered throughout different software, mediated through multiple expressions of self through various platforms. These range from the mundane but new arenas of loss for the living to negotiate—automatic bill payment systems, rewards programs— to the spaces between a LinkedIn profile and a throwaway Reddit account. Together they are kaleidoscopic metadata, a composite self that the digital allows us to affirm, attenuate, and—with great effort—destroy.

While Buntin refrained from overwriting her friend's digital estate, she observed others do so as the space shifted from one of production to stillness.

Perhaps the most remarkable thing about the dead online is their relative quiet compared to the hundreds of messages our networks produce in a day. Those connected to the deceased fill that silence with memorial communication. Digital estates are restless, haunting the everyday. A web developer for an academic library writes about the paradox of public and private grief: "I've learned that the hardest part about losing someone 'digitally' close to you, is that the physically present folks around you have no idea why you are upset. They can't grieve with you or feel empathy, because they don't 'get it.' My loss is invisible, yet my loss is just as devastating."[24]

Gaming

Repurposing technology to process grief is not unique to social media. Players have extended these practices into virtual realms since their inception, with Multi-User Dungeons holding text-based funerals for dead players as early as the 1970s.[25] Funerals and memorials for dead players are common to most massively multiplayer online games.

Sometimes in-game memorials are significant enough to draw attention from outside the game's community, as was the case with EVEOnline in 2012. Following the attack on the U.S. consulate in Libya, thousands of players memorialized Sean Smith, a Foreign Service officer killed in the attack, who they knew as the famous diplomat Vile Rat. Vile Rat's obituary appeared in *Harper's Magazine* and the *Huffington Post*. Both highlighted his role with the consulate and his life as an avid gamer.

In addition to screenshots and recorded game play, survivors collect chat logs, e-mails, and game artifacts in order to remember deceased players. When players die, the bereaved should consider gaming avatars to be extensions and augmentations of the self, and should therefore be treated with the same level of attention and care.

TAKING INVENTORY

Information professionals can conduct a reference interview to see which of the starting points offered in the appendix of this chapter may be available to the bereaved, with the caveat that these are offered as entry points to generate conversation and should not be seen as exhaustive. Because these reference interviews may be more intense than usual, maintaining distance without appearing clinical is important. Patrons will have varying degrees of comfort with technology, and defining what they believe is meaningful to the digital estate will determine the scope of the assistance we can provide. We have no power over how others will mourn, nor over what they find significant during the investigation of an estate.

To keep interactions manageable, information professionals can borrow from the Library of Congress's guidelines for personal digital archiving for the living:[26]

1. Identify what potentially exists in the digital estate. Patrons may return to this stage of discovery throughout their grieving process as new objects are found.
2. Define the scope of the interaction and maintain those boundaries throughout.
3. Determine what can be accessed for preservation.
4. Decide which objects are meaningful.
5. Save the objects.
6. Describe the objects in a useful way: 00001.jpg is less helpful; Smith-Graduation.jpg is more helpful.
7. Make copies. If patrons choose to upload them to a storage service, they should consider granting access to more than one person.

Together, a primary e-mail account and current cell phone are the best tools available for mapping a digital estate. Deceased persons with an interest in security potentially enabled two-factor authentication.[27] In these cases, our ability to see an estate more fully relies on access to both e-mail and a cell phone.

In the absence of these tools, we can still assist the recovery of other significant objects. Converting from one format to another—reformatting a VHS tape, for example—is usually outside the scope of the estate, but public libraries and the Library of Congress's personal digital archiving resources can be helpful here.

Librarians and information professionals working in any capacity with digital estates must be prepared to refer patrons to additional resources within and outside the library, depending on the nature of the information uncovered as a result of exploring a digital estate.

A survivor's loss can be mediated through vast estates of multiple personas, identity performances, platforms, and objects. These manifest in a variety of ways:

- A trans woman is out to her community and family of choice but estranged from her family of origin at the time of her death.
- The scholar who changes her surname throughout her career. The scholar maintains distinct professional, public, and private identities. She may or may not have a unique identifier linking her professional works, such as ORCID.
- A young woman who adopted her childhood nickname as an adult because no one in her elementary school could pronounce her legal name.

These scenarios and their endless variations hold clues to identifying the user's estate. User names may be reused in certain contexts. We may have a user name we consistently use for our professional identity (smith85), another for our personal interests (smith_loves_bikes), and still others for platforms where user names communicate information about us explicitly, like dating apps (stillseeking85).

In searching for these accounts, there may be links between platforms and identity performance in particular if a "throwaway" or "anonymous" account is uncovered. These accounts are in some ways misnamed—"throwaway" suggests an easily discarded portion of the self, a peripheral piece of representation. On Reddit, for example, it's trivial to create throwaway accounts for information-seeking and confessional use. To *throw away* those comments is a deliberate attempt to disassociate them from the primary digital estate because of the comments' often profoundly personal nature. When patrons ask how to recover "everything," we need to educate patrons on what *everything* might mean.

LEGAL ISSUES AND ACCESS

Limited attempts to address the lack of protocol for digital estate management exist. *The Digital Beyond* lists several dozen posthumous data and digital heirloom services. The majority of these services were founded after 2007, and none appear to have data sharing agreements or interoperability standards. A brief review showed no metadata standards between services, a foundational component of digital preservation.[28] Preserved objects without metadata cannot be discovered without considerable intervention. Such objects run the risk of becoming massive, hidden collections of the dead, assuming these estates survive at all.

Gaining access through Google's Inactive Account Manager is one solution, but not everyone uses Gmail accounts. E-mail can provide a vital access point, but it is not the whole of a digital estate. Lack of policy addressing death on the part of many providers is a growing problem.[29] Although early research on digital estates predates the linking of YouTube, Picasa, Drive, Gmail, and other Google products to a single identity in 2013, the issues of access and inheritance of digital estates remain problematic.

In 2005, Yahoo! was compelled by a court ruling to provide the family of Justin Ellsworth, a United States marine killed in Iraq, with his e-mail records. Yahoo! still maintains terms of service that do not permit transference or access.[30] Facebook fielded several controversial cases before and after instituting their memorial policy, one concluding after a two-year court case,[31] and another after court orders were issued to Facebook and Google for parents to gain access over a deceased child's digital estate.[32]

Five states have passed laws to assist digital estate management: Connecticut, Idaho, Oklahoma, Rhode Island, and Indiana. Several other states have legislation pending.

EMERGING ROLES AND SERVICES

The frequency of legal action against providers suggests that the needs of survivors are not addressed through profile memorialization alone and that many are not aware of Google's Inactive Account Manager. This is unsurprising, given the number of people without end-of-life care plans, advanced directives, and living wills.[33]

Perhaps the most important part of acknowledging the information professional's role is that it allows the bereaved to locate themselves in a future where estates are discoverable and grief consented to, not a series of random, disruptive encounters. Because this kind of work involves a high level of emotional labor for professionals with service-centered orientations, the library must decide the scope and investment it is willing to commit to these kinds of questions and services.

Library patrons have the opportunity to see the files they create as part of a greater cultural narrative; this is one of the talking points that the Washington, DC, Public Library offers for its Memory Lab. This allows information professionals to frame events and services in the context of producing a relevant part of cultural history rather than death.

Conversely, the death-positive movement and its various incarnations can offer guidance for how to initiate often-difficult conversations about death and dying in the context of the library or similarly positioned host institutions. Indeed, because death and dying affect everyone, the opportunities for information professionals who might not otherwise collaborate are exceptional. Unexplored collaborations between departments, experts, and the community are possible within the tensions offered by digital estates. Information professionals have countless avenues to explore connecting project management, inheritance and benefits, preservation, technology education through enabling the creation of digital memorial objects for survivors, the maintenance of digital estates for the living, and the justice work implicit in narrative correction, holding space for mourning, or archiving those digital estates.

APPENDIX

Starting Points for Reference Interviews and Mapping Digital Estates

Physical Components of the Digital Estate

- Current and old cell phones
- SD cards
- Portable storage like USB memory and zip drives
- Tablets
- E-readers
- Laptop and desktop computers
- Cameras

Task-Based Components

- Password managers
- Calendars
- Automatic withdrawals from primary banking accounts
- Direct deposits
- Tax information
- Insurance policies

Digital Components

- User names and other potential unique identifiers
- Photos, video, audio—both *saved* and *created* by the deceased user
- Streaming media accounts
- Text messages and voice mail
- Activity through apps
- Social media presence
- Blogs
- Avatars/player characters in virtual environments
- Communication directed to or about the deceased

NOTES

1. See, for example, Will Odom et al., "Technology Heirlooms?: Considerations for Passing Down and Inheriting Digital Materials," in *Proceedings of the SIGCHI Conference on Human Factors in Computing Systems* (New York: ACM, 2012), 337–46; Michael Massimi, Will Odom, David Kirk, and Richard Banks, "HCI at the End of Life: Understanding Death, Dying, and the Digital," in *CHI'10 Extended Abstracts on Human Factors in Computing Systems* (New York: ACM, 2010), 4477–80; Jamie Patrick Hopkins and Ilya A. Lipin, "Viable Solutions to

the Digital Estate Planning Dilemma," Iowa Law Review Bulletin 99 (2014): 61; Damien McCallig, "Facebook after Death: An Evolving Policy in a Social Network," International Journal of Law and Information Technology 22, no. 2 (2014): 107–40; Patrick Stokes, "Deletion as Second Death: The Moral Status of Digital Remains," Ethics and Information Technology 17, no. 4 (2015): 237–48.

2. Warren Smith, "Organizing Death: Remembrance and Re-collection," Organization 13, no. 2 (2006): 225–44.

3. For in-depth discussion of the physical "memory" of inherited objects, see Stacey Pitsillides, Janis Jefferies, and Martin Conreen, "Museum of the Self and Digital Death," in Heritage and Social Media: Understanding Heritage in a Participatory Culture (New York: Routledge, 2012): 56.

4. For example, the analysis of spontaneous, roadside memorials in Holly J. Everett, in Roadside Crosses in Contemporary Memorial Culture (Denton, TX: University of North Texas Press, 2002); or the growing body of literature on the "ghost bike" memorial phenomenon. A digital example which predates the memorialization feature on Facebook is the number of memorial "groups" and "pages."

5. Natalie Pennington, "Grieving for a (Facebook) Friend: Understanding the Impact of Social Network Sites and the Remediation of the Grieving Process," Mediating and Remediating Death (New York: Routledge: 2016): 233–50.

6. I use paratext to describe memorial communication toward the deceased as part of their digital estate; for example, the posting of goodbye messages or other expressions of grief within a particular platform. These are not necessarily a part of the original estate.

7. Consider the once common practice of saving an answering machine message tape or voice mail recording.

8. Robert Fox, "Forensics of Digital Librarianship," OCLC Systems & Services: International Digital Library Perspectives 27, no. 4 (2011): 264–71.

9. Stokes, "Deletion as Second Death," 238.

10. Jeffrey Bennett and Jenny Huberman, "From Monuments to Megapixels: Death, Memory, and Symbolic Immortality in the Contemporary United States," Anthropological Theory 15, no. 3 (2015): 338–57.

11. Robert Hirsch, Seizing the Light: A History of Photography (New York: McGraw-Hill Education, 2008), 33.

12. Bethany Nowviskie, "Digital Humanities in the Anthropocene," Digital Scholarship in the Humanities (2015): https://doi.org/10.1093/llc/fqv015.

13. Candi K. Cann, "Tweeting Death, Posting Photos, and Pinning Memorials: Remembering the Dead in Bits and Pieces," in Digital Death: Mortality and Beyond in the Online Age (Santa Barbara, CA: Praeger, 2014), 69–82, 69.

14. Safiya Umoja Noble, "Teaching Trayvon: Race, Media, and the Politics of Spectacle," The Black Scholar 44, no. 1 (2014): 12–29.

15. Noble, "Teaching Trayvon," 13. Coverage was so widespread that two images surface as visual shorthand for the event itself: black people wearing hoodies to challenge the narrative that Martin was inherently threatening, and Skittles candy with Arizona tea, the items Martin purchased from a convenience store before his death.

16. *Ebony Magazine,* www.ebony.com/news-views/ white-supremacist-hacks-trayvon-martins-email#axzz2ez1v2e83.

17. See the coverage of Emmitt Till's death for an example of this predating social media. Much like the Martin and Brown families sought to create a more "whole story" of their children, Till's mother deliberately showed the brutality of her son's death.

18. Cann, "Tweeting Death," 71.

19. Noble, "Teaching Trayvon," 14.

20. Penelope Papailias, "Witnessing in the Age of the Database: Viral Memorials, Affective Publics, and the Assemblage of Mourning," *Memory Studies* 9, no. 4 (2016): 437–54.

21. Anna Haverinen, "Memoria Virtualis—Death and Mourning Rituals in Online Environments," *J@rgonia* (2014).

22. Julie Buntin, "She's Still Dying on Facebook," *The Atlantic,* July 6, 2014, www .theatlantic.com/technology/archive/2014/07/shes-still-dying-on-facebook/ 373904/.

23. For more on this concept, see Susan Stewart, *On Longing: Narratives of the Miniature, the Gigantic, the Souvenir, the Collection* (Durham, NC: Duke University Press, 1984). Applied to the digital, see Elisa Giaccardi, *Heritage and Social Media: Understanding Heritage in a Participatory Culture* (New York: Routledge, 2012).

24. Leah Root, e-mail message to author, October 30, 2016.

25. Kevin Kelly and Howard Rheingold, "The Dragon Ate My Homework," *Wired,* March 1, 1993, https://www.wired.com/1993/03/muds-2/.

26. These steps are adapted from the Library of Congress's digital preservation and personal archiving of website guidelines: www.digitalpreservation.gov/ personalarchiving/websites.html.

27. See thedigitalbeyond.com/online-services-list/.

28. Evan Carol, "Digital Death and Afterlife Online Services List," The Digital Beyond, www.thedigitalbeyond.com/online-services-list/.

29. Cyndi Wiley, Yun Wang, Ryan Musselman, and Beverly Krumm, "Connecting Generations: Preserving Memories with Thanatosensitive Technologies," in *HCI International 2011—Posters' Extended Abstracts,* edited by Constantine Stephanidis, *Communications in Computer and Information Science,* 173 (Berlin and Heidelberg: Springer, 2011), 474–78.

30. See Yahoo!'s terms of service here: info.yahoo.com/legal/us/yahoo/utos/utos -173.html.

31. M. Avok, "Karen Williams' Facebook Saga Raises Question of Whether Users' Profiles Are Part of 'Digital Estates,'" 2013, www.huffingtonpost.com/2012/ 03/15/karen-williams-facebook_n_1349128.html.

32. E. A. Epstein, (2013, June 6–13), "Family Fights to Access Son's Facebook Account after His Suicide," *The Daily Mail,* June 2013, www.dailymail.co.uk/ news/iirticle2153548/Family-ñghts-access-sons-Facebook-Gmail-accounts -suicide.html.

33. Jaya K. Rao, Lynda A. Anderson, Feng-Chang Lin, and Jeffrey P. Laux, "Completion of Advance Directives among US Consumers," *American Journal of Preventive Medicine* 46, no. 1 (2014): 65–70.

SELECTED BIBLIOGRAPHY

Bennett, Jeffrey, and Jenny Huberman. "From Monuments to Megapixels: Death, Memory, and Symbolic Immortality in the Contemporary United States." *Anthropological Theory* 15, no. 3 (2015): 338–57.

Buntin, Julie. "She's Still Dying on Facebook." *The Atlantic.* July 6, 2014. www.theatlantic.com/technology/archive/2014/07/shes-still-dying-on-facebook/373904/.

Cann, Candi K. "Tweeting Death, Posting Photos, and Pinning Memorials: Remembering the Dead in Bits and Pieces." In *Digital Death: Mortality and Beyond in the Online Age,* 69–82. Santa Barbara, CA: Praeger, 2014.

Carol, Evan. "Digital Death and Afterlife Online Services List," *The Digital Beyond,* www.thedigitalbeyond.com/online-services-list/.

Costello, Matthew W. "The 'PEAC' of Digital Estate Legislation in the United States: Should States 'Like' That?" *Suffolk University Law Review,* Summer 2016.

Dougherty, William C. "Preservation of Digital Assets: One Approach." *The Journal of Academic Librarianship* 35, no. 6 (2009): 599–602.

Frank, Jeffrey. "The Impact of Hurricane Katrina on Gulf Coast Libraries and Their Disaster Planning." Master's Thesis, 2011. http://scholarworks.sjsu.edu/etd_theses/3925.

Hopkins, Jamie Patrick, and Ilya A. Lipin. "Viable Solutions to the Digital Estate Planning Dilemma." *Iowa Law Review Bulletin* 99 (2014): 61.

Kelly, Kevin, and Howard Rheingold. "The Dragon Ate My Homework." *Wired.* March 1, 1993. https://www.wired.com/1993/03/muds-2/.

Lingle, Virginia A., and Dorothy L. Malcom. "Interlibrary Loan Management with Microcomputers: A Descriptive Comparison of Software." *Medical Reference Services Quarterly* 8, no. 2 (1989): 41–64.

Massimi, Michael, and Andrea Charise. "Dying, Death, and Mortality: Towards Thanatosensitivity in HCI." In *CHI'09 Extended Abstracts on Human Factors in Computing Systems,* 2459–68. New York: ACM, 2009.

Massimi, Michael, Will Odom, David Kirk, and Richard Banks. "HCI at the End of Life: Understanding Death, Dying, and the Digital." In *CHI'10 Extended Abstracts on Human Factors in Computing Systems,* 4477–80. New York: ACM, 2010.

McCallig, Damien. "Facebook after Death: An Evolving Policy in a Social Network." *International Journal of Law and Information Technology* 22, no. 2 (2014): 107–40.

Notess, Greg. "Surviving Rot and Finding the Online Past." *Online Searcher* 38, no. 2 (March/April 2014): 65–67.

Nowviskie, Bethany. "Digital Humanities in the Anthropocene." *Digital Scholarship in the Humanities* (2015). https://doi.org/10.1093/llc/fqv015.

Odom, William, et al. "Technology Heirlooms?: Considerations for Passing Down and Inheriting Digital Materials." In *Proceedings of the SIGCHI Conference on Human Factors in Computing Systems,* 337–46. New York: ACM, 2012.

Papailias, Penelope. "Witnessing in the Age of the Database: Viral Memorials, Affective Publics, and the Assemblage of Mourning." *Memory Studies* 9, no. 4 (2016): 437–54.

Pennington, Natalie. "Grieving for a (Facebook) Friend: Understanding the Impact of Social Network Sites and the Remediation of the Grieving Process." *Mediating and Remediating Death* (2016): 233–50.

Pitsillides, Stacey, Janis Jefferies, and Martin Conreen. "Museum of the Self and Digital Death." *Heritage and Social Media: Understanding Heritage in a Participatory Culture.* New York: Routledge, 2012. 56.

Smith, Warren. "Organizing Death: Remembrance and Re-collection." *Organization* 13, no. 2 (2006): 225–44.

Stokes, Patrick. "Deletion as Second Death: The Moral Status of Digital Remains." *Ethics and Information Technology* 17, no. 4 (2015): 237–48.

Weaver, Stephen D., and Mark Gahegan. "Constructing, Visualizing, and Analyzing a Digital Footprint." *Geographical Review* 97, no. 3 (2007): 324–50. www.jstor.org/stable/30034175.

Wiley, Cyndi, Yun Wang, Ryan Musselman, and Beverly Krumm. (2011). "Connecting Generations: Preserving Memories with Thanatosensitive Technologies." In *HCI International 2011—Posters' Extended Abstracts.* Constantine Stephanidis (ed.). Berlin and Heidelberg: Springer, 474–78.

Wright, Nicola. "Death and the Internet: The Implications of the Digital Afterlife." *First Monday* [online] 19, no. 6 (May 21, 2014).

About the Contributors

RACHEL APPEL is the digital collections librarian at Bryn Mawr College (PA). Prior to Bryn Mawr, she worked at the University of Texas at Austin's Office of Communications and interned at both the Briscoe Center for American History and the Harry Ransom Center. Appel is interested in born-digital archives access solutions, software preservation, and personal digital archiving.

RYER BANTA is the information literacy and technology librarian at Centralia College (WA), where he manages digital resources and services, and helps learners develop information literacy and lifelong learning skills. His research interests include open education, instructional design, educational technology, information literacy, and user experience.

ISAIAH BEARD is digital curator at the Archibald Stevens Alexander Library at Rutgers, the State University of New Jersey. His research focuses on the long-term preservation of digital artifacts. He served on the external advisory committee for the Media Preservation Team at Indiana University Bloomington as they embarked on their massive university-wide digital preservation project. He also consults with cultural heritage institutions throughout the state of New Jersey on their preservation projects, as part of his work through the New Jersey Digital Highway project.

AMY BOCKO is the digital initiatives librarian at Emerson College in Boston. Previously, she created a digital initiatives program at Wheaton College (MA) and was part of the digital library team at Vassar College (NY). Bocko has overseen large-scale digitization projects and digital library platform implementations, and she is active in the digital library community.

MELODY CONDRON is the resource description and management coordinator at the University of Houston Libraries. She is responsible for the quality control of library data, and is passionate about information organization. She recently taught a "PDA for Librarians" class for the Library Information Technology Association, and she writes about such topics as file management, photo organization, and digital media archiving.

CAMERON COOK is the digital curation resident librarian for the General Library System at the University of Wisconsin-Madison, where she also received her MLIS degree in 2016. Her professional interests center on the intersections of the production, dissemination, and curation of many forms of digital scholarship.

JOANNA DIPASQUALE is the head of digital scholarship and technology services at Vassar College (NY), where she works to create, maintain, and preserve the digital collections of the college and to foster digital scholarship initiatives on campus. She holds degrees in history and mathematics, and received her MA degree from New York University and her MLIS from Rutgers University.

CELIA EMMELHAINZ is the anthropology and qualitative research librarian at the University of California, Berkeley. She has an MLIS degree from Kent State University and an MA in anthropology from Texas A&M University. Emmelhainz advises faculty and students on managing and archiving text and images as gathered from around the world.

ANGELA GALVAN is the digital resources and systems librarian for the State University of New York, Geneseo. Among her responsibilities are the reclamation of library systems for the user and strategic digital initiatives for the Milne Library. Her research interests include critical algorithm studies, decay in technology/infrastructure, and digital estates.

CHELSEA GUNN is a doctoral student at the University of Pittsburgh's School of Computer and Information Science, in the department of Information Culture and Data Stewardship. Her research is centered in archival studies, digital preservation, and personal and family papers. She earned her MLIS degree at Simmons College in Boston, concentrating on archival management, and has worked in archives, libraries, and historical societies.

SARA MANNHEIMER is the data management librarian at Montana State University in Bozeman, where she helps researchers manage, store, and preserve their data. She is an advocate for open science and open data. Her research interests include data preservation; discipline-specific data practices; and the social, ethical, and technical issues surrounding data-driven research.

SARAH WALDEN MCGOWAN is the digital collections and preservation librarian at Amherst College (MA). Prior to her current position, she was the digital projects librarian at Amherst. She supervises digitization operations, contributes to digital preservation strategies and policies, and runs an internship for undergraduate students interested in digital scholarship.

JAIME MEARS is an administrative assistant for the National Digital Initiatives division at the Library of Congress. She was a 2015 National Digital Stewardship Resident and helped create a public-focused lab, tools, and instruction on personal digital archiving for the Washington, DC Public Libraries. Mears has a BA degree in English literature from the University of Virginia and an MLS from the University of Maryland.

NATALIE MILBRODT leads the Queens Library's Metadata Services Division, and is responsible for the system's cataloging and digitization efforts as well as the Queens Memory program. Milbrodt graduated in 2000 from Michigan State University with a BA in interdisciplinary humanities and a specialization in film studies. She earned her MLIS degree in 2011 from Queens College, CUNY. Before joining the library profession, she worked for film production, design, and marketing firms in both creative and management roles.

YVONNE NG is the senior archivist at WITNESS. She is the coauthor of the "Activists' Guide to Archiving Video," and has led numerous workshops and trainings on video archiving. She has also co-taught a course on personal digital archiving at New York University, and has been a member of the XFR Collective and the AMIA Community Archiving Workshop.

LOTUS NORTON-WISLA is the tribal digital archives curriculum coordinator at Washington State University's Center for Digital Scholarship and Curation. She also works with the Mukurtu CMS platform and the Sustainable Heritage Network at WSU. Before relocating to Washington, she worked with cultural heritage, project planning, digitization, and preservation in projects at the Wisconsin Historical Society and the American Folklife Center.

COLIN POST is a doctoral candidate in information and library science at the University of North Carolina at Chapel Hill, where he is also pursuing an MA in art history. His research interests include artists' personal archiving practices, digital art preservation, and the history of art conservation. He also holds an MFA in poetry from the University of Montana.

MAGGIE SCHREINER is a project archivist at New York University. Previously, she was the Queens Memory outreach coordinator at the Queens Library (NY), where she facilitated mobile digitization and developed partnerships with local community organizations. She is also a longtime volunteer with the Interference Archive and with Librarians and Archivists with Palestine. Schreiner holds an MA degree in archives and public history from New York University.

MATT SCHULTZ is the metadata and digital curation librarian at Grand Valley State University Libraries (MI). Prior to his work at GVSU, he was program manager for the award-winning MetaArchive Cooperative, one of the first international library-led digital preservation networks. In conjunction with his curatorial and data management work at GVSU, he engages in research and publication aimed at solving organizational and technical challenges to preserving digital content.

SARAH SEVERSON is the coordinator of digital library services at the McGill University Library & Archives. Prior to joining McGill, she worked as the digital archivist at Moment Factory and was the media librarian at the Canadian Broadcasting Corporation. Her research interests include digital archiving, and new media and digital and special collections outreach.

CAMILLE THOMAS is the scholarly communication librarian at Texas Tech University. Her research is focused on the connections between scholarly communication, emerging library services, and broader impact.

JAMIE WITTENBERG is the head of scholarly communication and is the research data management librarian at Indiana University. Previously, she was the service manager for the University of California at Berkeley's Research Data Management program. Her current research includes data management curricular design and data enrichment for time-based media. Wittenberg's recent publications include "Building a Research Data Management Service at the University of California, Berkeley" and "Selection in Web Archives: The Value of Archival Best Practices."

MICHAEL WYNNE is the digital applications librarian at Washington State University, where he primarily provides training and support for Mukurtu CMS. He is a recent graduate of the iSchool at the University of British Columbia, within the First Nations Curriculum Concentration, and while there he worked as a student librarian at Xwi7xwa Library and helped with previous Indigitization cohorts.

Index

Lightning Source UK Ltd.
Milton Keynes UK
UKHW02f1051281117
313492UK00003B/4/P